The Japanese Legal System: An Era of Transition

STUDIES IN COMPARATIVE LEGAL HISTORY

The Japanese Legal System: An Era of Transition

Edited by
Tom Ginsburg
and
Harry N. Scheiber

The Robbins Collection 2012

Robbins Collection Publications
School of Law (Boalt Hall)
University of California at Berkeley
Berkeley, California 94720
(510) 642-5094 (510) 642-8325
http://www.law.berkeley.edu/robbins

This book is printed on acid-free paper.

ISBN 978-1-882239-20-7

Library of Congress Cataloging-in-Publication Data

The Japanese legal system : an era of transition / edited by Tom Ginsburg and Harry N. Scheiber.
p. cm.—(Studies in comparative legal history)
ISBN 978-1-882239-20-7 (hardcover : alk. paper)
1. Law—Japan. 2. Law reform—Japan. 3. Justice, Administration of—Japan. I. Ginsburg, Tom. II. Scheiber, Harry N.
KNX470.J37 2012
349.52—dc23

2012037429

Editors' Dedication

For Professor Sanford Kadish
Mentor, colleague, and treasured friend

Contents

Part I
General Views

Part II
Transforming Legal Institutions: Empirical Perspectives

Part III
Transforming Legal Practices

Preface

This book is the latest in a series of studies analyzing historical, contemporary, and comparative aspects of legal change in Japan, under sponsorship of the Sho Sato Program in Japanese Law of the University of California, Berkeley, School of Law. Like previous Sho Sato Program publications, this book contains papers originally presented at a major international conference on the Berkeley Law campus. Subsequent to the conferences, the papers have been edited and revised for publication as formal scholarly studies. It might be said that these volumes track, or at least run parallel to, the course of debate in Japan concerning the substantive, procedural and institutional reforms that have been going forward since the late 1990s. As in the Program's previous publications, this book seeks to analyze the changes already accomplished, to compare the progress and direction of change with the goals originally articulated for them, and to open new lines of inquiry as to the character of innovations—and, not less important, resistance to them—manifested in what we call here an era of transition. The roots of Japanese legal culture run deep and full. There have been dramatic discontinuities in the history of Japan's legal system, being, as is well recognized, the Meiji reforms, the overturn of many civil institutions and laws by the militarists, the 1946 Constitution adopted during the Occupation, and, now, the new wave of reform across a broad spectrum of subject areas and institutions. Movement on the several fronts of innovation and change has been uneven, in many regards either overtly contested or subject to the ravages of bureaucratic and political inertia. Yet, it has also been the source of truly dramatic departures in the texture and content of the legal culture.

As in earlier Sho Sato Program studies, the essays in the present volume variously illuminate significant dimensions of the scope, the dynamics, and the effectiveness of changes that have been achieved. Historical examples of adaptation and innovation in Japan's law and legal have also been of interest to some of our authors, most notably in this volume with regard to the Japanese response to Western concepts and applications in diplomacy of international law.

The first of the Sho Sato Program conference volumes appeared in 2002, with publication of the book *The Japanese Adversary System in Context: Controversies and Comparisons*, edited by Professors Malcolm Feeley and Setsuo Miyazawa. It was followed by a set of papers on Japan's legal culture, from a conference co-organized by Sho Sato Program Director Harry N. Scheiber and Professor Kahei Rokumoto, published in a 2001 symposium issue of *The American Journal of Comparative Law,* Volume 49. In the same year, a symposium on comparative administrative law and regulation, organized by Professor Robert A. Kagan, appeared in the journal *Law and Policy,* Vol. 22. In cooperation with the Japanese Association of Sociology of Law, the Sho Sato Program sponsored UC Berkeley scholars who presented papers at an international symposium in Tokyo that led to book publication under title *The Role of the Judiciary in Changing Societies* (Kyoto, 2001).

Under collaborative sponsorship of the UC Berkeley Law School's Robbins Collection in Religious and Civil Law, later Sho Sato Program conferences produced papers collected in books coedited by Harry N. Scheiber and Professor Laurent Mayali in the Robbins Collection's distinguished series, *Studies in Comparative History:* The first, *Emerging Concepts of Rights in Japanese Law* (Berkeley, 2007), presented studies of the ideological and jurisprudential character of new rights being contended for as they were reflected in specific aspects of the mobilization of law and of institutional reforms. The second book to appear in the Robbins publication program was *Japanese Family Law in Comparative Perspective* (2009), featuring monographic studies of constitutional issues, divorce law, mediation and other dispute resolution structures, medically assisted reproduction, educational policies, and inheritance law, but in addition also theoretical approaches to family law issues and systematic comparison with European legal developments. The present volume is thus the third to appear in the Robbins Series.

In addition to the foregoing activities, the Sho Sato Program has hosted an international meeting at Berkeley on Japanese and comparative tax law, coorganized by Scheiber and Professor John W. McNulty, and featuring a major overview of Japanese tax policy issues by Professor Hiroshi Kaneko along with monographic papers by scholars from Japan, Australia, Canada, the United States, and the Netherlands. It was published on-line, on the Program's website, in 2009. An earlier web-based symposium publication presented papers from a special conference honoring the scholarship of Professor Takao Tanase (on the Program's website, 2005). Waseda University's law faculty and the Sho Sato Program collaborated meanwhile in 2006 in sponsorship of a two-day conference at Berkeley Law, co-organized by Propfessor Charles Weisselberg, featuring papers on Japanese and American experience and new directions in clinical legal education.

During the last decade, moreover, the Program has hosted annually, to be in residence at Berkeley Law for specialized legal studies, an early-career lawyer interested in public interest law. These visits are made under terms of a joint program with the Japan Federation of Bar Associations. The anniversary of this joint program was celebrated at a JFBA symposium held in Tokyo in 2011. At the present writing, the Sho Sato Program is also collaborating with Meiji University and the Japan Foundation in sponsorship of three conference meetings and a project publication on the subject of responses of law and lawyers to the nuclear and natural disasters that Japan experienced a year ago. Professor Masayuki Murayama is principal organizer, and Berkeley Law professors Weisselberg and Daniel Farber are sharing in the project's leadership.

In the realm of international law of the sea, the Sho Sato Program has also been involved for more than fifteen years as collaborative sponsor with the Law of the Sea Institute of our own Law School and with the Japanese Ocean Policy Research Foundation, the Inha University-Incheon, and the Korean Ocean Research and Development Institute (KORDI) in Korea, the Fridjtof Nansen Institute in Norway, Academia Sinica of Taiwan, the U.S. Coast Guard, Wollongong University in Australia, and other U.S. and foreign institutions in the co-organization and collaborating sponsorship of international symposia and conferences on varied aspects of contemporary ocean law and policy. Major publications from these programs include three books already published by the Nijhoff/Brill company; and three more are in preparation or in press at this writing.

The Program and the entire faculty of Boalt Hall are deeply indebted as well to the interest and support given to us over many years by Mrs. Masako F. Sato—who has honored our conferences with her presence, too—in our activities that honor the memory of her late husband, our colleague and friend Sho Sato. He was a pioneering figure in American legal scholarship, the first Japanese American to hold a senior professorship in a leading American law school, and the cofounder with Dean Sanford Kadish of the program that today bears his name.

For constant institutional support and enthusiastic encouragement of the Sho Sato Program development, a great debt is owed to Dean

Christopher Edley, Jr., of the UC Berkeley School of Law. Professor Yasuhei Taniguchi has been generous with his time and attention to the Program, in addition to making frequent scholarly contributions to our publications. Intellectual debts are owed to many others, but special mention must be made of Professors Kahei Rokumoto, Setsuo Miyazawa, Tom Ginsburg, Masyuki Murayama, Aya Yamada, Eric Feldman and Charles Weisselberg. Professor Mayali has been a pillar of support both for the conferences and the publications. The structure of inquiries and whatever success our Program's projects have achieved owe much to the advice and counsel of these scholars, all of whom have contributed chapters to our symposium publications.

In editing and production of this volume, indispensable assistance was given by Karen Chin and Toni Mendicino of the Sho Sato Program staff; Benjamin Jones and James Phillips, graduate assistants at Berkeley; and Max Withers of the editorial staff of the Robbins Collection. Co-editor Tom Ginsburg gratefully acknowledges the support of the Russell Baker Scholars Fund at the University of Chicago Law School. He extends his thanks also to Ingram Weber and Kenneth Young of the University of Chicago for research assistance.

Professor Sanford Kadish is preeminent for his scholarship in criminal law and jurisprudence. He has also taken a major role of leadership in the academic world, having served as president of both the American Association of Law Schools and the American Association of University Professors. At the University of California, Berkeley, he was dean of the School of Law and (with Philip Selznick) co-founder of the School's doctoral program in Jurisprudence and Social Policy. His deep interest in Japanese and comparative law, and his success in launching and nurturing the Sho Sato Program, connect him with the present work in a vital way. For the editors of this volume, he has been a mentor and a deeply valued friend. Our dedication of the book to him acknowledges the personal and institutional debts that we and others in the Berkeley academic community owe to him.

Harry N. Scheiber
Berkeley, October 2012

Introduction: Accelerating Change from the Bottom Up

Tom Ginsburg and Harry Scheiber

Japan's legal system has entered its second decade since the adoption of the Justice System Reform Council Report in 2001, and its third decade of what have been called the Heisei reforms, after the current Imperial reign. This period has seen what must be characterized as steady restructuring of legal institutions, with the intention of producing a more responsive legal system. The most dramatic changes—those to legal education, to civil procedure, and to the criminal trial process with the introduction of the jury system—have now had several years to operate. Yet it is becoming clear that in numerous other areas of law there have been substantive changes, and that these may have significant consequences for Japanese society in the decades ahead. This volume seeks to provide a snapshot of many of these areas of legal change, and to explore how innovations are operating in practice.

Part I begins with a birds-eye view of Japan. Lawrence Friedman takes a grand historical and comparative perspective. While there are no doubt interesting differences between Japan and other modern societies, what stands out at the general level is a great deal of convergence with other advanced industrial societies. The crux of convergence theory is that similar societies produce similar legal systems; and as a modern nation, Japan is subject to the same powerful forces that affect the legal systems of rich, democratic nations. We thus see common pressures for change. From this perspective, the recent round of legal reform is simply part of a long historical trajectory of legal systems becoming more similar. Friedman finds this natural, since law always reflects underlying social realities.

In their contribution, Tom Ginsburg and Tokujin Matsudaira also consider the legacy of the nineteenth-century legal reforms, but they focus on continuity rather than the convergence process identified by Friedman. The nineteenth-century reforms borrowed heavily from legal thought in authoritarian Prussia, including an organic theory of the state constitution that, in the authors' view, continues to inform Japanese judges to this day. This adherence to organic theory underpins what many observers have identified as a judicial branch that is relatively deferential to the political authorities. Ginsburg and Matsudaira trace recent high-profile constitutional cases to argue that Japan is somewhat of an outlier when it comes to the "judicialization" of public policy. While they demonstrate that subtle changes have occurred, they argue that the pace has been slow.

The theme of historical convergence is once again prominent in Jon Van Dyke's chapter on the introduction of international law into Japan in the nineteenth century. Although public international law is often seen as a product of the Western world, Van Dyke argues that this assertion ignores Asian and African systems of international practices and their contributions to the modern state of International Law. The history of Japanese interaction with "Western International Law" is one interesting example of this contribution, as it has synthesized western ideas into Japan's own system. Although the "Western" concepts of "law" and "rights" are historically alien to Japan, the country made a concerted effort to join the world of "civilized nations" through a reform of its legal system in the mid-nineteenth century. From the late nineteenth century to the early part of the twentieth century, Japan enjoyed a reputation for scrupulous adherence to international law, both in and out of war. Japan thus internalized an important body of western law to great effect.

Part II of the volume turns to empirical studies of specific legal institutions since the Heisei reforms began. Masayuki Murayama continues the grand tradition of studies of litigation behavior that originated with Takeyoshi Kawashima. Presenting new empirical evidence derived from surveys, Murayama shows that Japanese are no less willing than Westerners to bring disputes to courts and other formal dispute resolution processes. International differences in litigation rates, he shows, derive more from institutional structure than traditional cultural values. His data provide an important contribution to the ongoing debates over legal consciousness and disputing behavior in Japan.

Kota Fukui and Yusuke Fukui focus their attention, in Chapter 5, on practicing lawyers (*bengoshi*). Lawyers in Japan have traditionally been like British barristers in that they focus on courtroom litigation or dispute settlement. As such, corporations have long relied on a bevy of non-lawyers who are nonetheless legal professionals to handle a variety of corporate legal needs. They do this in lieu of hiring either in-house lawyers or having lawyers on retainer. In recent years, however, the changing nature and demands of global business have led to pressures to increase the number of Japanese lawyers and to expand their scope of practice. Although recent data suggest that lawyers in Japan retain their traditional self-image, the utilization of lawyers in everyday business and the number of corporate in-house lawyers has increased drastically since 2000. If this trend continues, the self-image of lawyers in Japan is likely to change as well. A more entrepreneurial profession, playing a wider range of roles, may ultimately result.

Surely one of the most commented-on reforms in the Heisei period has been the introduction of lay participation in serious criminal trials through the so-called *saiban-in* system from 2008. Many commentators, including the members of the Justice System Reform Council, theorized that lay participation in the justice system would transform the Japanese legal system and Japanese society as a whole. Takayuki Ii analyzes data from *saiban-in* trials' first two years of nationwide use, reporting on extensive personal observation of the first twenty cases to be determined by *saiban-in* trial in the Aomori District Court. He argues that, although the *saiban-in* jurors appear to bring a fresh perspective to court proceedings, they generally defer to judges in difficult cases. Judges and prosecutors retain their inquisitorial habits. The author thus suggests that professional attitudes can form a barrier to ambitious reforms, implying the need to draw a longer perspective on the transformation of the Japanese criminal justice system. True reform may ultimately require on changes in the stance of legal professionals

Hiroshi Fukurai provides an analysis of a less well-known mode of lay participation, the Prosecutorial Review Commissions (*Kensatsu Shinsakai*, or PRCs). These institutions, established in the post-war period as analogues to common-law grand juries, were historically quite passive, but recent reforms have strengthened them. Fukurai provides an overview of the recent high-profile cases in which the PRCs have forced prosecutors to reverse non-indictment decisions. He then conducts a detailed study of such cases with regard to members of the U.S. military, also examining the role of *saiban-in*. Fukurai is much more optimistic about the impact of public participation than is Ii, perhaps a result of their different research methods.

Part III of the volume turns to specific areas of law. Eri Osaka examines the issues of environmental and worker safety through the lens of asbestos regulation. Environmental issues were long ignored in the early years of rapid growth. Beginning in the 1960s, when various industrial diseases became manifest, the government reacted by creating pollution-related health compensation systems. When these have proven inadequate, victims of environmental pollution have successfully found redress through tort liability. Osaka identifies asbestos-related injury as a major category of future environmental illness, and argues that the government should learn from past mistakes to produce a compensation system that is both fair and effective. This is an argument for greater legalization of public policy in the interests of justice and fairness.

Zenichi Shishido in Chapter 10 turns to the venture capital industry in Japan. One might expect a vigorous market for venture capital in Japan given the country's technological and financial development; but, as Shishido pithily summarizes "law matters". While Japanese corporate law has recently been reformed to accept a more Silicon Valley-type of venture capital investment, Shishido contends that tax law, labor law, and labor market norms continue to inhibit the growth of venture industry in Tokyo. Reform of these collateral areas of law will be necessary in order to expand the role of venture capital in the Japanese economy. (Such developments, one may speculate, might in turn trigger greater demand for law in Japanese society, fulfilling the Justice System Reform Council's vision.)

Junichiro Makita tackles the very important question of privacy law in Japan, a topic that has been increasingly debated in recent decades. This debate initially revolved around the tort system as the primary mechanism for privacy protection, for example, through the development of a doctrine of recovery for public disclosure of embarrassing facts. Another central issue in recent years has been Japan's Act on the Protection of Personal Information. Makita argues that it requires significant updating in light of technological advances in the storage and accumulation of personal information. He proposes the adoption of Privacy by Design, a revision of the Act on the Protection of Personal Information to allow for the free circulation of information that would not directly restrict personal autonomy, and the establishment of a third party entity for privacy protection that resembles the Federal Trade Commission of the United States.

Manabu Wagatsuma describes recent developments in two areas related to medical ethics, reproductive technology and organ transplantation. Both of these areas are strongly connected to Japanese culture;

and so it is found that attitudes, and law more formally, respond only loosely to rapid changes in technology. As technological possibilities have increased, traditional legal rules are under pressure, as many Japanese have been able to take advantage of access to other jurisdictions to obtain desired medical technologies. This is just another example of how global interactions put pressures on traditional rules.

While it is beyond the scope of any one volume to provide a complete image of a field as broad as the changes in Japanese law, the studies presented here provide an overall sense of a system in which subtle tectonic shifts are at play. Some of the authors, such as Shishido, Ii, Ginsburg and Matsudaira, emphasize continuity; others, such as Fukurai, Fukui and Friedman, emphasize change. Change is certainly afoot, and the only real debate is about pace and directions. Whether the aftermath of the horrific earthquake and tsunami that occurred just prior to our conference in 2011 will accelerate these changes, it is too early to say. But the tools are beginning to develop for a greater role for law in Japanese social ordering.

Japanese Law in the Modern World

Lawrence M. Friedman[1]

Japan has fascinated law and society scholars for many years. Here is a major non-Western country that became a fully developed, rich, modern society, and did so in a short space of time. Indeed, Japan became the second largest economy in the world, until China (with more than ten times the population) recently overtook it. There is a huge literature, of course, on Japanese culture and Japanese society. There is also a large literature which advanced an idea we might call *Japanese exceptionalism*, a good deal of it written by the Japanese themselves. This literature argues that despite all the recent and massive changes in Japan, despite its raging modernity, its rich technological culture, there is a core, an essence, which remains simply and stubbornly Japanese; that Japanese society is by culture and tradition unique; and that the vast oceanic forces of modernity cannot and have not been able to touch or impair this essence at the heart of Japanese society.[2]

I am going to offer a modest sort of dissent. I should begin by pointing out that there is nothing unique about the Japanese claim. There is also a literature about so-called American exceptionalism, and no doubt a case can be made for French exceptionalism, and, for all I know, Estonian exceptionalism as well.

Let me also, at the outset, make it clear that I have no right to pass myself off as a Japanese specialist. Nonetheless, I am going to be so bold as to make a few general comments, which I hope are relevant to Japanese legal history and Japanese society.

Japanese legal history is particularly interesting because it contains a significant discontinuity. In the course of the Meiji Restoration, in the

1. Marion Rice Kirkwood Professor of Law, Stanford University School of Law.

2. For example, there is the literature on the (supposed) Japanese reluctance to go to court and sue people. On the other side, see John Owen Haley, "The Myth of the Reluctant Litigant," *Journal of Japanese Studies* 4 (1978), 359.

middle of the nineteenth century, Japan adopted western codes of law. This move turned Japan into a civil law country. It aligned Japan with a legal tradition that, in some regards, harked back to the days of the Roman Empire. Obviously, Julius Caesar and the Roman emperors never quite got to Japan. Nonetheless, Japan opted to join the civil law family. The government was in the process of modernizing Japanese society, and it was plausible to include the legal system in their plans. And the ruling circles looked, not unnaturally, to advanced European countries as models. Of course, after more than a century and a half, Japanese lawyers I suppose do not really see their legal system as some sort of alien intrusion, any more than they would consider tempura an alien intrusion, despite the fact that they owe this marvelous food to Portuguese Jesuits.

I would like to suggest a kind of thought experiment. Suppose the ruling circles of Japan during the Meiji period had decided *not* to adopt European codes but rather to keep their native legal system. What would Japanese law be like today? Of course, nobody knows, but I suspect it would not be *that* different from the present form of Japanese law, in many if not most essential ways. There would be rules about taxes, computer software, rules about corporations, rules about commercial contracts and banking, air traffic control, cartels, land-use planning, and so on; these rules and doctrines would have at least a family resemblance to the rules in other modern, rich, developed countries, whether or not they belonged to the civil law family of systems.

Of course, you might object to this. You might point out that Japanese law before the Meiji restoration was simply not suited to modern life and the modern world. No doubt this was true. But as Japan modernized, as it developed, as it entered the club of rich and industrial nations, the law would necessarily evolve. The Diet would pass new statutes. The courts would develop new doctrines. In the end, the system would adapt.

There is a kind of natural experiment that points in this direction. The natural experiment is the common law itself. This was an old, old system, dating back centuries in England. Historically considered, it was completely unfit for modern society. It developed essentially as law for a feudal society. But as England became capitalist, industrial, and more democratic, the common law evolved along with it. Nobody ever sat down to modernize it. Nobody enacted English versions of European codes. But the common law was able to change, to conform to modern conditions as the years went by. And this is no surprise. All legal systems do tend to adapt to the conditions of their society. How could it be otherwise? Indeed, the civil law systems themselves, in many ways, despite their elegant codes, have undergone quite a parallel evolution. This would have been the trajectory of Japanese law as well, whether it had adopted the civil law or not.

This brings me to my main point and the reason I brought up this imaginary history. There are powerful forces in the modern world that are pushing all legal systems in the same direction—at least all legal systems of rich, developed, and more or less democratic countries. I am a strong believer in what one might call the theory of *convergence*. The basic idea is a simple one. Similar societies tend to produce similar legal systems. It follows, then, that modern, developed, technologically advanced and democratic countries will develop legal systems that are in many ways alike. Not entirely alike, of course. Each legal system is unique. Each society is unique. The societies themselves are convergent, but never totally so. The same must be true of their legal systems as well.

Modernity, then, can be compared to a single language, made up of a number of closely related dialects. Their legal systems, too, would converge, though of course with more or less variation from society to society. A theory of convergence, then, tends to play down the role of legal tradition—membership in civil law or common law family, for example. Traditions do matter; but the question is, how much? If we embrace the idea of convergence, the answer is: not all that much.

Not everybody agrees. Some scholars reject the central notion of convergence. Shmuel Eisenstadt, in particular, has put forward the idea of what he calls "multiple modernities." Modernity, he argues, takes a number of fundamentally different forms. There is a Western form, a Chinese or Confucian form, a Hindu form, an Islamic form, and so on.[3]

My problem with the concept of "multiple modernities" focuses on the word "modernity." This is of course derived from "modern," a word that has a number of meanings; it is, among other things, a synonym of "contemporary." Bhutan and the Chad Republic are "modern" in this sense. But I use "modern" in a different sense. There are modern societies and not-so-modern societies. Maybe "modern" is not the best word, but offhand it is hard to think of a better one. When I say modern, I am

3. Shmuel N. Eisenstadt, "Multiple Modernities," in Shmuel N. Eisenstadt ed., *Multiple Modernities* (New Brunswick, 2002), chap. 1.

referring to the club of rich, wealthy, democratic societies: the countries of the EU for the most part, the United States and Canada, Australia and New Zealand, South Korea and Taiwan, and, very definitely, Japan. The other "multiple modernities" are simply not modern enough, in this second sense. And this explains why they are fundamentally different—so far.

Anybody who visits Japan from the United States or from Europe is admittedly struck by sights, sounds, and customs that do seem strange and different. This includes the orange and purple vending machines and, above all, the writing system. It is distressing for foreigners who have advanced degrees, have written books, and consider themselves intellectuals, to visit a country and become instant illiterates.

On the other hand, a great deal is completely familiar. The streets are filled with cars. Tall urban buildings look like tall urban buildings everywhere else. If you go inside one of these buildings—an office building, say—you take an elevator much like elevators everywhere. Suppose you get off on the fifteenth floor and visit the offices of an insurance company. Inside, men are working at computers, dressed in business suits and ties; women are in other cubicles, wearing blouses and skirts. On the street people are talking on cell phones. Young people in blue jeans, some of them with dyed hair, are listening to rock-and-roll music on their iPods. At night you can eat pizza or go to McDonald's, or have fine French cuisine. You can even have sushi, just like you can in the United States. You can go to a kabuki theater; but you can also go to the movies, and perhaps see an American movie, or visit a concert hall, where a symphony orchestra is playing Mendelssohn and Brahms. In a drug store, you can get aspirin and Kleenex. Yes, there are differences in the street scene. But the similarities—the convergences—are also overwhelming: the cars, the trains, the clocks, indeed, the whole machinery of life.

No one denies that every society, even closely related societies like Norway and Sweden, has its own peculiarities; and the same goes for the legal systems that govern these societies. The question is: are the differences between, say Japan and Finland, or France, or the Irish Republic, greater than the similarities—in ways of life, in technology, in habits of thought? Of course there is no way to count and measure similarities and differences. I feel quite strongly, however, that the similarities outweigh the differences and are, perhaps, more fundamental.

Convergences in ways of life and in habits of thought *follow* from convergences in technology and in the structure and rhythm of life in a modern, developed—and democratic—society. But is there some inner core, some essence, some uniquely Japanese mentality, which has survived all the ups and downs of Japanese history, which has persisted through the Meiji Revolution, the Second World War, and the post-war recovery? A similar question can be asked about any society. How much of the England of William the Conqueror, or of Henry VIII, survives in a definitive way in modern England? When patterns of life become modern, when the tools at hand become modern, when all the conditions of daily life are modern, then the core personality cannot help but be affected. Attitudes toward time, money, sex, career, marriage, family—and law—cannot help but reflect the essential structures of life.

There is of course no obvious way to test the convergence theory. What I say strikes me as plausible; but nobody can talk about "proof" in the scientific sense. There do exist what we might call natural experiments, which at least shed light on this issue. I mentioned one of these earlier. It also seems obviously true that political systems have been converging. At the end of the Second World War, many people thought it was hopeless to try to make democratic societies out of Japan and Germany. These countries were completely lacking in democratic traditions. One weak experiment in Germany—the Weimar Republic—had been a disastrous failure. Imperial Japan looked like an even more dubious prospect for democracy. Had it not taken centuries in the West to achieve genuine democracy? Yet both Germany and Japan are resounding success stories—not only economically, but in terms of political democracy. Japan's political system has many flaws—which country does not?—but it is nonetheless a vibrant democracy with full freedom of speech, free elections, freedom of religion, and freedom to travel. Taiwan and South Korea have followed a similar trajectory. The notion that democracy is "Western" and cannot be transported to Asia is obviously wrong.

The convergence issue also bears on an important debate among scholars of human rights. There is a conventional list of fundamental human rights, and the question is: are these "universal" or are they not? Some scholars and others, right and left, have argued that the menu of human rights, embodied in various declarations, treaties, and constitutional documents, is not "universal" at all; rather, these are lists of strictly

"Western" concepts, which do not embody "Asian values" or "African values," or the like.[4]

But this argument strikes me as profoundly wrong. The history of human rights suggests that these rights are not "western" at all; rather, they are modern. They were equally lacking in the West for most of the history of the West. Take women's rights, for example. Women did not vote, hold office, or possess legal equality with men until quite recently. In the United States before the 1860s, there were millions of black slaves. Catholics could not hold office in England, supposedly a democratic country, until well into the nineteenth century. If we go back further, we reach periods in which European countries burned heretics at the stake. Torture, too, was a recognized instrument of procedure in the middle ages. The idea that there are basic, universal rights, which everybody shares or ought to share, forms part of the culture of modernity. Yes, it started in the West. But so did the automobile and the computer. Human rights are no more alien to Japan than they are to France or Italy—or to the United States, for that matter.

Of course, each country has its own slightly different dialect of human rights. But the fundamentals are the same all over the developed world. These countries typically also have constitutions with bills of rights, and most of them have some sort of system of judicial review. Judicial review is, to be sure, a western invention. It may even be an American invention; it has been part of the American constitutional system for the last two hundred years. But these institutions have now spread all over the world—as the world modernizes and globalizes. Not every country has embraced judicial review, but most of them have. Nor does it work the same in every country. The Japanese Supreme Court does not have the same record of activism as the German Constitutional Court. The United Kingdom and the Netherlands still lack judicial review, but both of these countries adhere to international human rights treaties and to the European Court of Human Rights.

The foregoing remarks of mine were presented at a conference on the Japanese legal system, held at Berkeley, California. The conference itself is a sign of globalization and convergence. The mere fact that people

4. See the discussion in Neil A. Engelhart, "Rights and Culture in the Asian Values Argument: The Rise and Fall of Confucian Ethics in Singapore," *Human Rights Quarterly* 22 (2000), 548.

from different cultures can talk to each other, understand each other, exchange ideas, is itself a sign of convergence. We have so much in common. Imagine a samurai warrior who came back to life in modern Tokyo. How totally baffled he would be; how strange he would find it. Nothing would be familiar except the Japanese language itself, and even here, there would be hundreds of words he could not understand at all. And what would Henry VIII make of modern London? Yet moderns can feel pretty much at home in London or Berkeley or Tokyo, or indeed any contemporary city.

I do not want to carry this thesis too far. Differences among societies are important. We have a lot to learn from each other, on all levels of culture. Convergence is not a one-way street. It is mutual and interactive. The Japanese gave us sushi. We gave them the Big Mac. I leave it to you to decide who is ahead on this exchange.

The Judicialization of Japanese Politics?

Tom Ginsburg[1] and Tokujin Matsudaira[2]

Are Japan's politics judicializing? Certainly Japan has been somewhat of an outlier among advanced industrial democracies, in which scholars have documented a strong trend toward greater scope and authority of judicial decision-making.[3] The largest political and social questions of the day—abortion, gay marriage, the status of religion, even who can take power—are regularly decided by national and supranational courts in North America and Europe,[4] but studiously avoided by Japan's Supreme Court. Closer to home, the Korean and Taiwanese constitutional courts routinely decide major issues of social policy, but Japan's courts seem to be much more quiescent.

At the same time, Japan has just experienced a decade-long period of major reforms of legal institutions. The declared goal of these reforms, as articulated in the 1998 launch of the Justice System Reform Council, was nothing less than the transformation of Japanese society into one that was more law-governed, in which "ex post" judicial remedies replaced "ex ante" planning as a mode of allocating rights and duties. Japan has also experienced major political change, with the emergence, however tentative, of what appears to be a two-party system. These factors would lead one to expect a degree of judicialization, as scholars have long predicted that an alternation in political power is a basic factor underpinning judicial power and independence.[5]

1. Spitz Professor of Law, University of Chicago and Research Faculty, American Bar Foundation

2. Assistant Professor of Law, Teikyo University.

3. C. Neal Tate and Thorsten Vallinder, *The Global Expansion of Judicial Power* (New York, 1995).

4. Ran Hirschl, "The Judicialization of Mega-Politics and the Rise of Political Courts," *Annual Review of Political Science* 11 (2008): 1–44.

5. J. Mark Ramseyer, "The Puzzling (In)dependence of Courts," *Journal of Legal Studies* 23 (1994): 721–47; Tom Ginsburg, *Judicial Review in New Democracies* (New York, 1994).

In this paper we examine the status of judicialization in Japan, showing that, while some areas have experienced an increased role for judicialized governance, others have not. Relative to other advanced industrial societies, we find the level of judicialization to be low. We then examine the reasons for this state of affairs, and find that conventional explanations rooted in politics and institutional structure are not fully adequate to account for the phenomenon. Instead, we find that a full understanding requires an inquiry into the institutional self-understanding of Japanese courts, rooted in the nineteenth-century Meiji adaptation of Prussian legal thought. Political theory, rather than political structure, seems to be the key to the puzzle.

Our account is consistent with recent work that emphasizes the role of ideational factors in judicial behavior. Lisa Hilbink, for example, in her recent account of Chilean judicial quiescence during the Pinochet regime, focuses on a particular institutional self-conceptualization of judicial apoliticism.[6] Rooted in a conservative positivism of the nineteenth-century modernizing state, she finds that apoliticism is far from apolitical: indeed, by refraining from getting involved in "political" issues, Chilean judges end up reinforcing the status quo. Similarly, Japan's relatively limited levels of judicialization mean that the political process gets to play the dominant role in the allocation of rights and responsibilities. This is precisely the idea behind the nineteenth-century theory that we elaborate.

In its emphasis on ideational and institutional factors, our story is also consistent with recent work by David Law, who has provided a thick description of the behavior of the Japanese Supreme Court.[7] But the approach is somewhat at odds with the prevailing views among Western scholars of Japanese law. Western scholars have tended to emphasize institutional factors over ideational ones in understanding Japanese judicial behavior. John Haley, for example, has emphasized the institutional weakness of the Japanese judiciary to explain its particular role in Japanese society. J. Mark Ramseyer has focused on the importance of political pressures from the long-ruling Liberal Democratic Party (LDP), which in his view indirectly controls judicial promotions. These and other scholars have played an important role in providing a corrective to simplistic

6. Lisa Hilbink, *Judges Beyond Politics in Democracy and Dictatorship* (New York, 2007).

7. For a similar approach, see also David S. Law, "Anatomy of a Conservative Court: Judicial Review in Japan," *University of Texas Law Review* 87 (2009): 1541–93.

cultural accounts of Japanese law. But institutional analysis, in particular its sociological variant, also takes into account internal understandings by actors who populate institutions, and so we ultimately see the present argument as complementing the dominant narrative rather than replacing it.

A word is in order on the concept of judicialization, by which we mean the expansion of judicial involvement in the formation and regulation of public policy. Our emphasis is on decision-making within the direct control of judges, rather than decisions by other political actors made in the shadow of judicial processes. Even focusing on the simple concept of judicialization, it is apparent that it is multidimensional and complex for several reasons. Judicialization may affect different policy areas, institutions and regions differently even within a single country. Judicialization can also ebb and flow, and so we thus should speak of degrees of judicialization, relative to some baseline.

Our chapter is organized as follows. Part I briefly introduces the concept of judicialization. Part II introduces the Japanese judiciary, and proceeds to examine the status of judicialization in Japan, considering historical and contemporary cases. Part III reviews theories that purport to explain the low levels of judicialization, finding that those associated with the rational choice school do a much better job of explaining the long period under LDP rule than the contemporary period. We then turn to the ideational factors that are our primary interest in Part IV. Part V concludes.

I. The Concept of Judicialization

There is a growing literature on the judicialization of politics, defined as an expansion of the role and authority of courts to make and influence policy decisions.[8] By judicialization of governance, we have in mind a broad conception of the expansion of judicial involvement in the formation and regulation of public policy. Expanded judicial power may come at the expense of bureaucratic power, as in the establishment of vigorous systems of judicial review of administrative action and judicially-policed

8. Martin Shapiro and Alec Stone Sweet, *On Law Politics and Judicialization* (New York, 2002); Tom Ginsburg and Albert Chen, eds., *The Judicialization of Administrative Governance in Asia* (New York, 2008); Ran Hirschl, "The New Constitutionalism and the Judicialization of Pure Politics," *Fordham Law Review* 75 (2006), 721.

processes of sub-legislative rule formation. It may come at the expense of politicians, so that political decision-making is shaped and constrained by higher order principles articulated by judges. And it may come at the expense of private actors, who find their own freedom to create and organize rules is constrained by judicially created or enforced public policies.

Our emphasis is on decision-making within the direct control of judges, rather than decisions by other political actors made in the shadow of judicial processes. We also do not focus on the alternative concept of juridification, which concerns the penetration of legal discourse and procedure into new realms.[9] Japan strikes us as a society that is highly juridified but not judicialized, in which legalism and rule-following play an important role, but courts do not.

Even focusing on the simple concept of judicialization, it is apparent that it is multidimensional and complex for several reasons. Judicialization may affect different policy areas, institutions and regions differently even within a single country. Judicialization can also ebb and flow. Notwithstanding Sweet's triadic model of governance, which seems to imply that judicialization is a one-way street, we can and do observe processes of "dejudicialization" in some times and places.[10] We thus should speak of degrees of judicialization, relative to some baseline.

In the discussion that follows, we will be comparing the levels of judicialization in Japan longitudinally, that is over time, and also comparatively with other advanced industrial societies. Notwithstanding extended writing on judicialization in Europe and Latin America, there have been few if any previous works explicitly applying the framework to Japan. We turn to that task in the next section.

II. The Status of Judicialization in Japan

The Japanese judiciary consists of some 3000 individual judges. There is a Supreme Court of 15 justices, eight High Courts located around the country, 50 judicial districts and some four hundred summary courts. Most judges join the judiciary as Assistant Judges and are appointed after completing their training at the Legal Training and Research Institute, which

9. Hirschl, "The New Constitutionalism," at 723.

10. Randall Peerenboom, "More Law, Less Courts: Legalized Governance, Judicialization and Dejudicialization in China" in Ginsburg and Chen, eds., *The Judicialization of Administrative Governance in Asia*, 175–201.

is run by the Supreme Court. This Institute is also the gateway to careers as prosecutors and practicing attorneys. Judges spend their careers in a series of jobs, rotating around the country, and occasionally being seconded to other organizations such as the Ministry of Justice. After ten years as an Assistant, a judge is appointed as a full Judge. Formally speaking, judges are subject to reappointment every ten years, though this is generally a routine matter. The members of the Supreme Court are selected by the Cabinet, and will typically include prosecutors and academics as well as career judges.

A key institution in the Japanese judiciary is the General Secretariat of the Supreme Court, staffed by judges themselves. Among other tasks, this body makes the decisions about judicial rotation and promotion. It thus serves as a central institution for internal management and discipline within the judiciary.

In recent years, there has been a push toward including judges appointed from the ranks of practicing attorneys. The Justice System Reform Council, a high level government commission that recommended a series of major reforms in 2001, called for diversification in the background of judges, greater transparency in systems of appointment and promotion. The major result was the establishment of a lower court nomination commission, a majority of whose members are non-lawyers, with responsibility for approving nominees to join the courts. This body has rejected a small number of candidates in recent years. But the basic bureaucratic structure of the Japanese judiciary has remained intact.

It is a commonplace among English-language scholars of Japanese law that the Japanese judiciary is a relatively weak actor. In his recent analysis of the Supreme Court, David Law, describes it as the most conservative court in the world.[11] It is seen as passive to a fault, and incapable of enforcing its decisions. This no doubt stems from the low rate of overturning statutes, and some prominent cases in which the political branches seemed to ignore the court. The major exception is John Haley, who sees the judiciary as highly autonomous but not powerful; even Haley

11. Law, "Anatomy of a Conservative Court," 1545–93. See also Jun-ichi Satoh, "Judicial Review in Japan: An Overview of the Case Law and an Examination of Trends in the Japanese Supreme Court's Constitutional Oversight," *Loyola of Los Angeles Law Review* 41 (2008): 603–27.

acknowledges the conventional wisdom is that it has been seen "as by far the least influential, much less dangerous, branch."[12]

There is much disagreement about the sources of institutional quiescence. Shigenori Matsui advances argues the judges of the Supreme Court tend to view the Constitution as being more of an articulation of political principles than as a source of law, and hence are reluctant to enforce it.[13] J. Mark Ramseyer, writing alone and with various co-authors, has marshaled an array of evidence suggesting that the judiciary conforms to the preferences of the long-dominant Liberal Democratic Party (LDP), which he argued was able to influence the Supreme Court Secretariat.[14] Haley has challenged this view, arguing instead that Japanese judges "are among the most honest, politically independent, and professionally competent in the world today."[15]

We do not want to wade into this debate directly, but rather to examine the evidence. As Haley's comments suggest, statements about the Japanese judiciary tend to involve, at least implicitly, a comparative metric. Typically this is the courts of the United States, especially those of the activist Warren Court era, which is perhaps an unfair vantage point for any constitutional court. Even if one broadens the comparative metric, however, it is apparent that Japanese courts are relatively insulated from major issues of social and political controversy. This section traces a number of the major cases in Japanese history.

Courts in The Meiji and Taisho Era

The Japanese judiciary has its origins in the nineteenth-century Meiji modernization of Japan. Because the lack of independent adjudication was one of the main criticisms of the foreign powers that imposed unequal treaties on Japan, modernizers made the legal system a focus of reform, and within two decades had created a judicial system that was formally autonomous of the Ministry of Justice. In the famous incident at

12. John Haley, *The Spirit of Japanese Law* (Athens, Georgia, 1998), 90.

13. David Law and Shigenori Matsui, "Why is the Japanese Supreme Court so Conservative?" *Washington University Law Review* 88 (2011): 1375–1423.

14. J. Mark Ramseyer and Eric B. Rasmusen, *Measuring Judicial Independence* (Chicago, 2003).

15. John Haley, "The Japanese Judiciary: Maintaining Integrity, Autonomy, and the Public Trust," in Daniel Foote, ed., *Law in Japan: A Turning Point* (Seattle, 2007), 99. For more on the debate, see Frank Upham, "Political Lackeys or Faithful Public Servants? Two Views of the Japanese Judiciary," *Law and Social Inquiry* 30 (2005): 421–54.

Ōtsu in 1891, the Supreme Court resisted political pressure to sentence a rogue policeman to death for his attempt on the life of the Russian crown prince, a crime punishable only by life in prison. This ruling established the principle of judicial independence in the Japanese context, and remains a touchstone of the traditions of institutional autonomy.[16]

Autonomy, however, is hardly equivalent to the exercise of power. Indeed, reviewing the history of the Japanese courts in the pre-World War II era, one sees relatively limited involvement with the major social and political issues of the day. It was not that there were no problems to solve: Japan's industrialization and social change threw up a host of new and novel issues. Furthermore there were intra-elite struggles to resolve. But Japanese courts did not adjudicate disputes among the ruling elites known as the *genrō*, and *hosei-kanryo* who were the lawmaking bureaucrats in *Sumitsuin* [the Privy Council] and the Cabinet,[17] even though courts in other authoritarian have played such a role.[18] Nor did the courts play much of a role in resolving major social struggles, even if they were willing to uphold individual rights in some cases.

Take the issue of rural landlord-tenant disputes caused by rapid urbanization, one of the major issues in the early twentieth century in Japan. Landlords and tenants had historically negotiated their relationships in the context of semi-autonomous villages, which served both to reinforce social hierarchies but also to place limits on landlord exploitation. With urbanization, the landlords were less frequently in ongoing relationships with tenants; the social pressures that restrained their exercise of formal rights were breaking down, and there was a concomitant increase in exploitative behavior and formal assertion of rights.[19] The courts' role in these cases, as in others involving ongoing relationships, was to encourage private bargaining, sometimes by invoking the "consensus of the commu-

16. See discussion in Tom Ginsburg, "Studying Japanese Law Because it's There," *American Journal of Comparative Law* 58 (2010): 19–20. The incident also illustrates the control of senior judges over lower ranked judges.

17. See Shinichi Yamamuro, *Hosei-Kanryo no Jidai [Time of Legislative Bureaucracy]* (1984); Kenneth Colegrove, "The Japanese Privy Council," *American Political Science Review* 25 (1931): 589–614, 881–905.

18. See, e.g., Robert Barros, *Constitutionalism and Dictatorship* (New York, 2002) (discussing Chile).

19. Dimitri Vanoverbeke, *Community and State in the Japanese Farm Village: Farm Tenancy Conciliation (1924–1938)* (Leuven, 2004).

nity" in the place of the formal requirements of the Civil Code.[20] But the courts were not sufficient. Instead, the political leadership set up an alternative conciliation system to encourage the traditional values of harmony, and this became the major channel for adjudication of disputes.[21] Gradually, this conciliation system evolved from being an option to be suggested by the judge into a mandatory system in which parties had little power. The pattern was clear: the courts were not a proper forum for major social and political disputes. This pattern of channeling disputes away from the courts was to continue in the postwar era.[22]

Courts in the Postwar Era

The postwar courts continued to refrain from involvement in major social and political disputes. This was the case despite major issues of constitutional interpretation. One pattern was lower courts being relatively more aggressive, but then to be overruled by the more conservative Supreme Court. This was certainly the case in two of the more contentious issues in postwar Japanese politics, the interpretation of Article Nine of the Constitution of Japan, and the electoral malapportionment cases.

Article Nine. Perhaps the most well-known clause of the Japanese Constitution is the Article prohibiting the use of war materiel. The provision, drafted by the American bureaucrats of SCAP and modified by their Japanese interlocutors, was in place only a short time before the Korean War forced a revisiting of its provisions. Notwithstanding a clear provision on armed forces, the government has continuously sought to expand the role and responsibility of Japan's Self Defense Forces. In turn, constitutional literalists have sought to prevent Japan's rearmament.

Japan's Supreme Court was, early on, called to adjudicate between these positions in the 1959 *Sunakawa* Case.[23] The case concerned demonstrators who sought to challenge a special law regulating U.S. base fa-

20. John Haley, *Authority Without Power* (New York, 1991). The idea of "shakaitsunen" is a juridical concept interpreted by professional judges. It is distinct from mere deference to social customs, but rather is a mode in which the Japanese courts reshape the society by construing what is to be the customary law of the society in an artful manner

21. Ibid., 87–91; Vanoverbeke, *Farm Tenancy.*

22. Frank K. Upham, *Law and Social Change in Postwar Japan* (Cambridge, Mass., 1987).

23. Judgment of December 16, 1959, Supreme Court, Grand Bench, 13 *Keishū* 3225.

cilities under the 1952 Security Treaty. A lower court had decided that the treaty and the presence of U.S. forces in Japan were unconstitutional under Article Nine. In deciding that only "obvious" constitutional violations should be overturned by the Court, the majority stated that "there is a certain element of incompatibility in the process of judicial determination of its constitutionality by a court of law which has as its mission the exercise of the purely judicial function."[24] This abdication of judicial involvement in political questions set the tone for subsequent adjudication of Article Nine cases. Sometimes the courts relied on standing concerns to avoid reaching the constitutional questions. This was the approach of the Supreme Court in the Naganuma Nike Missile Site Case (1982), which reversed a lower court finding that SDF unconstitutional. [25]

The language of *Sunakawa* is telling on another dimension as well however. The Court's insistence on preserving its ability to exercise purely judicial functions suggests that it had, in its internal understanding, a concept of "pure" judging. We will return to this concept later on in Part III.

Electoral Malapportionment. Another prominent series of cases was that concerning the apportionment of electoral districts in Japan. Indeed, two out of the eight Japanese Supreme Court decisions holding legislative acts unconstitutional concern elections. The ruling Liberal Democratic Party (LDP) had long relied on a base of voters in the countryside and so sought to overweight rural votes. An early challenge to the malapportionment on equality grounds was rejected in a 1964 ruling by the Supreme Court in the *Koshiyama* case.[26] The *Koshiyama* court rejected the appeal before it and adopted language of deference to the Diet as the political body best able to balance competing considerations. In 1976 the question of the constitutionality of malapportionment was again an issue before the Court in *Kurokawa v. Chiba*.[27] In an election for the House of Repre-

24. *Sunakawa Case*, 13 *Keishū* 3225 (Sup. Ct., 1959), available at http://www.courts.go.jp/english/judgments/text/1959.12.16-1959-A-No.710.html (trans.) (Sec. 2, paragraph 4 of the majority decision).

25. *Naganuma Case*, (1982). See also David S. Law, *The Myth of Imposed Constitutionalism*, manuscript.

26. *Koshiyama v. Tokyo Election Management Commission*, 18 *Minshu* 279 (Sup. Ct. G.B., 1964).

27. *Kurokawa v. Chiba Prefecture Election Commission*, 30 *Minshu* 223 (Sup. Ct. G.B., 1976).

sentatives, the Grand Bench looked at the disparity in the malapportionment, which amounted to nearly 5 to 1 in the Chiba district in question, and decided that it constituted an unreasonable level of malapportionment proportion. In its decision the court asserted that "voting is a historically significant popular political struggle and equal protection under the constitution was aimed at equal voting rights." The Court, however, refused to set a precise allowable ratio for future cases, nor did it void the contested election in question.[28]

The *Kurokawa* decision strongly implied that the Diet should correct the malapportionment, but by most accounts it failed to do so. The LDP continued to rely on small farmers as a core constituency, and had little incentive to equalize rural and urban vote strength. This again became an issue in 1986, in *Kanao v. Hiroshima*.[29] The Diet had not made any changes to the ratio since the *Kurokawa* decision, and the question of a 4 to 1 ratio was discussed. This time the court looked at two questions: first, had there been a reasonable time for the Diet to make adjustments in the ratio? And second, was the ratio reasonably within the Diet's discretionary power? Because it had been several years since *Kurokawa*, the court reached the conclusion that the Diet had had sufficient time to revise the system. Still, the Court declined to establish a specific level to be deemed reasonable. Furthermore, as in the *Kurokawa* case, the election was not invalidated. This gave rise to the possibility of what was called a "circumstance decision," which allowed the election to stand, even if the election rules were held unconstitutional.

Since then, there have been several cases discussing the constitutionally appropriate or allowable ratio of malapportionment, but no definitive answer has been provided by the courts. The pattern here is an apparent hesitancy on the part of the Court to order the Diet to act. Rather, the Court has preferred to set loose standards for the Diet to follow and wait for cases to be brought. A major electoral reform by the Diet in 1994 reduced the number of districts, and suggested that the revised redistricting plan should achieve a ratio of no more than 2:1 between largest and smallest districts. But in a subsequent case, the Supreme Court held that, although the law sought to establish a 2:1 ratio of malapportionment,

28. Dissenting opinion of Justice Seiichi Kishi, in Hiroshi Itoh And Lawrence Beer, *The Constitutional Case Law Of Japan, 1961–1970* (Seattle, 1978) at 372.

29. *Kanao v. Hiroshima Election Management Commission*, 39 *Minshu* 1100 (Sup. Ct. G.B., 1985).

in the instant election a greater ratio was allowable, in part because of concern that residents of sparsely populated prefectures continue to have their views reflected in national politics.[30] It thus justified malapportionment on a theory of representation.

Corporate Donations Case. In 1970, in the Yahata Steel Company case, the Court rejected a derivative suit brought by a shareholder against two directors of Yahata Steel who contributed money to the LDP.[31] The argument was that the donation to political parties deviated from the business purpose prescribed in the company charter and violated the duty of loyalty and the duty of care. The court held that there was no distinction between these duties and that corporate contributions to political campaigns were legal. Companies like natural persons, had a right to participate in politics. This decision, which anticipated the U.S. Supreme Court case of *Citizens United* forty years later, was grounded in private rights of participation, and framed as a conflict among those rights.[32] This is an example of a case that appears to uphold liberty, but does so in a way that reinforced the existing political structure in Japan so as not to challenge political authorities.[33]

In short, Japan's courts have tended to reinforce the status quo in politically charged cases during much of the postwar era. It is not that law played no role in underpinning economic growth and ordering private affairs; on the contrary, the particular vision of law that Japan adopted facilitated the developmental state model by insulating the administration from private lawsuits and by rarely exercising the power of judicial review of legislation. At the same time, the courts were by all accounts fair and unbiased in resolving civil disputes among private parties. Contracts were enforced and property rights protected, key factors for contemporary un-

30. Supreme Court Grand Bench Decision of November 10, 1999, (1) 53 *Minshu* 8-1577, 1696 *Hanji* 48, *Hanta* 114, (2) 53 *Minshu* 8-1704, 1696 *Hanji* 46, 1018 *Hanta* 114 (dismissing approximately 31 appeals of citizen groups from lower court decisions seeking nullification of the House of Representatives election of October 20, 1996). The decision is available at www.senrei.com/const6.htm.

31. *Judgment of the "Yahata-seitetsu" Case*, 1966 (O) No. 444, 24 *Minshu*, no. 6, 625 (Sup. Ct. G.B., 1970).

32. *Citizen United v. FEC*, 130 S Ct 876 (2010).

33. Yoichi Higuchi, *Kenpō toiu Sakui [Constitution as Artificiality]* (Tokyo, 2009), 157, 160 (arguing that the Court is active in upholding government policies).

derstandings of the legal bases of economic development.[34] Indeed, there was substantial judicial creativity in these private realms, generally involving issues such as landlord-tenant relations or family law that did not enter the explicitly political sphere.

Courts in the Heisei Era

The Heisei era (1989–present) has been one of major institutional change in Japanese law. Beginning in the early 1990s and accelerating toward the second half of the decade, there has been a major movement in Japanese society to expand the role of law and, by extension, the courts in society. Much of this responded to a sense that the earlier developmental model had run its course, as Japan entered a long period of recession. As put by the Justice System Reform Council, Japan needed to move from an "ex ante planning society to an ex post, remedies society."[35] By this it was meant that the society should develop a more liberal basis, in which firms and individuals could pursue their vision of the good, subject only to limits imposed by the freedoms of others. When interests clashed, it would be up the courts, and the legal system with its expanded capacities, to resolve disputes. This vision was the basis of major reforms of Japanese legal institutions, including the establishment of a system of lay participation in criminal cases (*saiban-in seido*), the creation of a new system of legal education, the expansion of prosecutorial review commissions, and many reforms to substantive law. For our purposes, changes to the system of appointing judges to encourage more practicing lawyers to enter the profession was a central one, as it seemed designed to ensure more links between the judiciary and society and to partially undermine the conservatism induced by the judicial hierarchy.

It has now been a decade since the reform process was blessed by the Justice System Reform Council, and many changes have been achieved. Have they been accompanied by judicialization? In the section below, we review many of the major cases of this era. Our argument is that Japanese courts systematically distinguish between issues involving statutory and constitutional rights, which are the proper province of judicial decision-making, from cases involving public policy issues. What we show is that the courts are independent and even activist as far as rights issues are con-

34. Douglass North, *Institutions, Institutional Change, and Economic Performance* (New York, 1991).

35. Shiho Seido Kaikaku Shingikai, Final Report, 2001.

cerned, but are systematically averse to any issue that potentially involves the court in "political" issues.[36] It is this pattern that marks the distinct approach of Japanese courts, and distinguishes them from other judiciaries that have willingly taken on a greater role in public policy.

The Shrine Visit Cases. Tokyo's Yasukuni Shrine, where Japan's war dead are enshrined, has long provoked controversy among Japan's Asian neighbors. With the rise of the revisionist faction of the Liberal Democratic Party, politicians have sought to visit the shrine in their "private capacity" to honor the war dead. These controversies came to the fore after the election of Junichiro Koizumi as Prime Minister in 2001, and his visits in 2001 and 2002 provoked serious challenges in relations with Korea, China and other countries.

The shrine visits led to several legal cases. A group of citizens joined by Shin Buddhists, Protestants and the war bereaved sought to enjoin the visit as a violation of the separation of church and state guaranteed by Article 20 of the Constitution. The Supreme Court held, on the merits, that the Prime Minister's visit alone did not constitute a tort, as the plaintiff could not show that his claim was within the zone of legally protected interests. The Court thus decided the issue on a non-constitutional basis, even though it raised interesting questions about the liberty of a politician to act in his private capacity. Justice Shigeo Takii suggested in his concurrence that the case might implicate Article 20, but the Court did not reach the issue, instead framing it as a private matter and using a civil law "zone of interest" test to dismiss the case.[37]

Several other cases were brought in district courts surrounding these visits, many by survivors of Japan's wartime atrocities in other Asian countries. In only one of six cases, the Yamaguchi Case heard in Fukuoka, did the judges rule in April that the pilgrimages were unconstitutional. But the court dismissed the suit.

36. We recognize that the distinction between political and non-political issues, like that between public policy and the private sphere, is hardly self-evident. We are not arguing that the distinction is a real one; rather it is an artifact of positivist legal theory, which has influenced Japan among other states. Our contention is that Supreme and Constitutional Courts in other jurisdictions have been willing to decide against the government in the kinds of cases we consider.

37. Sup Ct 2nd Bench decision of June 23, 2006, 1940 *Hanji* 122 (2006).

Recent SDF Cases. The first Gulf War marked the beginning of renewed pressure, both within Japan and from abroad, for its Self Defense Forces to participate in collective self-defense efforts. Recent deployments in Iraq and Afghanistan have stretched the limits even further. The Cabinet Legislation Bureau, which has a formal role in issuing constitutional interpretations for the government, has taken the lead, and its decisions have generated constitutional challenges.

Even when the lower courts have become involved in determinations of the constitutionality of military operations, they have shied away from major constraints on government. For example, when the Nagoya High Court heard a 2008 challenge to SDF deployment in Iraq, it denied relief based on the lack of ripeness, even though it found in dicta a violation of Article Nine.[38] In short, the courts have made some suggestive statements but have played no effective role in shaping policy in this central area, in which constitutional language is fairly clear.

Adjudicating History. Japan's war legacy continues to be a major issue in Asian politics, and there have been attempts by some victims to pursue legal claims. These include challenges from foreign "comfort women," from Chinese forced laborers and from Taiwanese soldiers. In the cases brought by Chinese citizens who had been forced to labor in wartime Japan, lower courts refused the plaintiffs' claims for compensation on the grounds that the claims were barred by the Joint Communique between Japan and the People's Republic of China, but acknowledged the victims' suffering at the hands of the Japanese authorities.[39] The Supreme Court ultimately rejected the appeals. In the "comfort women" cases, several lower court rulings found that the Japanese government ought to bear responsibility but concluded that the postwar peace treaties bar the victims who are now Korean or Chinese citizens from suing the Japanese government in Japan. The rationale of the Court's 2007 decision on Chinese

38. Nagoya High Court, Apr. 17, 2008 (unpublished decision), http://www.hahei-sashidome.jp/hanketsu_kouso; discussed in Craig Martin, "Binding the Dogs of War: Japan and the Constitutionalizing of Jus Ad Bellum," *University of Pennsylvania Journal of Constitutional Law* 30 (2008): 267–357.

39. See Judgment, http://www.courts.go.jp/english/judgments/text/2007.04.27-2004.-Ju-.No..1658.html; see also "Chinese Forced Labor Case Rejected," *The Japan Times*, available at http://search.japantimes.co.jp/cgi-bin/nn20090310a6.html.

forced labors applied.[40] On the other hand, Taiwanese soldiers who had served in the Japanese military were successful in obtaining compensation after the Court ruled that the Diet should indeed pay their pensions.

Hansen's Disease. Japan retained very severe policies toward those with Hansen's disease, commonly known as leprosy, late into the twentieth century. Mandatory quarantine laws were only repealed in 1996, long after similar policies disappeared from Europe.[41] Victims were kept isolated from society, and many forced to undergo sterilization, even though reliable treatments were available by the end of the 1950s. The victims sought greater inclusion in society, and began to use the courts in the late 1990s, seeking compensation for denial of constitutional rights.[42] In 2001, a large group of Hansen's disease sufferers won a district court case against the government in Kumamoto. The court ruled that the 1953 Leprosy Prevention Law had encouraged discrimination, and that the government should have encouraged integration of Hansen's patients after drug therapy became available in the 1950s. To the surprise of many, the government of Prime Minister Koizumi decided not to appeal, even though many bureaucrats had hoped that it would. Koizumi also apologized, helping to establish his reputation as a reformer.[43] This represented a very different tack from that taken with the prominent AIDS related-litigation by hemophiliacs, which had led to settlements without a government admission of wrongdoing.[44] The Diet subsequently passed a compensation bill, and concluded settlements with various victims not directly covered.

These cases generated some litigation in Korea and Taiwan from people who thought they should also be eligible for abuses that had taken place during the colonial period. These cases were encouraged by members of the Japanese bar, but they had different levels of success. The Japanese colonial regime had not directly applied Japanese law in Korean territory and so the hospital statute did not apply there. In Taiwan, in contrast,

40. See Nagoya High Court ruling May 31, 2007, 54 *Shomu Geppo* 287. The Supreme Court refused to hear the appeal (Sup Ct decision Nov. 11, 2008).

41. The 1996 repeal was pushed by later Prime Minister Naoto Kan during his time as Minister of Health and Welfare.

42. Jeffrey Kingston, *Japan's Quiet Transformation* (London, 2004), 188.

43. Ibid., 192.

44. Ronald Bayer and Eric Feldman, eds., *Blood Feuds: AIDS, Blood, and the Politics of Medical Disaster* (New York, 1999); Kingston, *Japan's Quiet Transformation*, 168.

there was direct application of some Japanese rules, and the court held that a reasonable reading of the statute, which gave coverage to "any establishment" set up under the law, would include a Taiwanese hospital.[45] The Diet subsequently amended the compensation law to cover Korea as well, and both Taiwanese and Korean victims were compensated.

Equality Cases. Two recent Supreme Court cases regarding equality are worth mentioning.[46] In 2005, Japanese citizens living abroad won the right to vote in national elections.[47] In 2008, the Supreme Court invalidated a provision in the Nationality Law that effectively disqualified children who were born by Japanese father and non-Japanese mothers from acquiring Japanese nationality.[48] After the Supreme Court decision, such children now are recognized as Japanese. This decision has been described as "epoch-making."[49] In reviewing the decision, it is clear that the Japanese justices take the rights of individuals seriously. The interpretive statement of the *chosakan* (the staff judge who serves as a clerk in the case) cited other countries' jurisprudence, and Justice Izumi's concurring opinion sought to articulate a kind of intermediate scrutiny standard in the

45. Tokyo District Court Ruling, Oct. 25, 2005, 1910 *Hanrei Jiho* 69; see also 1910 *Hanrei Jiho* 36 (on Korea).

46. Craig Martin, "Glimmers Of Hope: The Evolution of Equality Rights Doctrine in Japanese Courts from a Comparative Perspective," *Duke Journal of International and Comparative Law* 20 (2010): 167–246.

47. In 1998, the Diet amended the Public Offices Election Act to make it possible for Japanese nationals living overseas to vote in Diet elections. However, a Supplementary Provision allowed overseas voters to vote only in the proportional representation component of the lower house electoral system, and not in the single-member elections for the House of Representatives or for councilors elected from prefectures. See Case to seek declaration of illegality of deprivation of the right to vote of Japanese citizens residing abroad, 2001 (Gyo-Tsu) No. 82, 2001 (Gyo-Hi) No. 76, 2001 (Gyo-Tsu) No. 83, 2001 (Gyo-Hi) No. 77, 2005.09.14. For the text in English, see http://www.courts.go.jp/english/judgments/text/2005.09.14-2001.-Gyo-Tsu-.No..82,.2001.-Gyo-Hi-.No..76,.2001.-Gyo-Tsu-.No..83,.2001.-Gyo-Hi-.No..77.html.

48. See Judgment concerning whether a child who was born, out of wedlock, to a native Japanese father and mother from the Philippines, 2000 (Gyo-Hi) No. 149, English judgment: http://www.courts.go.jp/english/judgments/text/2004.07.08-2000-Gyo-Hi-No..149.html. See also *The Japan Times*, http://search.japantimes.co.jp:80/cgi-bin/nn20080605a1.html.

49. Martin, "Glimmers of Hope," 223, n. 149 (citing Hasebe Yasuo, "Kokusekiho ikkenhanketsu no shisoyoshiki [The Pattern of Thought in the Judgment Holding the Nationality Act Unconstitutional]," *Jurist* 77 (2008), 1366.

case, which if adopted might have more widespread implications of equality jurisprudence. The case was significant in that issues of nationality go to the core of Japan's self-conception as a nation. The Diet was somewhat reluctant to amend the law after the case, though it eventually did so to excise the unconstitutional provisions.

Other Constitutional Rights. Courts in Japan have been willing to find violations of individual rights when the violations are clear. A major issue in involving free expression concerned schoolteachers who refuse to honor the Japanese flag or sing the national anthem, the *kimigayo*, because of its association with wartime militarism. With the election of nationalist demagogue Shintaro Ishihara in 1999, the Tokyo City Government became more vigorous in pressuring teachers to participate in such activities. In September 2006, the Tokyo District Court found that the city had violated the constitutional guarantee of freedom of thought, but the decision was recently reversed by the Tokyo High Court.[50] In February 2008, the same District Court found that the city had exceeded its discretion in punishing a set of activist teachers.[51] Relying on their past refusal to honor the flag and anthem at graduation ceremonies, the City had cut their pay and refused to re-hire them on a part-time basis after they had retired. The Court held that, although its directive making the patriotic displays mandatory was constitutional, the City had exceeded its discretion in punishing the plaintiffs and awarded roughly US$258,000 in damages. But this case too was reversed by the High Court, in January 2010.[52] Similar lawsuits elsewhere have failed or been overturned on appeal.

Are There Any Signs of Judicialization? There has not been a major shift toward judicialization in the Heisei era, which is somewhat puzzling given the major social and political effort to expand the role of courts. We should perhaps expect this self-conscious effort at institutional design to bear some fruit in the form of a higher profile for the judiciary. But to date there have been relatively few appointments from outside the judiciary.

50. Associated Press, "Japanese Teachers Win Patriotism Suit," *New York Times*, February 7, 2008; Reversal was by the Tokyo high court, Jan. 28, 2011. See also http://www.courts.go.jp/english/judgments/text/2007.02.27-2004.-Gyo-Tsu-.No..328.html.

51. Ibid.

52. http://search.japantimes.co.jp/cgi-bin/ed20110208a1.html.

Material incentives keep the best private attorneys from seeking to join the courts, and so the traditional structures remain intact.

There are some tentative hints that increasing public involvement in the judicial system may affect the decisions of legal actors. One example comes from Prosecutorial Review Commissions (PRC), in which 11 citizens review decisions of non-prosecution, and have the power to recommend prosecution. Japanese prosecutors have always been willing to go after corrupt politicians: indeed, some of the major figures of postwar politics, such as Tanaka Kakuei and Kanemaru Shin, have felt the sting of criminal prosecution. This speaks to the integrity of the judicial process and the rule of law, and suggests that the view that Japanese judicial actors "avoid politics" is too simple a formulation. In this regard, one recent case of significant interest concerns Ozawa Ichiro, the opposition kingpin who stepped down from his position with the Democratic Party of Japan in summer 2010 after a financial scandal. Prosecutors initially decided that there was not enough evidence to indict him; but a prosecutorial review committee (PRC), a subgroup of eleven anonymous citizens that examines cases of non-prosecution, recommended another look.[53] At the end of January 2011, Ozawa was indicted by private attorneys—recommended by the second Tokyo Bar Association and appointed by the Tokyo District Court to represent the PRC—for misreporting political funds.[54] The story suggests that public pressure can, on occasion, lead to action on the part of judicial actors. Increasing transparency of the legal system might lead to renewed pressures in this regard. But it is far from a sure thing, notwithstanding the major reform process.

Another sign on the horizon are certain statements by ex-Justices that the court should play a more active role in electoral cases.[55] Finally, it is worth noting that in March 2011, the Supreme Court ruled that the 1994 electoral system was "in a state of unconstitutionality" because of vote disparities and called on the legislature to fix it.[56] This was the first time the Court had issued such a ruling on the 1994 electoral reform, having previously upheld the system on three occasions. Because the un-

53. NHK World, 27 April 2010.

54. Jun Hongo and Masami Ito, "Ozawa charged over funds misreporting," *The Japan Times*, 1 February, 2011, 1.

55. Tokuji Izumi, "Concerning the Japanese Public's Evaluation of Supreme Court Justices," *Washington University Law Review* 88 (2011): 1.

56. *Mainichi Daily News*, March 24, 2011.

constitutional vote disparity of 2.3 was in the range that had previously been ruled constitutional, one has a quantitative indication of creeping expansion of the court's doctrine in this area, though it is too early to say if it constitutes a trend.

III. Explanations for Limited Judicialization

The overall picture of this survey is one of relatively limited judicialization. What might explain this pattern? One might attribute the limited level of judicial involvement to the non-existence of a Japanese Constitutional Court, which can authoritatively restrain political actors in the name of higher law. Yet this explanation is clearly insufficient. Other countries with a unified judicial system have been part of the trend toward judicialization. And the Japanese Supreme Court does have the formal power of constitutional review.[57] To be sure, it has used the power sparingly, striking government action in a total of eight cases on constitutional grounds since 1946. But judicialization involves more than constitutional review; and so the claim that timidity in constitutional adjudication limits the courts in other areas is not convincing.

Furthermore, the claim that constitutional timidity drives the courts ignores the significant gap between lower courts and the Supreme Court on various matters. Lower courts have at times been willing to make controversial anti-government rulings, though these are with some frequency overturned by the courts of appeals.

Other conventional explanations do not seem to fully account for the pattern. In recent years, political explanations rooted in rational choice theory have had a good deal of influence in comparative understandings of judicialization. J. Mark Ramseyer, who pioneered these theories in the Japanese case, emphasized electoral alternation as a key factor.[58] Ran Hirschl has a theory of judicial empowerment that he calls "hegemonic preservation" focusing on departing elites who want to preserve their policies into the future.[59] One of us has a version of this argument that he calls political insurance.[60] All of these influential theories have a common flaw in the Japanese case: they all predict that the de-

57. Japan Const., Art. 81.
58. Ramseyer, "Puzzling (In)dependence."
59. Ran Hirschl, *Towards Juristocracy* (Cambridge, Mass., 2004).
60. Tom Ginsburg, *Judicial Review in New Democracies* (New York, 2003).

cline of the LDP would lead to significant judicial empowerment. And although we have observed some increased resources devoted to the judiciary, the judges have not fundamentally changed their passive approach to deciding public policy issues. Hirschl's theory would predict a major effort by the LDP to empower the courts to preserve its policies in the future; Ginsburg and Ramseyer would predict that both major parties would have a shared interest in such a policy. It may indeed be the case that such an effort has been made. But without a court willing to take the football, it is hardly worth trying to make the pass. As such, the insurance and hegemonic preservation theories do not seem to fit well in understanding contemporary Japan. And it appears that judicial attitudes may form a key constraint.

We also have theories that focus on institutional structure. It is certainly the case that the hierarchical structure of the Japanese judiciary discourages public policy innovation. But this is, in many ways, an outcome to be explained rather than an independent reason for non-judicialization. Why is it that Japanese judges stay away from public policy issues even when they might be able to be more involved? The next section focuses on a particular legal theory as the key factor.

IV. The Role of Ideas

The Organ Theory: Prussian Origins

Like other recent accounts of Japanese judicial conservatism, we emphasize the importance of ideas and institutional self-understandings.[61] We differ from other accounts in our emphasis on a particular set of ideas, German in origin, which have received greatest institutional expression in Japanese constitutionalism. These are the ideas underlying the so-called "organ theory" of Japanese constitutional interpretation. Western scholars of Japan may be familiar with the organ theory in light of debates over the constitutional status of the emperor that arose in the drafting of the 1946 Constitution.[62] But the theory extends beyond the question of whether or not the emperor was the embodiment of sovereignty or an organ of the constitution itself.

The organic theory draws on a broader set of nineteenth-century German ideas that saw the state as an inherent central part of the con-

61. Law and Matsui, "Why is the Japanese Supreme Court so Conservative?"

62. Ray Moore and Donald Robinson, *Partners for Democracy* (New York, 2004).

stitutional order. The purpose of constitutionalism was not so much a political movement to guarantee democratic self-governance so much as a set of auto-limitations established by the state in the name of the *Rechtstaat*. Within the constitutional state, the polity is analogized to a body composed of different organs, each of which must exercise its proper role to ensure proper functioning of the system. Power in this conception is spread throughout the system, and not dependent on a higher authority. Just as the brain cannot order the heart not to beat, so it is impossible for coequal organs to be superior to each other. Instead, each organ receives its power from the source of constitutional authority, whether the emperor as in the Meiji Constitution, or the people under the theory of the 1946 document.

This approach is quite distinct from French and American theories of the separation of powers. In the American tradition, the separation of powers jurisprudence focuses heavily on drawing the line between executive and legislative activities, and many of the cases concern *legislative* over-reaching.[63] In the French tradition, the separation of powers was targeted differently;[64] after the Revolution, it has historically been targeted at the judiciary and the historically rooted fear of *government du juges*. Under the Fifth Republic, there has been the additional twist of seeking to ensure, through the creation of the *Conseil Constitutionnel*, that legislative lawmaking power does not interfere with that of the executive. In each case, the conception of power is essentially Montesquiean in character. Power comes in three flavors, and only three, and there is little room for the modern administrative state. In each case, a neutral third party—the courts in the U.S. case, the *Conseil* in the French—is set up as a guardian of the separation of powers scheme.

The German tradition is quite different. As a late-developing state, Germany (and Japan) was in the position of organizing a state before it really had a modern economy, and so there was a sense of necessity to the state-building enterprise. Naturally, this led to interest in providing constitutional legitimacy to the administrative apparatus. As one of us has written elsewhere, "Prussian-German constitutionalism is an imitation of, and reaction against, its French counterpart. Its basic concern is

63. See, for example, *Bowsher v. Synar*; *Buckley v. Valeo*; *INS v. Chadha* (Opinion of Powell).

64. George Athan Billias, "American Constitutionalism and Europe, 1776–1848," in G. A. Billias, ed., *American Constitutionalism Abroad* (Westport, Conn., 1990), 13, 18.

the creation, not the division, of a sovereign power."[65] Instead of viewing society as the ultimate legitimator of the state, the state has an independent organic vitality and is a proper bearer of rights and duties within the polity. The ultimate right of the state is to govern. There is room in the theory for the existence of rights and liberties of citizens, but rights are not the starting point or ultimate criteria of constitutional legitimacy, and indeed democracy is in some tension with the statist theory. The people are not the source of rights. Instead, private rights and duties are granted by the state, rather than the other way around. For example, property rights are interpreted not as delegations of sovereign power to individuals by the state, but as rights of acquisition and utilization granted to citizens.[66] This is not to say that the state dominates private life; instead it must respect the public-private distinction. In the realm of private law the state can distribute rights to citizens, in accordance with what Carl Schmitt called as "principle of distribution."[67] If the government violates that principle, the proper redress for a politically powerless citizen is the judicial enforcement of his or her rights.[68] Thus, depoliticized private law empowers zones of pluralistic autonomy, and the state too is strictly limited by the *Rechtstaat* concept.

Courts are not central in this tradition. Whereas the Anglo-American tradition of the rule of law emphasizes the common law heritage of external judicial controls on administrative action, the *Rechtstaat* tradition focuses more on internalization of norms by government officials and structural constraints. The state itself is defined and empowered through law, and law is the tool to structure its internal relationships, strictly limiting the role of any one actor.

As mentioned above, this organic theory of constitutionalism has its origins in nineteenth-century German thought and fit the needs of developmental Meiji authoritarian state. In the Japanese context, the most influential thinkers were Otto von Gierke and Georg Jellinek.[69] Gierke's

65. Tokujin Matsudaira, "Judicialization of Politics and the Japanese Supreme Court," *Wasington University Law Review* 88 (2011), 1559.

66. Carl Schmitt, *The Concept of the Political*, trans. George Schwab (Chicago, 2006), 62–63.

67. Ibid.

68. Ibid.

69. Others included Paul Laband and Gerhard Anschutz. Frank O. Miller, *Minobe Tatsukichi: Interpreter of Constitutionalism in Japan* (Berkeley, 1965), 9.

great book, *Das Genoßenschaftsrecht*, was an exploration of the law of communal associations.[70] As part of the historical school associated with Friedrich von Savigny, von Gierke sought to develop normative theory out of historical inquiry into the development of German legal institutions. According to von Gierke, it was in the possibility of forming collective organizations that human society flourished, and the state emerged only out of a very long process of evolution of such associations. Though rooted in a logic of voluntary associations, the state had distinctive qualities as it encompassed all other collectivities. As he put it, "the state alone cannot be subordinate as sovereign collective person to any organized will power external to and above it, and consequently it cannot be limited in its will and action by a higher community participating in its decisions."[71] This theory was organic in that it did not rest on a fundamental opposition between individual and state.

While the concept of the *Genoßenschaft* focused on the state *qua* state, as opposed to the government, the theory was quite compatible with a meritocratically selected, insulated government bureaucracy. Of course, that institution has a long history in East Asia, and provided some means for people of ordinary birth to influence government in the absence of democratic legitimation. The emergence of the modern civil service in Germany and Japan fit well with the organ theory: the bureaucrats had a legitimate role to play in national affairs, in contrast with an Anglo-American distrust of the modern administrative state. The bureaucracy was not seen as sovereign or dominant in the organ theory, but within its realm of expertise, was an autonomous actor free from the vagaries of democratic politics. Meritocracy is itself representative in that it is anti-aristocratic, and this provided some mode of participation.

The theory was attractive to Japanese thinkers who found themselves in a similar developmental imperative to that of Germany. The bottom-up character of von Gierke's theory and its communitarian focus fit well with the Japanese tradition of the self-regulating village or *mura*. The romantic overtones of ethnic solidarity were also a better fit than, say the French ideas of equality of citizenship and natural rights. The Chinese tradition, in which the state was itself seen as a natural phenomenon, and

70. Sobei Mogi, *Otto von Gierke: His Political Teachings and Life* (London, 1932); Rupert Emerson, *State and Sovereignty in Modern Germany* (New Haven, 1928), 129–42.

71. Otto Von Gierke, *Die Genoßenschaftstheorie*, 641–42, quoted in Mogi, *Otto von Gierke*, at 185.

in theory unlimited by higher authority, was powerful in the Japanese consciousness in the early years of Meiji, which had adopted the *Ritsuryo* structure as a stopgap before Western structures could be effectively imported. The German model became even more attractive after the defeat of France in 1871, imbuing the theoretical compatibilities with an aura of objective superiority as well.

The organic theory entered the Japanese academic context through Ichiki Kitokuro, who was a bureaucrat and Professor of Law at Tokyo University. He in turn was the mentor of the great constitutional theorist Tatsukichi Minobe.[72] Minobe tried to rationalize the popular concept of the *kokutai*, or national polity. Under this theory, the emperor himself was only an "organ of the State" rather than himself being an embodiment of sovereignty beyond the state itself. The relevant provisions of the Meiji Constitution held that the Emperor was "sacred and inviolable" (Article 3) but also "the head of the Empire, combining in Himself the rights of sovereignty, and exercises them, according to the provisions of the present Constitution" (Article 4). This latter provision, according to Minobe, brought the emperor within rather than outside the constitutional framework. He drew on the analogy of the head of the human body to describe the role of the emperor: the Emperor was the supreme organ, but an organ nonetheless.

Minobe's view was opposed by imperial absolutists like Shinkichi Uesugi, a student of Jellinek and the Japanese scholar Hozumi Yatsuka, whose views diverged. Rooted in the German historical school, Uesugi promoted ideas of imperial supremacy and absolute monarchy that proved attractive to the militarists who seized power in the 1930s. As Minobe summarized the differences between the two views: "Among scholars who explain our state law there are those who frequently assert that the monarch is the subject of governmental power. This is an inadmissible error... the state alone is the subject of governmental power, and the monarch is an organ of the state."[73] Minobe himself was subjected to withering criticism, including investigation on charges of *lèse majesté* and political attacks in the Diet in 1935.[74] This led to his total withdrawal from public discourse. But in the aftermath of the military defeat, the organ theory

72. See Miller, *Minobe Tatsukichi*.

73. Ibid., 27.

74. Ibid., 196–253.

again proved useful to understand how a formerly divine emperor could become a constitutional monarch. Minobe's theory was redeemed during debates over the 1946 Constitution.[75]

Even before the militarist interlude, the organic theory developed deep roots in Japanese institutions. The organ theory served as theoretical basis for the fights among the different services in World War II. Each of these claimed responsibility for its own domain. Indeed, this was the source of some backlash against General Tojo, the military leader hanged after the Tokyo War Crimes Trial. Tojo was chosen as Prime Minister by Hirohito in late 1941, just before Pearl Harbor, after serving as Army Minister. During his tenure, he retained the post of Army Minister and also served at various points as the Minister of Home Affairs, Foreign Affairs, Education and Commerce. This embodiment of multiple posts was incompatible with the notion that each body had its own designated role, and this hastened Tojo's downfall in July 1944. Even a strongman like Tojo failed to concentrate organically distinct powers into a single person.

What did the organ theory mean for the judiciary? Recall that the modern judiciary is a creation of the Meiji era, a defensive move to free Japan from the yoke of the unequal treaties, rather than a long-standing institution with deep cultural roots. Yet, like any constitutional organ, it had a defined role to play. In the Japanese conception, this was mainly the realm of private law. The courts' role was to adjudicate private disputes involving legal rights; but it was not conceived of as enforcing a social contract or serving to protect the people from an overbearing state. The courts in the colonies played a similar role. Professor Wang Tay-sheng finds that the prewar courts in Taiwan tended to be fairly high quality with regard to ordinary civil cases, but were very reluctant to make any holdings that appeared to constrain Imperial authority. The judges found the "Movement for a Taiwan Parliament" not guilty.

Under the organ theory the state's legislative power was to be carried out first and foremost by the legislature, so the theory would sit uncomfortably with judicial review by ordinary judges.[76] This was not an issue under the Meiji Constitution, which did not provide judges with explicit power to supervise the parliament. But it may have hampered the postwar attempt to create a vigorous judicial oversight.

75. Moore and Robinson, *Partners for Democracy.*

76. Miller, *Minobe Tatsukichi,* at 127

The Postwar Retention of the Organ Theory

Precisely because of their notion of avoiding constraint of public authority, Japanese judges were relatively quiet during the militaristic period. At the same time, the military regime did not rely heavily on courts to carry out its policies. Rather, they seemed content to allow the courts to continue to operate in their own autonomous realm of governing private law.

Precisely because the courts had stayed out of public affairs, they were not targeted for purges after the war, as were the military and political organs. Like the rest of the Japanese bureaucracy, there was a good deal of continuity between prewar and postwar personnel, and hence no sharp ideological break. Nineteenth-century German positivism survived intact, and with it the organ theory. (To be sure, there was a large break in terms of the treatment of the Emperor, who we have already described as being outside the organic structure in the views of the militaristic faction. But with the triumph of Minobe's ideas after World War II, the organ theory encompassed the entire Japanese state structure.

This continuity has profound implications for the relationship of government, people and judiciary. The central government, representing the Japanese nation-state, still monopolizes all sources of political legitimacy and exercises powers with the presumption of constitutionality.[77] The state strips individuals and groups of *powers*, reassigning to them *rights* in return.[78] Property rights are interpreted not as delegations of sovereign power to individuals by the state, but as guarantees of freedom to citizens through juristic institutions in compensation for their de-politicization. By contrast, the self-binding state is free to meddle in the periphery of private autonomy so long as it does not disproportionately infringe on rights of citizens. The de-politicized citizenry enjoys private rights, but cannot rely on *judicial* enforcement of rights to displace *political* decisions.

Japan is now a democracy, so that citizens can assume public office and participate in the selection of representatives; but the Diet is also just one organ of the state among many, not in principle superior to the bureaucracy, the emperor, or any other within their own zones of constitutionally granted authority. The political and administrative branches

77. Japan Const., Art. 41 (making the Diet "the highest organ of state power").

78. Schmitt, *The Concept of the Political*, 62–63; see also Yasuo Hasebe, Book Review, *Journal of Japanese Studies* 30 (2004): 189, 192.

possess authority that is presumptively constitutional, and the judicial branch will overturn that action only when the government action immoderately violates rights of the citizen. U.S.-style judicial review fits uneasily with such a conception, though there is a vein of American constitutional scholarship that promotes a somewhat analogous view that legislative activity is presumptively constitutional.[79]

Postwar Japanese democracy creates no incentive for the high court to judicialize politics. Instead, the Court falls back on its traditional conception of a distinction between public political authority and a pluralistic private realm by ensuring that citizens enjoy their economic freedoms and equality of suffrage. When citizen's subjective rights are under serious and direct threat, as in the equality cases and many private law matters, the courts will respond. When, on the other hand, citizens are claiming to represent an objective interest common to anyone in the society, such as in the Article Nine cases, the court tends to find the case not justiciable.[80]

The persistence of the organ theory is nowhere better illustrated than in the Final Report of the Justice System Reform Council itself:

> When likened to the human body, if the political branches constitute the heart and arteries, the judicial branch shall be said to be the veins. The series of reforms... such as political reform and administrative reform, are, so to speak, an effort to restore and strengthen the functions to make blood flow swiftly by removing extraneous crudescence in the heart and arteries. According to this metaphor, justice reform shall be considered to be aiming at harmonizing the body and improving its health by expanding and strengthening the scale and function of the justice system as part of what the "shape of our country" should be in

79. James B. Thayer, "The Origin and Scope of the American Doctrine of Constitutional Law," *Harvard Law Review* 7 (1893): 129–156 (courts "can only disregard the Act when those who have the right to make laws have not merely made a mistake, but have made a very clear one, —so clear that it is not open to rational question... This rule recognizes that, having regard to the great, complex, ever-unfolding exigencies of government, much which will seem unconstitutional to one man, or body of men, may reasonably not seem so to another; that the constitution often admits of different interpretations; that there is often a range of choice and judgment; that in such cases the constitution does not impose upon the legislature any one specific opinion, but leaves open this range of choice; and that whatever choice is rational is constitutional.")

80. See also Upham, *Law and Social Change.*

> the twenty-first century, with fundamental reflection on whether or not the existing veins were excessively small.[81]

We see these ideas, essentially principles of legal theory, as being at the root of the judicial self-conception in Japan. Japan's judges surely *are* independent when judged by formal criteria, and their record in this regard is admirable. There are no credible reports of judicial corruption; and there has been no overt influence by members of the political class (notwithstanding Professor Ramseyer's convincing evidence about implicit influence through the process of appointment and promotion).[82] At the same time *the reverse is also true*: just as politicians do not interfere with judges, judges do not interfere with politicians. The organ theory goes a long way toward explaining *both* phenomena, while previous work has tended to focus only on one or the other aspect of this relationship.

The organ theory has been challenged by various others at different points in modern Japanese history, but is remarkably persistent. In the prewar era, it was challenged by Uesuki and Hozumi from the right as being too liberal, and by the liberal left for being too conservative. In the postwar era, liberal academics have challenged it as well. In the political sphere, one of the recent challengers was Ozawa Ichiro, the now disgraced DPJ politician. Ozawa sought to revolutionize Japanese politics after the DPJ took over. His basic theme was to make political practice match the actual text of Japanese constitution. For example, he argued that the cabinet was superior to the bureaucracy, surely a radical position from the point of view of the theory that sees each constitutional organ playing its own role. He also argued for the supremacy of the Diet in forming the cabinet, in accordance with classical parliamentarism.

Ozawa and the DPJ also argued that the Emperor (or rather Imperial Household Agency) did not have independent authority to refuse a visit of the Chinese Vice President Xi Jinping in December 2009, so long as he was requested to accept by the cabinet. Xi had requested the visit on very short notice, not within the traditional thirty day period demanded by the Agency. The Agency viewed the Constitution's provision that the Emperor "shall not have powers related to government" (Article 4) as insulating the Emperor from political requests from the government. In contrast, Ozawa argued that this provision meant that the Emperor had

81. Justice System Reform Council, Final Report, Ch. I, Part 2.1

82. Ramseyer and Rasmusen, Measuring Judicial Independence.

no independent authority to refuse a government request, for a refusal would be the exercise of a governmental power. This was, of course, consistent with the organ theory as reinterpreted for the postwar constitutional monarchy. After some political wrangling, the Emperor did accede to the request, leading to significant protest in Japan.

With the fall of Ozawa, however, it seems that the organ theory remains the dominant one. Until a suitable rival is found, Japan will remain an outlier among industrial nations: it simply does not have a judiciary that is interested in judicialization. And it has no prospect of getting one.

Conclusion

Compared to other advanced industrialized nations, including its close neighbors in Taiwan and Korea, Japan has experienced relatively little judicialization. The Japanese Supreme Court is not adjudicating issues related to who can serve as the head of government, as are its counterparts in Taiwan and Korea. It is not considering major issues of social policy, as are constitutional courts in Germany and Latin America. It is not setting aside major programs of the legislature, as has the *Conseil Constitutionnel* in France.

Why this situation obtains has been the subject of some controversy. Some point to cultural factors, including the preference for harmony that is often invoked in discussions of Japan.[83] Others emphasize the lack of a constitutional court; and the system of appointments and promotion, through which those who rise in the judiciary tend to reinforce the cautious approach. A related category of explanation emphasizes political controls. Because of continuity in the rule of the Liberal Democrats, and their ability to communicate with the Supreme Court Secretariat at the apex of the judicial branch, lower court judges tended to uphold policies that are consistent with the preferences of the Diet.. But the current situation, in which Japan is governed by the Democratic Party of Japan, poses a direct challenge to these theories. We should be witnessing at least tentative steps toward judicialization if the political theories are correct.

This chapter has argued that we are not yet seeing these signs. Despite a major program of judicial reform, continuity rather than change is the theme. We join recent analysts in emphasizing ideational factors as

83. See Law and Matsui, "Why is the Japanese Supreme Court so Conservative?," 23 (discussing views of former Justice Masami Itoh).

providing the explanation. But we focus on different ideas. While Professor Matsui's account relies on general ideas of positivism and a belief among judges that the constitution is more a political rather than legal document. In our view, regardless of political structure or positivism per se, Japanese judges are heir to a particular conception of law and the state that provides a limited role for the judiciary. This view survived the constitutional transformation of the Allied Occupation. As a discrete organ exercising the state's judicial power, Japanese judges *are* independent, but they are cabined within a small zone of activity, mainly the adjudication of private rights. The judges police other branches only when their violations of individual rights are truly egregious *and* when the violation does not reflect a strong interest of the state, in conformity with the organ theory. This zone of violations is small indeed.

This is not to say that the nineteenth-century German ideas are uncontested. There are bureaucrats and politicians in Japan who do want to move to a more liberal model, which presumably would facilitate a larger role for judicial protection. But even after a self-conscious effort to change the system, the ideas remain deeply rooted.

Japan is exceptional within advanced industrial democracies in its low level of judicialization. It illustrates that the general association between divided politics and judicial empowerment is a matter of tendency, not an iron law. Even when they have room to exercise power over important policy matters, judges may not always choose to do so if they do not conceive of the judicial role as a policymaking one. A self-conception of an activist role seems to be a necessary, if not sufficient, condition for judicialization.

The Introduction of Western International Law into Japan

Jon M. Van Dyke[1]

Introduction

Japanese officials and scholars were first exposed to and started to master principles of Western international law in the years that followed Commodore Perry's visit to Japan with his "black ships" in 1853. The United States and the European powers imposed "unequal treaties" upon Japan, and Japan was determined to renegotiate those treaties and become a member of the "family of nations." To accomplish this goal, Japan needed to establish a stable legal system that would protect foreign investment and allow Japan to join the world economy, and also to master the principles of international law that would enable it to function in the world community. Prior to this era, Japan did not utilize the concepts of "law" and the "rule of law" (in the Western sense) and operated primarily through hierarchy and relationships. Japan's understanding of "law" thus came in part through its mastery of international law.

What Is [Western] International Law?

International law has been evolving in the West for centuries to provide a framework for international and transnational activities. Like other areas of the law, its purpose is to allow participants to deal with each other with some level of predictability and thus to reduce misunderstandings and avoid conflicts and confrontations.[2]

1. The late Professor Jon Van Dyke was Professor of Law and Carlsmith Ball Faculty Scholar at the William S. Richardson School of Law, University of Hawaii at Manoa. He was Visiting Professor at Berkeley Law, University of California, Spring 2011.

2. "Law is an instrument for creating, maintaining, and changing a society. Law prescribes the behavior of the society's members so that social order—that is, regularity and predictability of social behavior—prevails, the survival of the society becomes

But international law is still a more primitive system of law than the domestic legal systems found in advanced nations. It does not have a legislative body with the capacity to enact laws binding on all nations, an executive branch or military or police force that can enforce the laws that do exist, or judicial tribunals that have broad jurisdiction or the power to issue binding and enforceable decrees. Although early versions of such bodies can be found in the United Nations and in emerging regional organizations, the process of constructing institutions that enjoy widespread support and can meet the challenges presented by a deeply divided world is just beginning.

Some have argued that because international law cannot be enforced by a superior body it is not law at all.[3] But most commentators contend that because most nations follow international law most of the time, and because those that violate its norms do frequently suffer consequences, it should be viewed as a system of law.[4]

International law is less developed than other systems of law because the larger and more powerful nations do not always accept that it is in their interest to subordinate their self-interest to an international or

---

possible, and the members can live in peaceful coexistence." Werner Levi, *Contemporary International Law: A Concise Introduction*, 2nd ed. (Boulder, 1991), 1.

3. John Austin defined a "law" as "a rule laid down for the guidance of an intelligent being by an intelligent being having power over him," and wrote that a "command" and a "sanction" are essential elements of a law. He put international law into the different category of "positive morality"—along with "the laws of honor" and "the laws of fashion"—because it consisted of "rules set and enforced merely by the opinion of an intermediate body of men." See John Bassett Moore, *International Law and Other Current Illusions and Other Essays* (New York, 1924), 292 (discussing John Austin, *Jurisprudence*).

4. The American scholar John Bassett Moore explained that: "In respect of actual observance, I venture to say that international law is on the whole as well observed as municipal law. Perhaps one would not go too far in saying that it is better observed, at any rate in time of peace. In time of war, when a contest by force exists, it is needless to repeat that the application of law, whether municipal or international, becomes more or less uncertain, and that, as turmoil and excitement grow, the uncertainty increases. In time of peace, however, the regard which nations are accustomed to feel for their reputation and dignity strongly influences them, perhaps quite as much as does the dread of retaliation to respect the rules by which their intercourse is confessedly regulated." Moore, *Illusions*, 300. A more recent study examining this question is Louis Henkin, *How Nations Behave* (New York, 1979).

multinational goal.[5] Although smaller nations will see the benefit of an international structure that protects the weak against the powerful, the stronger nations do not always agree that such a structure is beneficial.[6] The foundations of international law have always been, therefore, reciprocity and enlightened self-interest. "For example, the increasing cost of war, or perhaps the infeasibility of a major war, makes a legal settlement of conflicting interests more attractive. At any rate, war costs diminish the types of interests over which states are willing to fight a war."[7]

The primary sources of international law are treaties—bilateral and multilateral—and "customary international law," which emerges from the actual practices of states undertaken with an understanding that the practice is required by law (*opinio juris sive necessitatis*). The "practices" of states are usually found in actions taken by a country, but sometimes can be discovered in the statements their diplomats or leaders issue or in their votes at international organizations or diplomatic conferences. To become "custom," a practice must have the widespread (but not necessarily universal) support of countries concerned with the issue and must usually have continued for a period of time long enough to signify understanding and acquiescence. Occasionally a regional custom can emerge, if the countries of a certain part of the world order their affairs in a certain manner.

5. "There is little incentive for states to sacrifice their national interests to an international interest. Therefore, they have no incentive to create an effective international law, except insofar as this may serve their purposes." Levi, *Contemporary International Law*, 4.

6. When the United States was a small and weak country, for instance, its leaders enthusiastically embraced international law. The First U.S. Congress enacted in 1790 a statute giving aliens the right to bring claims in U.S. courts for violations of torts committed "in violation of the law of nations." Judiciary Act of 1789, ch. 20, sec. 9(b), 1 Stat. 73, 77 (1789), codified at 28 USC sec. 1350. In 1792, Attorney General Edmund Randolph issued in opinion explaining that: "The law of nations, although not specially adopted by the constitution or any municipal act, is essentially a part of the law of the land. Its obligation commences and runs with the existence of a nation, subject to modifications on some points of indifference." 1 Op. Att'y Gen. 26 (June 26, 1792). But now that the United States is the world's only superpower, it appears to have much less interest in multinational institutions and solutions to problems.

7. Levi, *Complementary International Law*, 4.

Most scholars[8] explain that "modern" international law emerged in Europe at the time of the Renaissance and Enlightenment through the Peace of Westphalia, which ended the Thirty Years War (1618–48) and gave formal recognition to the sovereign state system. This treaty-based system was designed, in part, to allow Catholic and Protestant states to coexist in Europe. International law became necessary to confirm the boundaries among these states and to bring some order to their dealings with each other. "These agreements also proclaimed the doctrine of *pacta sunt servanda* (treaties are to be observed)—a fundamental principle of international law—and established a machinery for the settlement of disputes arising between the signatories."[9]

The Final Act of the Congress of Vienna (1815), signed by Austria, France, Great Britain, Portugal, Prussia, Russia, and Sweden, which formally ended the Napoleonic Wars, was another significant event because it created a system of political and economic cooperation in Europe as well as delimiting norms of international law. Among the norms that emerged from this Congress were a set of rules governing diplomatic protocol, a condemnation of the slave trade, the principle of free navigation (not only for the riparian states but for all states) on the major rivers of Europe (the Rhine, the Neckar, the Main, the Moselle, the Meuse, and the Scheldt), and the neutrality of Switzerland.[10] Treaties, both bilateral and multilateral, began to cover a wide range of topics, supplementing and sometimes replacing custom as a source of law.

This agreement reinforced the notion that "states" are all equal to each other, with horizontal relationships among them and complete sovereignty over their own territory. Today, 192 "states" make up the world community.

In recent years, it has become accepted that some principles of customary international law are so important that they are called "peremptory norms" or "*jus cogens*" (commanding law) of international law and

8. A leading treatise on the history of international law is Arthur Nussbaum, *A Concise History of the Law of Nations* (New York, 1954).

9. Thomas Buergenthal and Sean D. Murphy, *Public International Law* (St. Paul, 2002), 15.

10. Buergenthal and Murphy, *Public*, 15–16; Moore, *Illusions*, 296; Nussbaum, *Concise History*, 186–87.

that no nation is permitted to depart from these principles.[11] Among these norms are the right to self-determination and the prohibitions on aggression, genocide, crimes against humanity, slavery, extrajudicial murder, prolonged arbitrary detention, torture, and racial discrimination.[12]

Although most historical summaries of the development of international law focus on its growth in Europe and the West,[13] the reality is more complex. Practices governing interactions among nations and peoples also developed in Asia and elsewhere,[14] and these norms have been merging with those that came to be accepted in the West.[15]

11. See, e.g., Article 53 of the Vienna Convention on the Law of Treaties, May 23, 1969, 1155 U.N.T.S. 331: "A treaty is void if... it conflicts with a peremptory norm of general international law... [A] peremptory norm of general international law is a norm accepted and recognized by the international community of States as a whole as a norm from which no derogation is permitted and which can be modified only by a subsequent norm of general international law having the same character."

12. See, e.g., Restatement of the Foreign Relations Law of the United States Sec. 702 (3rd ed. 1987).

13. "Today's international law is a product of modern European civilization." Yasuoki Onuma, "Moderator's Introduction," in Nisuke Ando, ed., *Japan and International Law: Past, Present and Future* (The Hague, 1999). "International law as it now stands is essentially the product of the European mind and has practically been 'received'... lock, stock and barrel by American and Asiatic states." J.H.W. Verzijl, "Western European Influence on the Foundations of International Law," in J.H.W. Verzijl, *International Law in Historical Perspective* (Leiden, 1968), 442. "There is no doubt about it: the traditional law of nations is a law of European lineage." B.V.A. Roling, *International Law in an Expanded World* (Amsterdam, 1960), 10. Professor Nussbaum wrote that the international law of the Western states overwhelmed the views of East Asia rather than merging with it, but added that Western concepts did later evolve as a result of the contact between the two systems: "The expansion of the Western law of nations to the Far East did not involve a fusion of European and Asiatic ideas. The European conception prevailed as to substance and form. The Oriental nations had small success instilling their cherished notions regarding ranks and ceremonials into the new agreements. Nevertheless, the process of expansion in itself divested the law of nations more and more of its "European" character..." Nussbaum, *Concise History*, 196.

14. Various treaties covering a number of topics were entered into between European and Asian nations beginning in 1547. See Jeremy A. Thomas, "History and International Law in Asia: A Time for Review?," in Ronald St. John MacDonald, ed., *Essays in Honour of Wang Tieya* (Dordrecht, 1994), 813, 823 (citing C. H. Alexandrowicz, *An Introduction to the History of the Law of Nations in the East Indies* [1967]).

15. Professor Onuma has explained that we need to look at "the history of international law from an intercivilizational perspective" because today's world is "a world of various civilizations' making which date back much further than modern European

The Sino-Centric System in East Asia

"In contrast with the European World Order characterized by horizontal relations among sovereign States, the East Asian World Order was based on hierarchical relations with a Middle Kingdom at its apex."[16] Under this different approach, the smaller nations around the periphery of China paid tributes to China and accepted China as the hegemonic power of the region. For the most part, China did not directly interfere with the internal affairs of its smaller neighbors, but the need to respect China and its role remained as a central feature of East Asian relationships.

The Westernization of Law in East Asia

After Commodore Matthew Perry came to Japan in 1853 with his "black ships," Japan entered into the 1854 Treaty of Peace and Amity with the United States.[17] This treaty was followed in 1858 with a Treaty of Commerce with the United States[18] and then similar treaties with other Western countries. These treaties were "unequal" and conveyed consular jurisdiction to the Western powers, established a conventional tariff, and gave

---

civilization." Onuma Yasuaki, "When Was the Law of International Society Born?—An Inquiry of the History of International Law from an Intercivilizational Perspective," *Journal of the History of International Law* 2 (2000): 7. He has explained that today's international law did not emerge until the end of the nineteenth century when global interaction became a reality. "What existed before were regional normative systems, each of which claimed its universal validity based on its universalistic world image. Sinocentric, Islamocentric, and Eurocentric systems were leading examples. Together with the subjugation of competing powers in other civilizations by European powers, European international law became the global standard." Onuma Yasuaki, "The Birth of International Law as the Law of International Society," *American Society of International Law Proceedings* 94 (2000): 44. Similarly, Georges Abi-Saab has explained that the European system had co-existed with other systems, which "it gradually managed to set aside or replace." Georges Abi-Saab, "International Law and The International Community: The Long Road to Universality," in *Essays in Honour of Wang Tieya*, 32. Professor Anand has written that the failure to appreciate "the contribution of Asian and African countries toward the development of modern international law... is more often than not based on ignorance of their history and lack of understanding of the cultures and cultural traditions." R. P. Anand, *Origin and Development of the Law of the Sea—History of International Law Revisited* (The Hague, 1982), 5.

16. Yoshiro Matsui, "Modern Japan, War and International Law" in *Japan and International Law*, 8.

17. 111 Consolidated Treaty Series 377.

18. 119 Consolidated Treaty Series 253.

to the Western country a unilateral most-favored-nation clause.[19] They also tended to restrict the movement of Westerners in Japan to identified treaty ports and prohibited them from moving into the interior.[20]

On Feb. 8, 1868, the new Meiji government in Japan declared that it would respect these treaties and conduct its foreign relations "according to the universal law of nations," but also indicated that it would seek to revise the burdensome unequal provisions of the earlier treaties.[21]

Politically and psychologically galling, though not often called upon, were the extraterritoriality provisions that permitted foreigners accused of crimes on Japanese soil to be tried by foreigners resident in Japan. The impetus to design a Western style legal system developed in part from the desire to remove the unequal treaties, especially these extraterritorial provisions.[22]

The breakthrough occurred in 1894 with the Anglo-Japanese Treaty of Commerce and Navigation, signed 16 days before Japan's declaration of war against China.[23] This treaty recognized freedoms of residence, travel, property, trade, and navigation for each country's subjects on an equal basis,[24] and it marked Japan's entrance into the "Family of Nations" as a "Civilized Nation." Japan thus moved out of the East Asia World Order and into the European sovereign state system, and it used force to bring an end to the Sino-Centric system that had operated in East Asia for centuries. Japan moved Ryukyu from being a tributary of China to being a part of Japan in 1874–79 and then defeated China in the Sino-Japanese War of 1894–95.[25] Japan also acted to break down Korea's tributary relationship with China in 1875–76, and then more decisively in the Sino-Japanese War of 1894–95, followed by the formal annexation of Korea in 1905–10 (after Japan defeated Russia in the Russo-Japanese War of 1904–05 and

19. Matsui, "Modern Japan," 9.

20. Ibid.

21. Ibid. at 10, citing Gaimusho [Ministry of Foreign Affairs], ed. *Nihon Gaiko Bunsho [Diplomatic Documents of Japan]*, Vol. 1, Book 1 (1936), 227.

22. Michael Young & Constance Hamilton, "Historical Introduction to the Japanese Legal System," *Japan Business Law Guide* (1988), chapter 1, reprinted in Curtis J. Milhaupt, J. Mark Ramseyer, and Mark D. West, *The Japanese Legal System: Cases, Codes, and Commentary* (St. Paul, Minn., 2006), 32.

23. 180 Consolidated Treaty Series 257.

24. Matsui, "Modern Japan," 10.

25. Ibid. at 11–12.

thereby secured Korea into its own sphere of influence).[26] The Japanese Association of International Law was established in 1897, nine years before the founding of the American Society of International Law in 1906.[27]

Japanese Adherence to International Law Principles

Japanese authors tend to emphasize that Japan engaged in "scrupulous observance of international law" from 1854 to the early 1930s.[28] This adherence was designed to earn acceptance into the "Family of Nations," and later to provide justification for Japan's expansionist activities.[29]

Some Japanese scholars found similarities between the natural-law roots of international law principles and "their own neo-Confucian metaphysical concept of the 'principles of the universe (*ten ri* or *ten do*)' which were applicable to the human relations in society."[30] Japan participated in five international arbitrations between 1873 and 1903, more than any other country during that period, but became demoralized when it lost the 1903 *Yokohama House Tax Case* before the Permanent Court of Arbitration.[31] This defeat led many Japanese to view international law as "not so much

26. Ibid. at 12–13.

27. Shigeru Oda, "Banquet Speech: One Hundred Years of the Japanese Association of International Law and Fifty Years of the International Court of Justice," in *Japan and International Law*, 235.

28. Matsui, "Modern Japan," 10. See also ibid. at 27 ("Until about the time of First World War, Japan maintained a good record in observing international law."); Oda, "Banquet Speech," 236 ("It is worth mentioning that Japan was at that time regarded as a nation which most faithfully adhered to the rules of warfare... [I]n the first years of this century, Japan was regarded as a law-abiding nation."); Hisashi Owada, "Japan, International Law and the International Community," in *Japan and International Law*, 347, 357 (referring to Japan's "faithful observance and application of international law"); ibid. at 359: "[W]ith the exception of a comparatively brief period of less than twenty years from the beginning of the 1930s until the end of the Second World War in 1945...Japan tended to observe quite meticulously and scrupulously the norms of international law in her conduct of foreign relations."

29. Matsui, "Modern Japan," 27; Owada, "International Community," 359.

30. Owada, "International Community," 347, 351; see also ibid. at 352.

31. Ibid. at 355. This case was brought by France, Germany, and Britain against Japan, after the unequal treaties had been negotiated and concerned whether a building built upon land conveyed in an in-perpetuity lease under the previous treaty could be taxed. Japanese officials and scholars accepted that the conveyed lands would not be subject to taxation, but were flabbergasted when the arbitrators ruled that the subsequently-built buildings were also exempt from taxation.

a body of principles based on natural justice which the East could share in common with the West," but rather "as a bunch of technical rules to be manipulated."[32] Many Japanese scholars developed a conservative approach toward international law, viewing it as in a state "in which the evolutionary process of the law ceased to be in motion and those rules tended to be fixed in Japan then and there."[33] Japanese scholars and international lawyers now tend to "interpret and apply [international] law almost as a pure analytical process rather than as a process of testing the validity of the law in the context of the social reality in which the case in question has to be weighed," i.e., applying "formal logic, almost divorced from the context of societal values of the international community in which the case has to be examined."[34] This approach has been criticized as "an excessively legalistic and technical approach to international law"[35] by Hisashi Owada, now the President of the International Court of Justice.

The State of "Law" in Japan in the early 1800s

Many writers have observed that Japan (and other East Asian communities) did not in the early 1800s recognize and utilize "law" and the "rule of law" in same way these concepts were used in the West. "In traditional China law remained a small and not very significant department of ethics. It was not considered worthy of study in itself, nor was there any interest in systematizing it."[36] Similarly, in Tokugawa Japan, "the idea of law and legal philosophy itself were absent."[37]

The Tokugawa Shogunate governed through a feudal structure, forbidding Japanese to travel abroad and permitting foreigners little access to Japan.[38] Japan's feudal structure was different from Western feudalism in that "contract played no role in the feudal system" in Japan and "the 'glue' that held the feudal system together was a kind of family or kinship relationship together with Japanese notions of neo-Confucianism."[39]

32. Ibid. at 356.

33. Ibid. at 361.

34. Ibid. at 364.

35. Ibid. at 367.

36. Richard H. Minear, *Japanese Tradition and Western Law: Emperor, State, and Law in the Thought of Hozumi Yatsuka* (Cambridge, 1970) 155.

37. Ibid. at 157.

38. Carl F. Goodman, *The Rule of Law in Japan: A Comparative Analysis* (The Hague, 2003), 12.

39. Ibid. at 13.

Control was exercised through "the notion that the peasant (or any subordinate Lord) owed obligations to his higher Lord."[40] Although rulers "had an obligation to justly rule," the primary concept connecting society was the concept of "obligation," and the ruler's subjects did not have "rights."[41] Throughout the Tokugawa period,

> Japan is still either following the commands of a centralized government with no formal legal system that would apply principled rules and allow persons to form their own governing law for their relationships or is following an informal system of dispute resolution which relies on compromise to re-establish harmony between the disputing parties.[42]

Some authors have explained that although "[d]uring the Tokugawa period there had been judicial law as well as standardized forms of action through which the government usually afforded remedies to parties whose legitimate interests were injured, ...a legal science, analogous to the European legal science, with which Meiji scholars were confronted, had not emerged."[43] Although claims could be brought during the Tokugawa period, the concept of a "right" as it was understood in Europe was lacking and therefore "Meiji students of Western jurisprudence had to coin a new term, *kenri* (power plus interest) in order to express the concept of a right."[44]

The hierarchical social structure was so rigid during the Tokugawa period that a dispute could not be taken to a higher level for resolution without the permission of the claimant's immediate superior. Officials were thus able to pressure potential litigants directly and could also "encourage other people, on whose good will the litigant were dependent, to discourage the litigant from continuing the dispute."[45] It was also difficult to pursue claims because it was challenging to identify "clear-cut rules" that applied to any given situation. "Personal entitlements and even du-

40. Ibid.

41. Ibid. at 14.

42. Ibid. at 16.

43. Kenzo Takayanagi, "A Century of Innovation: The Development of Japanese Law, 1868-1961," in von Mehren, ed., *Law in Japan* (Cambridge, Mass., 1963), 15–40, reprinted in Hideo Tanaka, ed., *The Japanese Legal System: Introductory Cases and Materials* 173 (Tokyo, 1976).

44. Ibid. at 174.

45. Young and Hamilton, "Historical Introduction," 31.

ties were apparently intentionally kept hazy and hidden from the view of the population."[46] In addition, "[r]ights and entitlements, such as they were, ...attached more to the group than to the individual."[47] Commentaries on legal principles were not generally published, and judges were not independent but were rather "functionaries of the shogunate government and slipped easily and quickly from judge to administrator and back."[48]

With the beginning of the Meiji period, it became clear that "Japan needed a legal system"[49] to overcome the unequal treaties and the exercise of consular jurisdiction by the Western powers. "Western law" came to be viewed "as the embodiment of civilized justice."[50] The concept of "the law of nations" invoked by the U.S. Consul-General Townsend Harris when negotiating the 1858 Treaty of Amity and Commerce "was totally alien and new" to the Japanese negotiators, but they came to understand that it was "an essential prerequisite for a satisfactory conduct of intercourse with these barbarian Westerners."[51] Japanese scholars were, therefore, sent to the West,[52] and Western advisors came to Japan.[53] Japan was seeking to understand Western legal concepts in general at the same time that it was seeking to understand Western international law, and some have stated that Japan received its understanding of "law" through its understanding and practice of Western international law.

Western International Law Around 1900

In the late nineteenth century, Western international law was even more primitive than it is today. No global institutions existed, and only a few special-purpose regional organizations had been created. Some topics—such as diplomatic immunity—were fairly well defined, and consensus had also been reached on the important goals of stopping piracy and slavery. War was still viewed by many as an acceptable instrument of foreign policy, but the dramatic increase in destructive weaponry resulting from the industrial revolution caused many to realize that some constraints

46. Ibid.
47. Ibid.
48. Ibid.
49. Goodman, *The Rule of Law*, 17.
50. Takayanagi, "Century of Innovation," 177.
51. Owada, "International Community," 347, 350.
52. See, e.g., Minear, *Japanese Tradition*.
53. Goodman, *The Rule of Law*, 17.

were needed on the use of force. Major international meetings were called, the most significant being the 1899 and 1907 Hague Conferences (which Japan participated in), which were designed to codify the laws of armed conflict and establish limits on certain types of military activities. The growth of daily newspapers in the industrialized countries had the effect of allowing common citizens to participate more fully in policy decisions, and led, in many countries, to a democratization of international politics.

Twenty-five nations attended the 1899 Hague Conference, which was convened by Czar Nicholas II of Russia, and a larger number ratified the documents produced by the meeting, which included conventions for the Peaceful Settlement of International Disputes, on the Laws and Customs of War on Land, for the Adaptation to Maritime Warfare of the Principles of the Geneva Convention of 1864, Prohibiting the Launching of Projectiles and Explosives from Balloons and declarations on the use of projectiles to transmit poisonous gases, and on the prohibition of dum-dum bullets.[54] Although European nations dominated the negotiations, 19 Latin American nations signed or ratified one or more of the documents, as did China, Japan, Korea, Persia, Siam, and Turkey.[55]

The 1907 Hague conference, called again by the Russian Czar Nicholas II upon the initiative of Theodore Roosevelt, produced conventions on the Pacific Settlement of International Disputes, the Limitation of Employment of Force for Recovery of Contract Debts, the Opening of Hostilities, the Laws and Customs of War on Land, the Rights and Duties of Neutral Powers and Persons in Case of War on Land, the Status of Enemy Merchant Ships at the Outbreak of Hostilities, the Conversion of Merchant Ships into War-Ships, the Laying of Automatic Submarine Contact Mines, Bombardment by Naval Forces in Time of War, Adaptation to Maritime War of the Principles of the Geneva Convention, Certain Restrictions with Regard to the Exercise of the Right of Capture in Naval War, the Creation of an International Prize Court (Never Ratified), and the Rights and Duties of Neutral Powers in Naval War.[56] The European nations again dominated the negotiations, but 18 Latin American nations signed or ratified one of more of the conventions (Honduras

54. See generally the website of The Avalon Project, http://avalon.law.yale.edu/subject_menus/haguemen.asp.

55. *Signatures, Ratifications, Adhesions and Reservations to the Conventions and Declarations of the First and Second Hague Peace Conferences* (Washington, D.C., 1914), 2–4.

56. The Avalon Project.

was missing) as did China, Japan, Persia, Siam, and Turkey (with Korea missing because it had been placed under a protectorate by Japan). Liberia also adhered to many of the conventions.[57]

The nature of the international legal system that was being built was thought by many to be one of consent—or "positivism"—wherein only those norms agreed upon by the states could be enforced against them.[58] But perhaps because of the theocracies that had governed many parts of Europe in previous centuries, the canon law that had developed during that period, and the religious fervor that still burned brightly for many, others contended that certain inherent principles also governed nations. Tension emerged between this "natural law" formula for the basis of international law and the perspective of "positivism" promoted by others, and this tension still exists today.

The Dutch diplomat Hugo de Groot, who wrote under the Latin name Grotius, is often called the "father"[59] or "founder"[60] of international law because he tried to reconcile the conflicting sources of international law, believing "that the foundation of international law is a combination of natural and positive law."[61] His analysis of the laws of war, the law of the sea,[62] and the protection owed to diplomats laid the framework for

57. *Signatures*, 8–11.

58. The Italian scholar Alberico Gentili (1552–1608) departed from the theological approach utilized by other writers of his time and "deduced the rules of the law not from some metaphysical source but from the practice of states and the writings of historians. He was thus the first representative of the 'positivists,' who argue that the law is created by humans for definite conditions and purposes rather than by some supreme being for all eternity." Levi, *Contemporary International Law*, 10. The next significant positivist was the British scholar Richard Zouche (1590-1660), who "was the first author to undertake a systematic treatment of the entire field of international law." His writings "simply sets forth the controversial issues as such, without venturing to offer a decision..." "[W]ith him international law is based distinctly on custom—supposing it is reasonable—and on treaties. While Zouche mentions natural law, he considers it to be knowable from the actual attitudes of men. Of the traditional natural-law doctrine, his book shows practically no mark." Nussbaum, *Concise History*, 166–67 (discussing Richard Zouche, *Juris et Judicii Fecialis, Sive Juris Inter Gentes et Quaestionum de Eodem Explicatio* (1650)).

59. W.S.M. Knight, The *Life and Works of Hugo Grotius* (London, 1925), 112.

60. Moore, *Illusions* (New York, 1924), viii.

61. Levi, *Contemporary International Law*, 11.

62. Grotius was particularly influential in promoting free access to the oceans and their resources and was undoubtedly influenced himself by the maritime practices of Asian nations in the East Indies and elsewhere. See, e.g., Anand, *Law of the Sea*, 124.

modern thinking on these topics. He believed that a "law of nature" could be deduced by logical reasoning, rather than by resort to divine sources, and thus tried to formulate a law that could be "acceptable to all, conceivably even to 'infidels.'"[63]

Another continuing issue has been whether international law is incorporated into national legal systems, and is thus part of the law applied by national courts ("monism"), or whether it is a separate and distinct legal system governing the nations but not accessible by normal citizens in disputes in domestic courts ("dualism").

Did Western States View International Law as Applying Equally Everywhere? European and U.S. scholars and judges viewed international law as applying only to "civilized nations,"[64] and this term referred almost exclusively to Christian nations.[65] Theodore Woolsey's influential *Introduction to the Study of International Law*[66] contains a typical Eurocentric and politically-incorrect explanation of this phenomenon, explaining that Christians were "the first to elaborate a system of international law" for the same reasons that "have enabled Christian states to reach a higher point of civilization than any other."[67] These reasons include "the high moral standards of the religion... which cultivates alike the sentiments of justice and humanity" as well as the Roman law heritage.[68] Christian nations, he explained, had shared "religious and jural views" and "a similar historical development," but "[n]o such common feeling, but quite the opposite,

63. Levi, *Contemporary International Law*, 10.

64. See, e.g., *The Paquete Habana*, 175 US 677, 686, 700, 709 (1900); *Hilton v. Guyot*, US 163, 228 (1895). This term remains in Article 38(1)(c) of the Statute of the International Court of Justice, T.S. No. 993, 59 Stat. 1055 (1945), which describes as one of the sources of international law "general principles of law recognized by civilized nations."

65. Oppenheim pointed out that "whenever a new Christian state made its appearance in Europe, it was received into the existing European community of states" but that until recently "international law was confined to those states." Sir Robert Jennings and Sir Arthur Watts, eds., *Oppenheim's International Law* 1, 9th ed. (London, 1997), 87. Wheaton explained that the law of nations "has always been, and still is, limited to the civilized and Christian people of Europe or to those of European origin." Henry Wheaton, *Elements of International Law* (The Literal Reproduction of the Edition of 1866 by Richard Henry Dana, Jr.) (Oxford, 1936), 15.

66. Theodore D. Woolsey, *Introduction to the Study of International Law*, 4th ed. (New York, 1874).

67. Ibid. at 22.

68. Ibid.

existed between them and their Mohammedan neighbors; and hence the latter were long shut out from the pale of their international law."[69]

One of the major disputes of the early colonial period was whether the colonized peoples had any rights of any sort under international law. The generally-accepted view was that "peoples overseas could be subjected to European rule and their territories annexed through effective occupation by the conquering state," and "[t]he territory then became subject to treatment or mistreatment without protection of international law or, indeed, with its approval. Rules legitimizing imperialism and its means... endured well into the twentieth century, until most colonies became independent."[70]

The first writer to oppose this view was a Spanish professor of theology Francisco Vitoria (1480–1546), who "defended Spain's right in principle to create overseas dependencies and to exploit them" but also "argued that Spain was obliged to treat the conquered Indians in the Americas humanely, and he even granted these Indians a limited right to conduct 'just wars' against their cruel conquerors."[71] He "considered that the Amerindians had a soul, and in consequence were part of the *societas gentium*, the expression of the fundamental unity of the human race, and were subjects of the *jus humane societatis* or *jus gentium* derived from natural law."[72]

During the Tokugawa period, strenuous efforts had been made to keep Christianity out of Japan:

> It is a well-known historical fact that, fearful of the devastating effect of Christianity on the moral base of its political power, the Tokugawa Shogunate strictly banned the spread of the Gospel in Japan, and this ban on Christianity formed the cornerstone of the Shogunate's policy of national seclusion.[73]

During the nineteenth century, Western states were forced to realize that non-Christian countries such as Turkey, Persia, Siam, Japan, and China needed to be included within the international legal structure. It

69. Ibid.

70. Levi, *Contemporary International Law*, 9.

71. Ibid. at 10.

72. Abi-Saab, *International Community*, 33 (referring to de Vitoria's book *De Indis*).

73. Yosiyuki Noda, "Nihon ni Okeru Hikaku-Hō no Hatten to Genjō [Comparative Jurisprudence in Japan: Its Past and Present]," *Hogaku Kyokai Zasshi* 89 (1972–73): 1244–87, reprinted in *The Japanese Legal System*, 196–97.

was never exactly clear what was needed to be admitted to the family of nations. The British scholar T.J. Lawrence wrote in 1895 that "a certain degree of civilization is necessary, though it is difficult to define the exact amount."[74] "It would, for instance, be absurd to expect the king of Dahomey to establish a Prize Court, or to require the dwarfs of the central African forest to receive a permanent diplomatic mission."[75] In 1856, the European nations formally admitted Turkey into their "family of nations" in Clause 7 of the Treaty of Paris, after the Crimean War, which had been concluded to maintain the balance of power in Europe.[76] Western countries started dealing with China as a "state" for at least certain purposes because of the relationships that developed after China's defeats in the Opium Wars of 1840 and 1856.[77] Japan forced itself in by defeating China in 1894–95 and Russia in 1904–05.[78] In 1900, the U.S. Supreme Court referred to "the Empire of Japan" as "the last state admitted into the rank of civilized nations."[79] Africa continued to be completely excluded in a formal sense, and at the Berlin Conference on Africa in 1884–85, "where European powers agreed on rules for dividing between themselves territories which they had not yet occupied or even explored,"[80] no African representative was invited. But the colonial process forced Europeans to come to grips with the rest of world, and, as Professor Anghie has explained, "[i]t was principally through colonial expansion in the nineteenth century that international law became universal..."[81]

74. T. J. Lawrence, *The Principles of International Law* (London, 1895), 58.

75. Ibid.

76. See Abi-Saab, *International Community*, 37; see generally Sir Travers Twiss, *The Law of Nations Considered as Independent Communities* (Oxford, 1884), 88–124 (discussing in some detail the status of the Ottoman Empire under international law).

77. China was not enthusiastic about the Western international law "concept of a community of equal States adhering to a common code for intercourse" and preferred their own customs and world order. Thomas, *History and International Law*, 826 quoting from Wang Tieya, *International Law in China: Historical and Contemporary* (The Hague, 1990), 203, 226.

78. A Japanese diplomat was quoted as having said that "[w]e show ourselves equal to you in scientific butchery, and at once we are admitted to your council tables as civilized men." Roling, *Expanded World*, 27.

79. *The Paquete Habana*, 175 U.S. 677, 700 (1900).

80. Abi-Saab, *International Community*, 37.

81. Antony Anghie, "Colonialism and the Birth of International Institutions: Sovereignty, Economy, and the Mandate System of the League of Nations," *NYU Journal of International Law and Politics* 34 (2002): 516.

Writing in 1905, Oppenheim declared that 72 European and 21 American states were in the family of nations but that "in Asia only Japan is a full and real member of the Family of Nations, Persia, Korea, China, Siam and Tibet are, for some parts, only within the family."[82] The British scholar T. J. Lawrence was more positive with regard to China, writing in 1895 that "Turkey, China and Japan were formally placed under International Law as soon as they expressed a desire to submit themselves to it."[83]

The Western countries negotiated a wide series of multilateral treaties in the second half of the nineteenth century, but Asian countries were not centrally involved in any of these negotiations.[84] China "did not adhere to the Universal Postal Union until 1897, 20 years after its inception, and this was the first public international organization in which she took part."[85]

The Content of International Law at the Time

Because international law was viewed as regulating activities among states, it covered only selected topics and left many issues unregulated. International law required that treaties be followed (*pacta sunt servanda*), it ensured the immunity of diplomats, it regulated the treatment of foreigners or aliens in some detail, it provided rules allowing for free use of the seas, and it had some principles governing the use of armed force. The Western books on international law that had the earliest impact in Asia were Henry Wheaton's 1836 book entitled *Elements of International Law*, which was translated into Chinese in 1864 and reprinted in Japan in 1865, Theodore D. Woolsey's *Introduction to the Study of International Law* (1864), James Kent's *Commentaries on International Law* (1826), and J. Bergeon's *Le Droit International de l'Europe* (1873).[86]

Woolsey was president of Yale College and his book was republished with editions several times.[87] His book begins with a discussion of the theoretical underpinnings of international law and then contains

82. Thomas, *History and International Law*, 822 (quoting from Oppenheim, *International Law*, 1st ed. (1905), 37).

83. Lawrence, *Principles*, 59.

84. Thomas, *History and International Law*, 828.

85. Ibid.

86. R. P. Anand, "Family of "Civilized States and Japan: A Story of Humiliation, Assimilation, Defiance and Confrontation," *Journal of History and International Law* 5 (2003): 19; Thomas, *History and International Law*, 832.

87. See, e.g., Woolsey, *Study of International Law*.

chapters on the sovereign rights of independent states, their rights in the oceans and rivers, the rights of aliens in foreign countries, the rights of diplomats to immunity, the law governing treaties, and the laws that apply in armed conflicts. The material on the use of force fills half of the volume, covering neutrality in some detail as well as the justifications for using force and the limitations on its use.

Other international law treatises of the time were similarly spare in the topics they covered. T. J. Lawrence's 1895 book[88] also devotes more than half its pages to the laws governing armed conflict, and otherwise covers diplomatic immunity, the equality of states, methods of acquiring territory, jurisdiction, maritime principles, and has brief references to piracy and slavery.

The late nineteenth century was a period of intense imperialism, with France, Britain, and Germany competing for colonies in Africa, Asia, and the Pacific, and the United States joining the fray with its acquisitions of the Philippines, Guam, and Puerto Rico in the Spanish-American War in 1898 and annexation of Hawaii that same year. Japan, in particular, learned the lesson that conquest of other territories was part of what it meant to be a "civilized nation."[89]

Japan Becomes a "Civilized Nation"

In 1900, Justice Horace Gray wrote the majority opinion for the U.S. Supreme Court in *The Paquete Habana*,[90] involving two small fishing vessels which were seized in 1898 as prizes of war during the Spanish-American War. President William McKinley had decreed that U.S. naval activities should be conducted consistently with "the law of nations applicable to such cases" and "upon principles in harmony with the present views of nations and sanctioned by their recent practice."[91] Justice Gray again explained that international law is part of U.S. law:

> International law is part of our law, and must be ascertained and administered by the courts of justice of appropriate jurisdiction as often as questions of right depending upon it are duly presented for their

88. Lawrence, *Principles*.

89. Anand, *Japan*, 25–27.

90. *The Paquete Habana*, 175 U.S. 677 (1900).

91. Ibid. at 712 (quoting from President McKinley's decrees of April 22 and 26, 1898).

> determination. For this purpose, where there is no treaty and no controlling executive or legislative act or judicial decision, resort must be had to the customs and usages of civilized nations, and as evidence of these, to the works of jurists and commentators who by years of labor, research, and experience have made themselves peculiarly well acquainted with the subjects of which they treat.[92]

He then engaged in an extensive survey of treatises, cases, and historical practices which led to the conclusion that:

> By the general consent of the civilized nations of the world, and independently of any express treaty or other public act, it is an established rule of international law, founded on considerations of humanity to a poor and industrious order of men, and of the mutual convenience of belligerent states, that coast fishing vessels, with their implements and supplies, cargoes and crews, unarmed and honestly pursuing their peaceful calling of catching and bringing in fresh fish, are exempt from capture as prize of war.[93]

Again, Justice Gray's survey is primarily of European and U.S. scholars, cases, and events, but the Argentine writer Carlos Calvo is included,[94] as is the Japanese scholar Sakue Takahashi.[95]

Twentieth-Century Developments

The interaction between Western and Asian approaches toward international relations and international law caused both to rethink some of their assumptions and led to renewed efforts to develop international law. During the twentieth century, international law developed substantially, with Asian countries participating actively in that development. Enormous strides have been made in codifying the law governing maritime matters, private transactional disputes, public economic relations, and the human rights that belong to all individuals.

But some important differences still exist between Asian and Western approaches to this subject. Perhaps the most striking concerns

92. Ibid. at 700.

93. Ibid. at 708.

94. Ibid. at 703–04, 708.

95. Ibid. at 700 (quoting Sakue Takahashi, *International Law 11*, 178, where he explained that Japan had exempted coastal fishing vessels from seizure in its 1894 war with China).

dispute-resolution procedures. Numerous international and regional tribunals have been developed, but Asian nations have been reluctant to use them. Only three cases involving East Asian nations have been adjudicated by the International Court of Justice.[96] In 1909, China rejected a Portuguese suggestion that their dispute over Macao's boundary be submitted to the Permanent Court of Arbitration in The Hague for decision. "European and American countries have a bias against East Asian people," the Chinese negotiator is reported to have stated. "Hague arbitration will definitely defend Portugal's interest... It is better for us to negotiate with Portugal directly so that we may yet have a fifty-fifty chance to succeed."[97] Japan apparently lost interest in utilizing international arbitration after it lost the *House Tax* arbitration in the Permanent Court of Arbitration in 1905. "It was suspected that the Western lawyers who made up the tribunal were strangers to Oriental ideas, principles and theories of jurisprudence and that they had little knowledge of legal and administrative concepts based on Oriental culture, and also that they might not be entirely free from racial or religious prejudices in dealing with disputes between European and Asiatic countries."[98]

This attitude and reluctance to use third-party adjudication remains today, and other differences between Western and Asian approaches toward international law can also be identified. Asian countries remain skeptical about certain aspects of customary international law because they view it as being formed by the practices and expectations of Western countries without active attention to Asian perspectives. They view international law as essentially instrumental in nature rather than normative and are skeptical that international law norms can be viewed as being neutral. They sometimes express skepticism about the "sovereign equality of states" because they are familiar historically with a sense of hierarchy among political communities, and they may believe that such hierarchies

96. *Temple of Preah Vihear (Cambodia v. Thailand)*, 1962 I.C.J. 6; *Sovereignty over Pulau Ligitan and Pulau Sipadan (Malaysia v. Indonesia)*, 2002 I.C.J. 625 (Dec. 17, 2002); *Sovereignty over Pedra Branca/Pulau Batu Puteh, Middle Rocks and South Ledge (Malaysia/Singapore)*, 2008 I.C.J. 14.

97. Thomas, *History and International Law*, 827 (quoting from Jerome Cohen and Hungdah Chiu, *People's China and International Law* [1974], 11).

98. Miyoshi Masahiro, "International Law in the Modern History of Japan," *Hohkei Ronshu (Journal of Legal and Political Studies)* 136 (1994), 15.

can still be found today. They view human rights through a different lens, and are more comfortable than Westerners with notions of "group rights."

But despite these important differences in perspective, international law has become part of the thinking and planning of East Asian nations. "Thus international law..., having started its life as a stranger to the country towards the end of the Tokugawa era, has come through some vicissitudes of sunny and rainy days to an age when it is treated [in Japan] as a matter of course by government officials and lawyers in general."[99]

Conclusion

Japan's orderly but cautious bureaucracy has meant that Japan has in recent years rarely taken bold initiatives in its foreign relations. Participants in the Third United Nations Conference on the Law of the Sea (1974–82) sometimes commented that Japan's delegates seemed to be about a year behind the other delegations with regard to the issues being discussed. Japan has made broad claims to extended maritime zones under the 1982 Law of the Sea Convention, which seems to many to go beyond the language in the Convention, and it has significant maritime delimitation disputes with its neighbors.[100]

When Japan's unilateral increase in the harvesting of blue fin tuna was challenged under the dispute-resolution procedures created by the Law of the Sea Convention by New Zealand and Australia in the late 1990s, Japan was able to avoid a decision on the merits by raising formalistic procedural objections to the proceeding.[101] More recently, however, Japan filed two prompt-release claims in the International Tribunal for

99. Ibid. at 20.

100. See generally Jon M. Van Dyke, "Disputes Over Islands and Maritime Boundaries in East Asia," in Seoung-Yong Hong and Jon M. Van Dyke, eds., *Maritime Boundary Disputes, Settlement Processes, and the Law of the Sea* (Leiden, 2009), 39–75.

101. The *Blue Fin Tuna Arbitration* adjudicated under the dispute-resolution procedures of the United Nations Law of the Sea Convention was dismissed on procedural grounds. *Southern Bluefin Tuna Case (Australia and New Zealand v. Japan)*, Provisional Measures Order (ITLOS), Aug. 27, 1999, http://www.itlos.org/fileadmin/itlos/documents/cases/case_no_3_4/Order.27.08.99.E.pdf; Award on Jurisdiction and Admissibility, Aug. 4, 2000, http://icsid.worldbank.org/ICSID/FrontServlet?requestType=ICSIDPublicationsRH&actionVal=ViewAnnouncePDF&AnnouncementType=archive&AnnounceNo=7_10.pdf. See Jon M. Van Dyke, "Louis B. Sohn and the Settlement of Ocean Disputes," *George Washington International Law Review* 33 (2000): 31–48.

the Law of the Sea in 2007 against the Russian Federation, thus trying to take advantage of these new procedures.[102] And in 2010, Australia filed a proceeding against Japan in the International Court of Justice arguing that Japan's "scientific whaling" violates the International Whaling Convention, the Southern Ocean Whale Sanctuary, the Convention on International Trade in Endangered Species of Wild Fauna and Flora, and the Convention on Biological Diversity.[103] This proceeding will test Japan's commitment to third-party dispute resolution procedures and will help define how Japan approaches international law in the coming generations.

102. *The Honshinmaru Case* and *the Tommaru Case* (both Japan v. Russian Federation) (ITLOS, 2007); see website of the International Tribunal for the Law of the Sea.

103. *Whaling in the Antarctic (Australia v. Japan)*, ICJ, filed June 1, 2010.

Reconsidering the Japanese Way of Dispute Resolution: What Is It and Why?

Masayuki Murayama[1]

Since Takeyoshi Kawashima wrote about modern Japanese legal consciousness, scholars have debated the theoretical significance and empirical validity of his arguments. Because his article "Dispute Resolution in Contemporary Japan"[2] dealt with the empirical question of why the Japanese do not litigate as frequently as Americans, foreign scholars tended to understand his work as presenting empirical arguments. However, his popularity among Japanese scholars owes much more to his normative arguments than to his empirical ones.

After clarifying Kawashima's arguments, this chapter will present findings from our recent survey to explore the extent to which his arguments can be sustained. Section I reviews his normative and empirical arguments and considers the empirical questions that they raise.[3] Section II presents patterns of problem solving behavior to see whether they support Kawashima's empirical arguments. Section III discusses possible causes for these patterns of problem-solving behavior.

1. Professor, School of Law, Meiji University. I thank Tom Ginsburg for editing the manuscript to make it more readable. I also thank Larry Repeta for reading the earlier version of the manuscript and correcting the English.

2. In Arthur Taylor von Mehren, ed., *Law in Japan: The Legal Order in a Changing Society* (Cambridge, Mass., 1963), 41–72.

3. Previous studies do not always distinguish these two aspects of Kawashima's arguments. Setsuo Miyazawa, "Taking Kawashima Seriously: A Review of Japanese Research on Japanese Legal Consciousness and Disputing Behavior," *Law and Society Review* 21 (2) (1987), 219–241, at 222.

I. Kawashima's Arguments on "Legal Consciousness" and Problem Solving Behavior

Two Meanings of "Legal Consciousness": A Normative Model and an Empirical Model

In his well-known article on the law-abiding spirit [*Junpo Seishin*], Kawashima argued that modern legal consciousness was necessary for modern law to function in a society, and that the lack of such consciousness was the real cause of the wide-spread evasion of economic regulation during and after the Second World War.[4] Kawashima explained his understanding of what would constitute modern legal consciousness and observed that normative expectations borne in traditional social relationships were not congruent with this consciousness.

Kawashima explained that modern legal consciousness consisted of two main factors: (1) the equality of people as individuals who have the sense of their own territory and inherent value and the respect of other individuals as such, and (2) unconditional voluntary compliance with the law.[5] He contrasted the patriarchal structure of traditional social relationships, such as the relationship between a landowner and a tenant farmer, with relationships based on modern legal consciousness.[6]

By contrasting an equal relationship based on modern legal consciousness and the traditional patriarchal relationship based on benevolence and piety, Kawashima urged readers to internalize modern legal consciousness so that modern law, epitomized in the postwar constitu-

4. Takeyoshi Kawashima, "Junpo Seishin [Law-Abiding Spirit]," in *Kawashima Takeyoshi Chosakushu [Collected Works of Kawashima Takeyoshi]*, hereafter *Works*, (Tokyo, 1982), vol. 4, 112. This article was first published with a slightly different title in 1946 and later included in *Kindai Shakai to Ho [Modern Society and the Law]* in 1959. Kawashima, Takeyoshi, "Junpo Seishin no Seishinteki oyobi Shakaiteki Kozo [The Mental and Social Structure of the Law-Abiding Spirit] (1) (2)," *Hogaku Kyokai Zasshi* 64 (1946), no. 7, 1–24 and no. 9, 1–29.

5. In the earlier version of the article, Kawashima referred to the Kantian notion of categorical imperative to explain what the unconditional voluntary compliance with the law means. He also emphasized that this normative consciousness was common both in law and in morality. (Kawashima [1946], 552–553).

6. Kawashima himself later wrote that his article on modern legal consciousness was not on the sociology of law, but on social philosophy. He also noted that he used the word "consciousness" to mean "the structure of the spirit" as a concept of cultural sociology or anthropology. *Works*, vol. 4, 403–405, 411.

tion, would become "living law" in Japanese society.[7] According to Kawashima, modern legal consciousness was an innovation that should be widely shared among the Japanese if they wanted to modernize their society. This was an appeal for social change toward modernization.

In his English-language article, "Dispute Resolution in Contemporary Japan," and later in *Nihonjin no Ho Ishiki [Legal Consciousness of the Japanese]*, published in 1967, Kawashima argued that the Japanese normative consciousness was the main cause of Japan's low litigation rate, though he acknowledged that delay and cost also discouraged litigation.[8] In this causal argument, he defined legal "consciousness" to mean attitudes toward law and argued that these attitudes led the Japanese to avoid litigation, resulting in a low litigation rate and a relatively small lawyer population.

Contemporary Significance of Kawashima's Arguments

What kind of empirical questions do Kawashima's arguments raise? In his article on modern legal consciousness, Kawashima used a normative model to contrast modern legal consciousness and contemporary normative expectations emerging from traditional social relationships. In the same way, we can use this normative model to assess whether and to what extent social order is based on law. In Kahei Rokumoto's words, the normative model indicates the quality of social order.[9] In his research on the legal resolution of traffic and rent disputes, Rokumoto expanded Kawashima's normative model to assess the quality of the social order in light of the law.[10]

7. It is true that Kawashima associated traditional normative consciousness with traditional social structure and that he assumed that industrial urbanization would transform the traditional consciousness into the modern one. But he also emphasized that the modernization of the living law should be the central agenda of postwar Japan. I suspect that the appeal of Kawashima's works to a wide range of contemporary readers came from this combination of the idea of historical development and the urge to join in social transformation.

8. Takeyoshi Kawashima, *Nihonjin no Ho Ishiki [The Legal Consciousness of the Japanese]* (1967).

9. Kahei Rokumoto, "'Nihonjin no Ho Ishiki' Kenkyu Gaikan—Ho Kannen wo Chushin ni shite [Overview of Studies on 'The Legal Consciousness of the Japanese': Focusing on the Legal Conception]," *Hoshakaigaku [Sociology of Law]* 35 (1983), 14–33.

10. Idem, *Minji Hunso no Hoteki Kaiketsu [Legal Resokution of Civil Disputes]* (1971).

The idea of consciousness necessarily focuses on individuals. According to the normative model of Kawashima and Rokumoto, individuals internalize legal rules and use universalistic norms to deal with problems based on reason. Behavior in compliance with the law does not always mean, however, that the individual unconditionally complies with the law. Therefore, one must also consider the motive for using law and the manner in which it is used. I will suggest a different approach below.

Suppose that a person faces a problem related to divorce. He does not know what to do and visits a fortune-teller for advice. The fortune-teller tells the man to consult a lawyer. He follows the fortune-teller's advice and the lawyer solves the problem by applying the law. According to Kawashima's normative model, the man does not use the law based on modern legal consciousness. However, I consider this to be an example of using the law. The normative model indicates how the institution of the law works. Such attitudes as the normative model demands are required for professional lawyers, but not for laypersons. When laypersons hire lawyers for advice, handling disputes, or direct negotiations involving legal provisions, this represents a use of the law, regardless of the layperson's motives. In other words, when a problem is dealt with based on the law, I consider that the law operates there.

By ignoring motive, we can focus on behavior in order to understand whether and to what extent we behave according to the law. From this perspective, the significant questions to be asked focus on actual experience of legal issues and on the ways Japanese people resolve them. Accordingly, we share the same goal as the empirical model: to describe and explain law-related behavior.

II. What is the Japanese Way of Dispute Resolution?

We conducted the "Dispute Behavior Survey" in 2005.[11] The sample was 25,014 randomly chosen Japanese men and women from twenty to seventy years-old. We visited and asked respondents whether they had experienced various types of problems in the previous five years and what they did to solve those problems (Behavior Survey). After obtaining answers to these questions, we asked the respondents to fill out a questionnaire concerning legal and social attitudes (Consciousness Survey). 12,408 per-

11. Masayuki Murayama, "Experiences of Problems and Disputing Behaviour in Japan," *Meiji Law Journal* 14 (2007), 1–59.

sons completed both oral and self-administered questionnaires, yielding a response rate of 49.6%.

The respondent group is not representative of the Japanese population in several respects. Women, rural residents, the elderly, self-employed and part-time workers, and people with higher education backgrounds are overrepresented compared to their counterparts. There is also an especially low number of respondents who are in their twenties.

Experience of Legal Problems in Japan, the U.S. and England

We listed ten types of legal problems with examples and asked respondents whether they had experienced any of these or similar problems in the previous five years. 2,343 persons (18.9% of the respondents) reported having experienced at least one problem in the previous five years. Because we were concerned with legal attitudes as well as experience and behavior, we asked about only individual experiences, not the experiences of other household members.

Similar surveys have been conducted in various countries and there are large variations in the problem experience rate, partly depending upon the survey methods employed. In this article we compare our data with the data on the U.S. and England and Wales (cited as England hereinafter). The U.S. data is taken from the Civil Litigation Research Project, conducted in 1980,[12] while the England data is taken from Paths to Justice Survey, conducted in 1997 and 1998.[13] The former listed eight types of legal problems and asked whether respondents or their household members experienced certain problems (money problems worth $1,000 or more or non-monetary problems such as discrimination) in the previous three years. The latter listed thirteen types of legal problems and asked respondents whether they or their partners had experienced problems in the previous five years in the screening survey (for problem types, see Table 1).

In the U.S. survey, 41.6% of the respondents reported having experienced a civil rights violation, a post-divorce, discrimination, social benefit, or zoning problem, or a problem worth at least $1,000. In Japan, the percentage of respondents who experienced problems worth at least ¥100,000 (US$1= roughly ¥100) or non-monetary problems in the previous

12. Richard E. Miller and Austin Sarat, "Grievances, Claims and Disputes: Assessing the Adversary Culture," *Law and Society Review* 15 (1980–81), 525–566.

13. Hazel Genn, *Paths to Justice: What People Do and Think about Going to Law* (Oxford, 1999).

Table 1. Types of Problems Shown to Respondents

Japan	The U.S.	England & Wales
Accident	Torts	Injuries and Health Problem
Accident	Torts	Negligent/Wrong Medical or Dental Treatment
Neighbor		(Owning Residential Property/ Living in Rented Accommodation)
Consumer	Consumer	Faulty Goods or Services
Employment		Employment
	Discrimination (Employment, Education, Housing, etc.)	Discrimination (Sex/Race/ Disability)
Family/Relatives	Post-Divorce	Relationship and Other Family Matters
Money	Debt	Money
Rent/Lease	Landlord	Renting Out Rooms or Property/ Living in Rented Accommodation
House/Land	Property	Owning Residential Property
Private Insurance		
Government (Pension, Insurance, Tax)	Government	
		Unfair Treatment by the Police
		Immigration
Others		

three years is 8.6% (problems involving unknown monetary amounts are excluded in the percentage; if included, the percentage would be 10.3%). Because the number of household members in the U.S. is 3.0 on average,[14] and because U.S. respondents were asked about household members, we can normalize the U.S. percentage to be equivalent to 13.9% in Japan. The Japanese percentage is lower than the U.S. percentage, but the difference

14. I thank Herbert Kritzer for providing the data.

is much smaller than the difference in the litigation rate between the two countries.[15]

In England, 40% of respondents reported having experienced at least one problem. However, interviewers asked follow-up questions of only 27.5% of the respondents because they excluded trivial problems that respondents explained as "not important", "no dispute" or "the other party was right." Researchers also excluded respondents whose partners had already reported the same problems.

When we exclude respondents in the same categories, the Japanese percentage becomes 17.8%. Given that the percentage of problems experienced in England includes the experience of partners, it would be difficult to say that the percentage of England is definitely higher than that of Japan.

These data on problem experience establishes the baseline for further comparison on subsequent problem solving behavior. It is to be noted that the Japanese rate of problem experience seems to be similar to the English rate and is not as small in comparison with the U.S. as the difference in the litigation rate indicates.

Are the Japanese Reluctant to Assert and/or Contest Claims?

When Kawashima argued that the main cause of Japan's low litigation rate was Japanese normative attitudes, he also argued that these attitudes were rooted in the traditional agrarian community, which suppressed conflict and valued harmony because collaboration among community members was vital for community life. Since people were averse to disputes, they were not willing to litigate problems because litigation frays critical social ties. This is a consistent explanation of behavior based on people's attitudes toward disputes.

If this explanation is valid, we should expect that the Japanese would be unwilling to contact the injuring party or to initiate legal claims. We should also expect that, when contacted by the other party, individuals would be unwilling to contest claims because such behavior could increase the likelihood of disputes. In order to test this hypothesis, we

15. For example, the Japanese litigation rate in traffic accidents was one-tenth of the U.S. Takao Tanase, "The Management of Disputes: Automobile Accident Compensation in Japan," *Law and Society Review* 24 (1990), 651–692.

compare the occurrence of contact/claims and disputes between Japan and the U.S.

Dispute pyramids can provide a clear image of the extent to which contacts or claims were made and how many disputes occurred after the contacts and claims. Figure 1 displays dispute pyramids for Japan and the U.S. related to all reported problems. Although the data is not exactly comparable, it gives reliable clues to test the hypothesis. In Japan, 80.5% of those who experienced problems contacted the other party and 43.3% faced disputes after the contact. In the U.S., 71.8% of individuals who experienced problems asserted claims and 44.9% faced disputes after the claim. The data appears to show that the Japanese tend to assert claims and face disputes just as frequently as Americans.

Figure 1. Dispute Pyramids for All Problems in Japan and the U.S.[16]

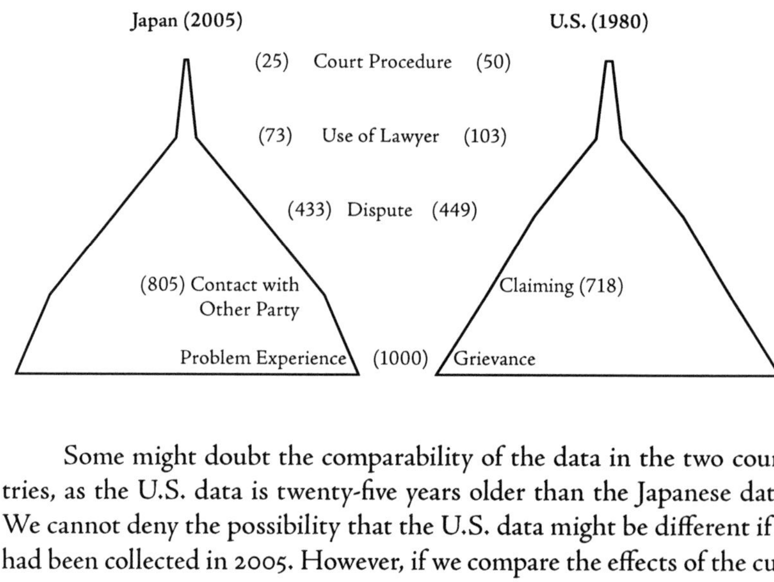

Some might doubt the comparability of the data in the two countries, as the U.S. data is twenty-five years older than the Japanese data. We cannot deny the possibility that the U.S. data might be different if it had been collected in 2005. However, if we compare the effects of the cul-

16. Note on the Japanese data: "Use of Lawyer" means retaining lawyers and "Court Procedure" means using a court procedure as plaintiff. The Japanese cases are those whose stakes are ¥100,000 or more and do not include the cases whose stakes are not related to money.

tural tradition of each country in this comparison,[17] the time difference can be considered insignificant.

Figure 2. Dispute Pyramids for Accidents/Torts in Japan and the U.S.[18]

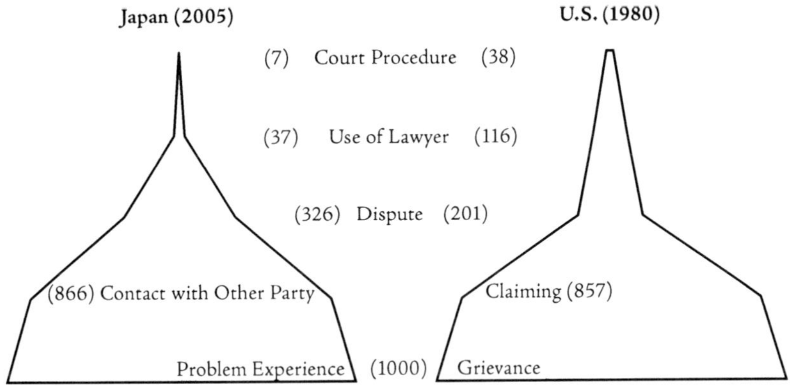

The Significance of Problem Type

Previous research has demonstrated that dispute behavior in the U.S. changes depending on the type of dispute.[19] Three problem types (torts, discrimination and post-divorce) generate different patterns of disputing behavior. People who experienced problems related to torts (primarily traffic accidents) often asserted claims and the tortfeasors did not contest these claims, resulting in few disputes. In discrimination cases, aggrieved parties tended to avoid asserting claims. When they did make claims, those were often contested. Claims were common in post-divorce cases, but these claims were often contested as well.

17. Rokumoto argued that Kawashima's idea of legal consciousness consists of two different elements: one can be called legal conception and the other legal consciousness in the narrow sense. Legal conception is a framework for perceiving law which is shared within a society and would not change easily (Rokumoto, 1983: 14). This is the core of his idea of legal consciousness.

18. Note on the Japanese data: "Use of Lawyers" means retaining lawyers and "Court Procedure" means using a court procedure as plaintiff. The Japanese cases include only those cases in which ¥100,000 or more was at stake and exclude the cases where plaintiffs did not seek money.

19. Miller and Sarat, 1980-81: 525–566.

Curiously, we find similar patterns of disputing behavior in the Japanese data. Figure 2 compares dispute pyramids for accidents/torts between Japan and the U.S. As in the U.S., in Japan, most people who experienced traffic accidents asserted claims. More often than not, the tortfeasor did not contest the claims. The percentage of disputes is higher in Japan than in the U.S., suggesting that either aggrieved parties or insurance companies are more willing to disagree in Japan than in the U.S.

Figure 3. Dispute Pyramids for Employment/Discrimination in Japan and the U.S.[20]

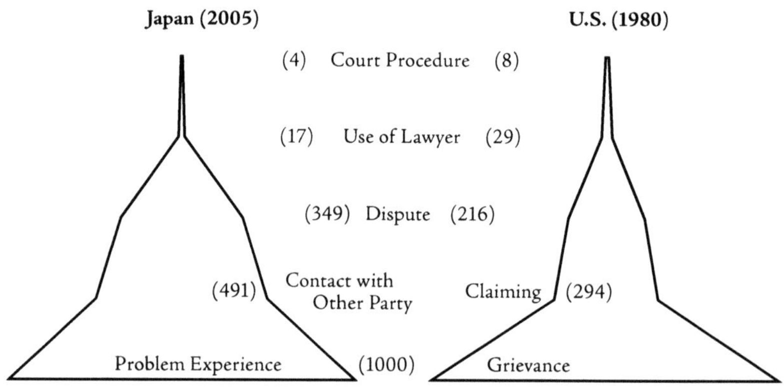

Figure 3 shows a comparison of the dispute pyramids for employment and discrimination cases in Japan and the U.S. The definition of "discrimination" used in the Japan and U.S. data differs in that the latter refers not only to employment discrimination, but also to housing and education discrimination. Nevertheless, problems related to discrimination demonstrate similar patterns of disputing behavior in Japan and the U.S. Japanese who experience problems in employment tend to avoid asserting claims. When they do assert claims, the claims are mostly contested. Lawyers and court procedures are rarely used in both Japan and the U.S.

Divorce/post-divorce as a problem type presents the third pattern of disputing behavior in Japan. Just like in the U.S., most people contact the other party and most parties reject these claims, leading to disputes.

20. Note on the Japanese Data: "Use of Lawyers" means retaining lawyers and "Court Procedure" means using a court procedure as plaintiff. All employment cases are included in the pyramid.

A salient characteristic of this problem type is that even in Japan, lawyers and court procedures are widely used.

In sum, dispute behavior in Japan and the U.S. differs depending on the problem type. There are clear and significant differences among the problem types, which are larger than differences between the two countries. In other words, nationality does not determine dispute behavior—problem type does. As the different patterns of dispute behavior in employment and divorce problems demonstrate, there is no typical Japanese dispute behavior which cuts across different problem types.

Figure 4. Dispute Pyramids for Divorce/Post-Divorce in Japan and the U.S.[21]

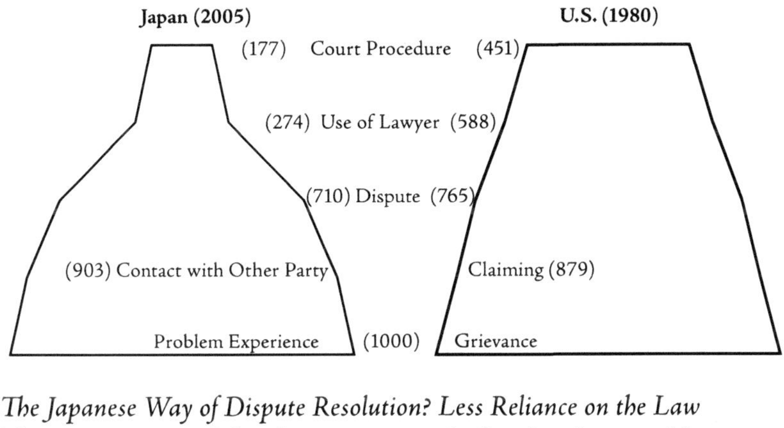

The Japanese Way of Dispute Resolution? Less Reliance on the Law

The comparison of the dispute pyramids for the three problem types shows that Japan consistently uses lawyers and courts less frequently than the U.S. Compared to England as well, Japan relies less on law. Table 2 shows that for all problems and particular problem types, such as accidents/injuries, employment and divorce/relationship, legal advice is less frequently sought and court involvement occurs less frequently in Japan than in England. This difference between Japan and England is especially striking, as the percentage of problems with a measurable monetary value is lower in England (51%) than in Japan (75%), while the amount of money

21. Note on the Japanese Data: "Use of Lawyers" means retaining lawyers and "Court Procedure" means using a court procedure as plaintiff. All of the divorce cases are included in the pyramid.

Table 2. Comparison of the Use of Lawyers and Court Procedure in Japan and in England & Wales

	Problem Experience	Legal Advice	Court Involvement
All Problems			
Japan	100	11	6
England & Wales	100	24	20
Accidents/Injuries			
Japan	100	6	3
England & Wales	100	50	14
Employment			
Japan	100	6	3
England & Wales	100	31	21
Family/Relationship			
Japan	100	46	43
England & Wales	100	82	62

Note: "Court Involvement" means the use of a court procedure either as plaintiff or defendant.

at stake tends to be higher in Japan than in England.[22] In other words, while problems in Japan are more amenable to legal resolution than problems in England, more problems in England are solved with lawyers and courts than are problems in Japan.

Why do people in Japan rely on law less frequently than people in the U.S. and England? One might follow Kawashima and argue that less reliance on the legal system is intrinsic to the Japanese way of dispute resolution. Kawashima argued that Japan's relative aversion to legal solutions stemmed from traditional attitudes, which valued harmony and avoided disputes. Yet as we saw above, Japanese people assert and contest claims as often as people in the U.S. Accordingly, social attitudes such as those described by Kawashima cannot explain Japan's low litigation rate.

22. Table A. Comparison of Amounts at Stake in Japan and in England & Wales.

Amount at Stake	£100 & less	£500 & less	£1,000 & less	£3,000 & less	£5,000 & less	£10,000 & less	£15,000 & less	Over £15,000
Japan	15%	23%	13%	18%	10%	8%	2%	10%
England & Wales	25%	30%	16%	16%	3%	5%	1%	4%

£1=¥200.

Instead, we should assume that the lower reliance on law is related to and probably caused by something inherent to the legal system.

III. What Encourages the Japanese to Use Lawyers and Court Procedures?

The Use of a Lawyer

Table 3 shows what variables are significantly correlated with the use of a lawyer to solve a problem. The use of a lawyer includes both obtaining advice from a lawyer and retaining a lawyer. It is intriguing to note that, setting aside three contextual factors, only four variables are significantly correlated with the use of a lawyer: Problem Type, Job, Connections with a Legal Professional, and the Use of a Lawyer in the Past.

When people experience problems concerning the purchase of real estate, their family, neighbors or their finances, they tend to use lawyers more frequently compared to when they face consumer-related problems. Apparently, the nature of some problems encourages the use of a lawyer because the stakes are too high to ignore or to handle without expert advice.

The other three variables implicate social connections in a broad sense. People in managerial positions have more opportunities to consult with lawyers related to their work. These lawyers are then also available for problems arising out of their private lives. If people know legal professionals they can consult, they are likely to use legal services when they face serious problems. Once people experience using lawyers, they have better understanding of how to use them. Individuals are also likely to return to the same lawyer if they have a positive experience during their first encounter.

In the U.S., Carlin et al. once argued that the use of lawyers and courts was directly correlated with socio-economic status and that the poor were unlikely to use the legal system.[23] They labeled "the ability to further and protect one's interests through active assertion of legal rights" as "legal competence"[24] and suggested that socioeconomic status influences the extent to which people possess legal competence. The development of legal aid has improved the situation of the poor, but that does not mean

23. Jerome E. Carlin, Jan Howard and Sheldon L. Messinger, *Civil Justice and the Poor: Issues for Sociological Research* (New York, 1967), at 81.

24. Ibid., 62.

Table 3. Logistic Regression Analysis of Lawyer Usage (Dispute Behavior Survey, 2005)

	The Use of a Lawyer	
Independent Variable	P Value	Odds Ratio
Problem Type (RC: Consumer Problem)	**.000**	—
Purchase of a House/Land	**.029**	**3.329**
Rent/Lease of an Apartment/House	.135	2.513
Employment	.167	2.105
Family	**.000**	**17.626**
Accident	.919	.951
Neighbor	**.047**	**2.702**
Money	**.006**	**4.172**
Private Insurance	.093	3.624
Pension/Public Insurance/Tax	.716	1.375
Age (RC: 20–39 Years Old)	.074	—
40–59 Years Old	.378	.800
60 Years or Older	.026	.448
Years of Living in the Same Area (RC: < 10 Years)	.079	—
10 to Less than 20 Years	.462	1.235
20 to Less than 30 Years	.849	1.058
30 to Less than 40 Years	.390	1.354
40 Years or Longer	.007	2.631
Urban-Rural (RC: Designated Cities)	.438	—
Cities with 200,000 or More Population	.234	.720
Other Cities	.329	.774
Towns and Villages	.123	.596
Individual Income (RC: Less than ¥4 Million)	.124	—
4 to Less than ¥8 Million	.041	1.816
¥8 Million or More	.345	1.525
Job (RC: Managerial)	**.045**	—
Fulltime Employee	**.037**	**.414**
Part-time/Temporal/Side Work	.827	.902
Self-Employed	.633	.807
Housewife/Househusband/Family Work	.838	1.107
No Job/Student	.386	.632

	The Use of a Lawyer	
Independent Variable	P Value	Odds Ratio
Education (RC: Junior High School)	.913	—
Senior High School	.734	.886
College/University/Graduate School	.669	.852
Study on Law (RC: None)	.625	1.133
Law-Related Work (RC: None)	.470	1.272
Connections with a Legal Professional (RC: None)	**.000**	—
Can Be Introduced	.087	1.632
Can Consult With	**.000**	**3.314**
Connections with a Insurance Agent	.080	—
Can Be Introduced	.741	.892
Can Consult With	.027	.601
Use of a Lawyer in the Past (RC: None)	**.000**	**4.370**
Use of the Court in the Past (RC: None)	.349	1.342
Gender (RC: Male)	.522	.841
Main Opponent: Organization (RC: Individual)	.052	.541
FAC_relation	**.005**	**1.334**
FAC_cost	**.000**	**1.760**
FAC_severity	**.000**	**1.731**
FAC_outcome	.428	.899
Constant	.002	.071
n=1,201, Hosmer & Lemeshow $p=.536$, Nagelkerke $R^2=.435$		

that socioeconomic status has become irrelevant. In the U.K., income was found to be significantly correlated with seeking advice from solicitors.[25] One survey suggested that legal knowledge was one factor that influenced whether people took legal action,[26] though in another survey education did not appear to correlate with seeking legal advice.[27] In contrast, Table 3

25. Genn (1999), 136.

26. Pascoe Pleasence, et al., *Causes of Action: Civil Law and Social Justice* (Norwich, 2004), at 107.

27. Hazel Genn and Alan Paterson, *Paths to Justice Scotland: What People in Scotland Do and Think about Going to Law* (Oxford, 2001), at 107.

demonstrates that Individual Income,[28] Education, and Legal Knowledge do not significantly correlate with the use of a lawyer. In other words, variables related to social stratification do not seem to correlate with the use of a lawyer. Instead, personal relationships seem to be one important factor influencing whether people use lawyers.[29]

The contextual factors which consist of Situational Variables cannot always be considered to be independent variables. Because Situational Variables were measured retrospectively, it is likely that the decision to use or not use a lawyer affected how respondents perceived or considered their problems and their resolution. Yet it is interesting to note that the direction of the two correlations is contrary to what we would expect. We usually expect that the more concerned people are with their relationships and how others view a problem, the less they would try to further their own interest. We also expect that the more concerned people are with money and time, the more they would try to avoid incurring costs. However, concern with relationships and with others' views of a problem, and concern for money and time, positively correlate with the use of a lawyer: The more concerned respondents are with such things, the more likely they are to use lawyers.

The third important factor is the perception of a problem's severity. The more serious a respondent perceives a problem to be, the more likely he is to use a lawyer. The findings regarding these three significant factors indicate that when people perceive their problems to be serious they are likely to consider using a lawyer. Although they become concerned with the effects and cost of using a lawyer, these concerns do not seem to deter them from using a lawyer.

Nevertheless, cost concerns are real. People who use lawyers tend to have two kinds of concerns when they consider seeking advice from lawyers: fees and approachability. According to findings from our research on people who used legal advice, 43.9% of them felt hesitation before their

28. In the Dispute Behavior Survey, we found Household Income less reliable as an income indicator, as respondents often did not know how much other members of their households earned.

29. This does not mean that socioeconomic status does not have any effects on the use of a lawyer. Private Income, Education, Job all correlate with Connections with a Legal Professional. In Japan, socioeconomic status affects the use of a lawyer indirectly.

visits,[30] 53.5% of the visitors to legal advice centers hesitated because they did not know how much the advice would cost, and 23.2% of them hesitated because they thought that fees were too expensive. Moreover, 36.3% hesitated because they felt it too difficult to approach a lawyer and 20.7% hesitated because lawyer's talk was difficult to understand. Although these concerns are even more pronounced among visitors to law offices, this anxiety is mollified by the fact that most visitors are usually introduced to the lawyers by those who know the lawyers personally.

Lawyers are often reluctant (and in some cases even decline) to meet potential clients without personal introductions. Lawyers say they cannot trust that a potential client will tell the truth unless there is a personal introduction. They say that a client who knows little about the law sometimes demands that a lawyer do what cannot legally be done. When a client comes to a lawyer through a personal introduction, the client tends to make more reasonable requests. The person introducing the client to the lawyer can also serve as an intermediary in case any disputes arise between the lawyer and the client. Although the number of lawyers who accept visitors without introductions has increased in recent years, most clients visit law offices only after a third party introduces the client to the lawyer.[31]

Accordingly, it is not surprising that the variables related to social connections with a lawyer significantly correlate with the use of a lawyer (as was shown in Table 3). However it is also important to note that Prob-

30. In cooperation with the Japan Federation of Bar Associations, we conducted questionnaire surveys in June to September, 2007 of people who visited either legal advice centers managed by the bar associations or law offices The sample size of visitors to the advice centers is 1,500 and the response rate is 92%. In the survey of visitors to law offices, we sent out questionnaires to all registered lawyers, but only 282 of around 20,000 lawyers responded. Masayuki Murayama, Akira Moriya, Kyoko Ishida, Tomohiko Maeda, Tsuneo Niki and Rie Ono, "Wagakuni ni okeru Horitsu Sodan Riyo no Jittai [The Use of Legal Consultation in Japan]," *Horitsu Ronso* 83, no. 1 (2010), 411–458.

31. According to the JFBA surveys, the percentage of clients without any introduction increased from 2.8% in 2000 to 18.2% in 2010. However, the percentage is especially high in rural cities (24.7%), while it is only 12.5% in Tokyo. Nihon Bengoshi Rengokai [Japan Federation of Bar Associations], "Bengoshi Gyomu no Keizaiteki Kiban ni kansuru Jittai Chosa Hokokusho 2010 [Report of the Research in 2010 on the Economic Basis of Lawyers' Activities]," *Jiyu to Seigi [Liberty and Justice]* 62, no. 6 (2011), 101–102. In rural areas, lawyers tend to have local knowledge and such knowledge helps to reduce the anxiety lawyers feel towards visitors. In big cities like Tokyo, it is more difficult to obtain such information.

lem Type has independent effects upon the use of a lawyer. Even without personal connections with a lawyer, people who face certain problem types tend to use lawyers. These clients may connect with lawyers by visiting municipal legal advice centers,[32] bar association legal advice centers, or the Japan Legal Support Center.[33] Nevertheless, it is more difficult to find lawyers through these centers than through personal introductions.

The Use of Court Procedures

Japanese court procedures include conciliation as well as litigation. As conciliation is very different from litigation, we ran multi-logistic regression analysis of the use of court procedures. As Table 4 shows, there are four categories of dependent variables: Conciliation, Litigation, Other than Litigation, and None. The reference category is None. As Other than Litigation includes different kinds of procedures, such as family court decisions and formal payment requests (*shiharai tokusoku*), we focus on conciliation and litigation.

Family Problem, Advice from a Lawyer and the Use of Courts in the Past significantly correlate with using both conciliation and litigation. However, the Family Problem and the Use of the Court in the Past correlate with conciliation much more strongly than with litigation, while Advice from a Lawyer correlates much more strongly with litigation than conciliation. Attending university or otherwise participating in higher education, cost concerns, and the Use of a Lawyer in the Past positively correlate with litigation, while concern about relationships and with others' views on a problem negatively correlate with conciliation. Here, too, income and legal knowledge itself do not affect the use of conciliation or litigation. However, it is apparent that litigation is much more related with lawyers than conciliation. Although conciliation is conducted in court and judges are appointed as chairs of conciliation committees, judges rarely attend conciliation ses-

32. Municipal governments set up legal consultation bureaus where residents obtain free legal advice. However, as demand is high, the time for consultation is often limited to within 30 minutes. Masayuki Murayama, "Rikon Mondai Tojisha no tameno Jichitai Sodan Network [Municipal Consultation Network for Divorcing Spouses]," *Horitsu Ronso* 83, no. 2–3 (2010), 375, 396–98.

33. The Japan Legal Support Center was established in 2006 and 100 local offices, including branch offices, have been set up all over Japan. The percentage of first-time clients who came through legal consultation to law offices was 10.8% nationwide and 5.2% in Tokyo, while the percentage of those who were referred by bar associations or Japan Legal Support Center was 13.9% for nationwide and 10.8% in Tokyo (JFBA, 2011, 102).

Table 4. Logistic Regression of the Types of Court Procedure Used as a Plaintiff (Disputing Behavior Survey, 2005)

	Dependent Variable (RC: None)					
Independent Variable	Conciliation Only		Litigation		Other Than Litigation	
	Odds Ratio	P	Odds Ratio	P	Odds Ratio	P
Dummy for Family Problem	**61.19**	**	**4.10**	*	**8.39**	**
Dummy for University Education	0.44		**3.27**	*	0.19	
Study on Law (RC: None)	1.20		0.32		**6.19**	*
Law-Related Work (RC: None)	0.37		1.27		0.72	
Advice from a Lawyer (RC: The Other or No Advice)	**7.88**	**	**59.15**	**	3.09	
Other Advice (RC: Advice from a Lawyer or Administrative Agency)	2.16		0.74		0.83	
FAC_relation	**0.48**	*	0.79		1.08	
FAC_cost	0.71		**3.88**	*	2.03	
FAC_severity	2.52	†	1.37		0.60	
FAC_outcome	2.36		2.84		6.23	†
The Other Side is Right	0.53		0.50		1.19	
The Use of a Lawyer in the Past	1.16		**6.25**	**	0.83	
The Use of the Court in the Past	**24.75**	**	**7.01**	**	**12.47**	**

n=884, Nagelkerke R^2 =.602. † $p<.10$, *$p<.05$, **$p<.01$
Note: Only dispute cases are used in the analyses.

The table is taken and translated from Ryo Hamano, Isamu Sugino and Masayuki Murayama, "Saibansho heno Kakawari to Sono Kitei Yoin [Involvement in the Court and Its Significant Factors]," in Yoshiyuki Matsumura and Masayuki Murayama, eds., *Ho Ishiki to Hunso Kodo [Legal Consciousness and Disputing Behavior]*, *Gendai Nihon no Hunso Shori to Minji Shiho [Civil Justice and Dispute Resolution in Contemporary Japan]*, Vol. 1 (Tokyo, 2010), 171–189, at 187.

sions. Thus, conciliation is not really a legal or judicial process. This is why legal advice and the use of a lawyer in the past affect the use of litigation much more strongly than the use of conciliation.

Conclusion

If Japanese disputing behavior is defined by traditional culture, people who experienced problems should have been reluctant to assert and contest claims. If such a pattern of behavior had been evidenced in the study described above, traditional culture could have explained the tendency not to use lawyers and court procedures. However, the study indicated that Japanese people are just as likely to assert claims and face disputes as Americans. Moreover, problem type tends to determine dispute behavior both in Japan and in the U.S. In this sense, the Japanese way of dispute resolution cannot be explained by traditional culture.

I believe that the less frequent use of lawyers and court procedures in Japan must instead be related to variables internal to the Japanese legal system. The result of the logistic regression analysis regarding the use of lawyers showed that problem type and connections with lawyers in a broad sense significantly affect the use of a lawyer. This result reflects the concerns of both lawyers and their clients. On the one hand, lawyers are reluctant to meet visitors without a personal introduction. On the other hand, people who consider visiting lawyers worry about the high fees and the unapproachability of lawyers. Connections with lawyers tend to facilitate their use because these connections can reduce concerns on both sides. Personal introductions remain the primary means for obtaining new clients because lawyers do not feel pressure to expand their client base. Insofar as lawyers have a sufficiently large client base, they can be more strict in screening out clients they deem to be inappropriate.

From the client's point of view, choices are limited. People who experience problems must choose the best available means for solving their problems. The fact that legal services are provided primarily through personal introductions indicates that an open market for legal services does not exist in Japan. Laypersons do not have much contact with lawyers and possess little information about what they do. This is why people feel lawyers are difficult to approach.[34]

Litigation rates in Japan are low for reasons that are similar to why lawyer usage in Japan is low. When there are few lawyers and judges, it should not be surprising that there is little litigation.[35]

34. According to results of a logistic regression analysis of Connections with a Legal Professional, people who have legal backgrounds in education or work and those who have "judicial connections" are likely to have Connections with a Legal Professional.

35. The recent increase in litigation was best explained by the increase of judges and then by the increase of lawyers. Tom Ginsburg and Glenn Hoetker, "The Unreluctant Litigant? An Empirical Analysis of Japan's Turn to Litigation," *Journal of Legal Studies* 35 (2006), 31–59, at 31.

There is no evidence that the public supports this situation. Laypersons with legal problems simply want the best existing solution. They are not interested in the legal system itself. Even those few who are interested are not organized into pressure groups.

As Kawashima once argued about the introduction of the conciliation system, the legal system is a product of political decisions. The limited availability of legal services is a product of decisions that have capped the number of new lawyers produced each year at no more than 350 or so for more than 20 years. We should ask what led to such decisions instead of why the Japanese do not use lawyers as often as people in the U.S. and U.K.

Lawyers and Changing Legal Practice: Regarding the Number of Lawyers in Japan[1]

Kota Fukui[2] and Yusuke Fukui,[3]
with assistance from Stacey L. Steele[4]

Introduction: The Changing Legal Profession in Japan

This paper aims to introduce the current legal needs, role, and image of lawyers in Japanese corporate society, utilizing three questionnaire surveys conducted by a research group at Osaka University. It sets out to clarify the reasons why Japanese corporations do not utilize lawyers for daily business activities and also discusses the future of lawyers in Japan. It claims that the increased number of corporate in-house lawyers is driving the change of corporate legal culture in Japan. This paper sets up some

1. This article is a revised version of an article that appeared in the *Australian Journal of Asian Law (AJAL)* in winter 2011 and is used with permission. The empirical data presented in this article was also used in an earlier Japanese publication (Kota Fukui and Yusuke Fukui, "Kigyō no Bengoshi Yakuwari Kan wa Kawaritsutsu Arunoka: Bengoshi Gyōmu ni Kansuru Mittsu no Ankēto Chōsa kara [On the Changing Role Images of Lawyer in Japanese Companies: From the Results of the 3 Questionnaire Surveys]," *Handai Hōgaku [Osaka Law Review]* 56(6) (2010): 1–48). Regarding this original paper, the preface and the final part were written by Kota Fukui and Chapters 1 through 4, the main empirical-analytical part of the paper, were written by Yusuke Fukui. The main translator from Japanese to English was Kota Fukui, with corrections and comments by Yusuke Fukui. The figures were translated by Yusuke Fukui. For the purposes of this article, we have substantially revisited the data with the assistance of our editor, Stacey Steele. We are also grateful for the support of our colleagues at Osaka University who assisted us with this research.

2. Professor of Law at the Graduate School of Law and Politics, Osaka University.

3. Foreign Teacher, Japanese Department, College of Foreign Languages, University of Shanghai for Science and Technology, China.

4. Senior lecturer of law and associate director of the Asian Law Centre at the Melbourne Law School, University of Melbourne, Victoria, Australia.

strong hypotheses and provides support using analysis of the data from three questionnaire surveys.

Problems Concerning the Number of Lawyers in Japan

According to the law governing the legal profession in Japan, a person who has obtained the qualification of a lawyer (*Bengoshi*) is authorized to deal with a wide range of legal matters.[5] Traditionally, however, the role of lawyers has been regarded as a barrister-like, specialized function, where s/he exclusively deals with court-related matters.[6] Lawyers are also regarded as highly independent professionals who do not work under the supervision of non-lawyers. Therefore, the number of lawyers has remained fairly low in Japan. When the Justice System Reform Council (JSRC) was established in 1999, the total number of Japanese lawyers was about 16,500,[7] approximately one lawyer for every 6,000 people in Japan. Presently, the total number of Japanese lawyers is still only 30,488 (as of June 1, 2011).[8]

Furthermore, functions which would generally be performed by lawyers in other developed countries are traditionally ascribed to other qualified professionals in Japan. The population of Japan's so-called "legal profession" would swell if it were to include professionals such as judicial

5. See the Attorney Act (*Bengoshi Hō*, Act No. 205, Shōwa Year 24 [1949]), art. 3 (1): "The duties of an attorney, upon the request of the party or the concerned parties, or upon the entrustment of public agency, shall be to engage in acts relating to lawsuits, non-contentious cases, and objections, request for re-examination, appeals, and other petitions against administrative agencies and other general legal services." Unless otherwise noted, translations of legislation in this article are taken from the legal-word database named "Japanese Law Translation," which is administered by the Ministry of Justice and is available at http://www.japaneselawtranslation.go.jp.

6. On the changing image of lawyers in Japan since the nineteenth century, see Ryo Hamano, "Bengoshi Zō wa Dō Kawatte Kitaka [How has the image of lawyers been changed?]," in Yoshitaka Wada, Shōzo Ota, and Masaki Abe, eds., *Kōshō to Funsō Shori [Negotiation and Dispute Resolution]*, (Tokyo, 2002), chap. 12 (248–273).

7. See the Japan Federation of Bar Associations (JFBA), "Statistics of the Year-to-Year Number Change of Lawyers from 1950 to 2009", available at: http://www.nichibenren.or.jp/en/about/whitepaper/whitepaper_2009.html.

8. Ibid.

scriveners (*Shihō Shoshi*),[9] administrative scriveners (*Gyōsei Shoshi*),[10] tax accountants (*Zeirishi*),[11] public consultants on social and labor insurance (*Shakai Hoken Rōmushi*),[12] and patent attorneys (*Benrishi*).[13] In the absence of plentiful qualified lawyers, these professionals fulfilled important legal needs, including conveyance work, property registration, preparation of legal or administrative documents, income tax returns, social and labor insurance submissions, and intellectual property filings. If the number of these specialist professionals were added to the population of lawyers in Japan, the so-called "legal professional" population would be approximately 200,000,[14] which would bring Japan into line with other developed countries.

There is also a general acceptance in Japan that employees in corporate legal departments may conduct legal matters concerning their employers' business during the course of their employment. Article 72 of the Attorney Act (*Bengoshi Hō*) prohibits the provision of legal services by non-qualified lawyers for the purpose of obtaining compensation, if it is not permitted by the Attorney Act itself or by other laws.[15] Based on

9. A specialized legal profession for conveyance and property registration, legal documentation and submission for judicial agencies, and, when certified, an attorney for the procedure of summary court. They call themselves "*Shiho Shoshi* lawyer[s]" on their English website. See their association homepage at: http://www.shiho-shoshi.or.jp/english.

10. A specialized law-related profession for administrative documentation and submission for administrative agencies. See their association homepage at: http://www.gyosei.or.jp/.

11. A specialized law-related profession for the documentation and submission of income tax returns, tax consultation, and consultation for tax review. See their association homepage at: http://www.nichizeiren.or.jp/eng.

12. A specialized law-related profession for documentation, consultation, and submissions relating to social and labor insurance. See their association homepage at: http://www.shakaihokenroumushi.jp.

13. A specialized law-related profession for the submission and consultation of patent, design and trademark filings. See their association homepage at: http://www.jpaa.or.jp/english.

14. See each law-related professional's association homepage above. As of June 1, 2011, there are 20,257 judicial scriveners, 41,584 administrative scriveners, 71,810 tax accountants, 8,724 public consultants on social and labor insurance (as of 30 September 2010), and 8,724 patent attorneys (as of 27 October 2010). Therefore, the sum of all "legal professionals," including lawyers (*Bengoshi*), is 208,161.

15. See Article 72 of the Attorney Act (*Bengoshi Hō*): "No person other than an attorney or a Legal Professional Corporation may, for the purpose of obtaining com-

the prevailing understanding of Article 72, however, legal work conducted by such employees does not contravene the Act because they do not receive compensation for their legal work from an external source; their legal work does not generate any independent profit as it would if they were to establish their own firm. The quality of work produced by these employees is high. They are often tertiary-trained law graduates and have passed one of the examinations relating to the professions mentioned above, such as the patent attorneys examination, or have business qualifications, such as as a financial planner,[16] small and medium enterprise (SME) management consultant (*Chusho Kigyō Shindanshi*),[17] or, in some cases, as a certified public accountant (*Kōnin Kaikeishi*),[18] which are also law-related in a broad sense. Therefore, traditionally, Japanese corporations have managed their own legal matters without the need to hire external or in-house lawyers. In the 1990s, however, the Japan Federation of Economic Organizations (*Keidanren*) changed its attitude. It perceived a need for more lawyers to enable Japan to compete globally.

Reform of the Legal Profession in Japan and the Need for Empirical Research

Criticism of the Japanese legal system and a desire for structural reform brought about by Japan's economic malaise culminated in the establish-

---

pensation, engage in the business of providing legal advice or representation, handling arbitration matters, aiding in conciliation, or providing other legal services in connection with any lawsuits, non-contentious cases, or objections, requesting for re-examination, appeals and other petitions against administrative agencies, etc., or other general legal services, or acting as an intermediary in such matters; provided, however, that the foregoing shall not apply if otherwise specified in this Act or other laws" (Japanese Law Translation).

16. A professional specializing in creating comprehensive financial plans based on data gathered from the client, including family profile, income and expenses, assets and liabilities, insurance, and the client's desires and goals. They are not certified by the national examination but are qualified by the Japan Association for Financial Planners (a non-profit organization). Though they are only financial consultants, they sometimes give law-related advice. See their association website at: http://www.jafp.or.jp/english.

17. A public qualification for SME diagnosticians and operational consults. Although they are corporate management consultants, they sometimes give law-related advice. See their association website at: http://www.j-smeca.jp/contents/018_english_contents.html.

18. A certified professional performing accounting and financial audits. Although they are corporate management consultants, they sometimes give law-related advice. See their association website at: http://www.hp.jicpa.or.jp/english/index.html.

ment of the JSRC by the Cabinet of Japan on 27 July 1999.[19] In June 2001, JSRC released its recommendations.[20] JSRC's fundamental findings for the creation of the ideal legal profession to "support Japan in the twenty-first century" included that: the "legal population" be "substantially increased," training for potential lawyers[21] should be comprehensively reformed, lawyers should be encouraged to focus on social responsibilities ("public interest" lawyering) and specializations such as business law and international transactions, and the status of people engaged in corporate legal affairs who have not been admitted to practice should be reviewed.[22]

A decade after the JSRC's final report, it is now useful to document by empirical research the changes in Japanese legal profession. This paper argues that the roles and perceptions of lawyers in Japanese corporations are changing, including as a result of the JSRC's watershed final report.[23] We also argue, however, that other reforms and developments in Japan's society and economy may bring about further and more fundamental change for lawyers working in corporate legal affairs departments. Our findings are based on empirical evidence collected by way of three questionnaire surveys conducted over the course of 2007–8. Our research was made possible by a grant from the Japan Society for the Promotion of Sci-

19. On the establishment of the JSRC, see *Shihōseido Kaikaku ni Mukete -Ronten Seiri- [The Points at Issue in the Justice Reform]* (1999), citing Article 2 of Shihōseido Kaikaku Shingikai Setchi Hō [the Law concerning Establishment of Justice System Reform Council] (Law No. 68, Heisei Year 11 [1999]).

20. *Shihōseido Kaikaku Shingikai Ikensho* [Recommendations of the Justice System Reform Council—For a Justice System to Support Japan in the Twenty-First Century] (12 June 2001), http://www.kantei.go.jp/foreign/policy/sihou/singikai/990612_e.html.

21. As discussed in more detail in this article, we use the English term "lawyer" to refer to the concept of a "*Bengoshi*," that is, a person admitted to practice law in Japan. The term "attorney" is also sometimes used. The Ministry of Justice (Japanese Law Translation) uses "attorney," but "*Bengoshi*" is a more independent actor than inferred by the term "attorney." See Japanese Law Translation.

22. *Shihōseido Kaikaku Shingikai Ikensho*, chap. 3.

23. The ideas and recommendations published by the JSRC in relation to the legal profession were not necessarily new, but the authority and public awareness of the JSRC, having been appointed by the Cabinet and promoted as a key reform initiative by the Liberal Democratic Party, gave its recommendations a new impetus. See, for example, Kahei Rokumoto, "Overhauling the Judicial System: Japan's Response to the Globalizing World," *Journal of Japanese Law* 10(20) (2005): 7–38.

ence (JSPS).[24] We were particularly interested in the roles given to lawyers in Japanese corporations and the perceptions of the need for lawyers held by corporate managers and lawyers themselves given the complicated and controversial debates about the population of lawyers in Japan.

Our main hypothesis was that the role-image of lawyers is changing dramatically, influenced by the increasing new legal needs of corporations. Accordingly, we conducted a questionnaire survey on corporations' legal needs ("Survey (a)"),[25] as well as questionnaires on the type of legal work currently being performed by private practice lawyers ("Survey (b)")[26] and corporate in-house lawyers ("Survey (c)"),[27] which provided us data to conduct a comparative analysis. We focused on the corporate legal needs fulfilled by lawyers because Japanese corporations are generating new needs for lawyers in response to global business competition.[28] The

24. Our research project is titled "The Construction of the Grand Design of New Fields of Legal Profession." Further details of our funding, data, and analysis may be accessed in Japanese at Osaka University, http://legalprofession.law.osaka-u.ac.jp. We collected information on various issues, but this article focuses on the perceived problem of the small legal population in Japan.

25. This questionnaire survey was conducted in February 2007. We distributed 2000 questionnaires to corporations from all over Japan selected randomly using Teikoku Data Bank, which is the biggest corporate data bank in Japan. We selected 1000 corporations which had over 100 employees and 1000 corporations which had less than 100 employees. The standard of 100 employees is a simple standard to classify relatively large companies and SMEs in Japan. The questionnaires were delivered by post. We received 320 responses, a response rate of 16.0%.

26. This questionnaire survey was distributed in August 2008 to 1500 members of the Osaka Bar Association (OBA), almost half of the private practice lawyers registered with the OBA. We selected private practice lawyers randomly by using the lawyers search engine on the website of the OBA. The questionnaires were delivered by post. We received 194 responses, a response rate of 12.9%.

27. This questionnaire survey was delivered in August 2008 to 259 corporate in-house lawyers in Japan, which we believe to be the entire population of corporate in-house lawyers at that time. We identified corporate in-house lawyers by using the lawyer search engine on the website of the JFBA, inserting keywords such as "*Kaisha* [Corporation]," "*Inku* [Inc]," "*Eru Eru Shī* [LLC]," "*Kabu* [Ltd]" etc. We received 68 responses, a response rate of 26.3%. The number of corporate in-house lawyers has risen to about 410 in 2010, a large increase from 2008 but still a small number.

28. An increase in the number of lawyers in Japan has also been supported on the basis of social justice reasons. See, for example, Setsuo Miyazawa, "Law Reform, Lawyers, and Access to Justice," in Gerald McAlinn, ed., *Japanese Business Law*, (Austin, 2007), 39–89.

Figure 1. Mapping the Formation of Legal Work

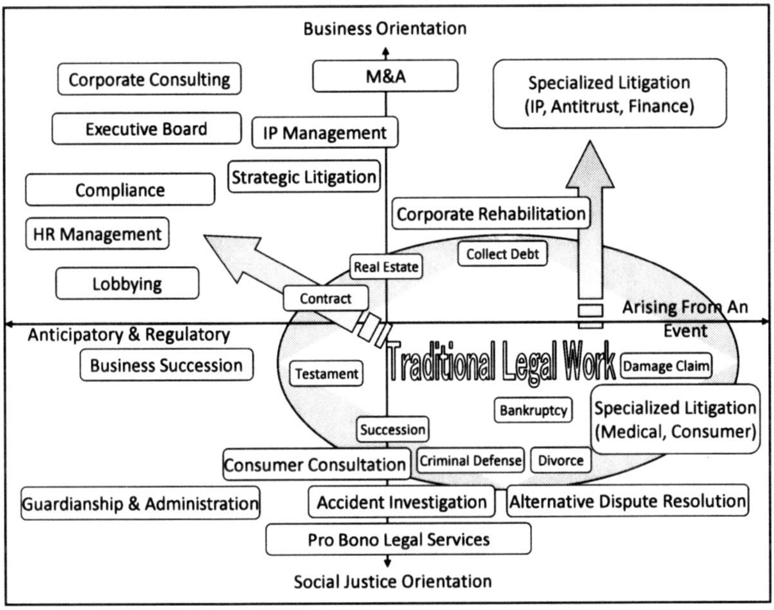

fields of legal work being performed for corporations are expanding due to internal and external pressure from "corporate compliance" demands and "corporate social responsibility (CSR)" requests, which have become common in the Japanese business world. Figure 1 maps many typical fields of legal work. The horizontal axis relates to the temporal stages of legal work (Anticipatory & Regulatory/Arising from an Event), and the vertical axis relates to the orientation of the legal work (Social Justice Orientation/Business Orientation). The map helps to plot the situation of legal work as of today and for the future.

Before conducting the questionnaire surveys, we assumed that the main fields for legal practice are shifting into both the upper left and upper right quadrants (more specifically, the upper left), which reflected a business-oriented shift from the lower right, which is the traditional jurisprudence zone.[29] The lower right quadrant is still very important, but it

29. For a discussion of how to measure the change brought by the legal reforms, see Bruce Aronson, "Changes in the Role of Lawyers and Corporate Governance in Japan—How Do We Measure Whether Legal Reform Leads to Real Change?" *Washing-*

is essential to analyze the movement toward the upper quadrant carefully, in light of our hypothesis that the increasing legal needs of corporations and the lure of lucrative work will see more lawyers engaged in that type of legal work.

The survey results, however, led us to slightly different conclusions from our first assumptions. According to the data, Japanese corporations were still largely expecting lawyers to play traditional roles related to litigation or dispute settlement.[30] Further, few think that they even need to employ in-house lawyers. The data suggested that the needs for lawyers in Japanese corporations are still located in the lower right quadrant in Figure 1. Per contra, our data also showed that roles mainly connected to corporate compliance matters, which are new to many Japanese corporations, were under consideration by Japanese corporations. We believe that the role-images of lawyers in Japan are in a transitional phase in which new fields of legal work, including compliance, may create traction for an increase in in-house lawyers.

Utilization of Lawyers in Japanese Corporations: Findings from the Questionnaire Survey on the Need for Lawyers in Japanese Corporations, "Survey (a)"

The Utilization of Lawyers in Japanese Corporations

Firstly, we asked respondents from Japanese corporations whether they retain their own external consultant lawyer by way of a retainer fee (*Komon Bengoshi*).[31] According to the results, half of the respondents (50.5%) answered positively to this question. There were, however, few corporations with a staff of less than 10 employees that retain their own external

---

ton University Global Studies Law Review 8 (2009): 223–240. Aronson adopts the expansion of the role of (elite) lawyers as a standard for the transformational change brought by the legal reforms in the field of corporate legal practice.

30. The first formal regulation of lawyers (*Bengoshi*) in Japan may be traced to February 1876, when the Attorney Rules [*Daigen Nin Kisoku*] were promulgated. Daigen Nin was a private court advocate in the early Meiji era. On this point, see the JFBA webpage at http://www.nichibenren.or.jp/en/about/us/profile/history.html.

31. A lawyer who is not employed by the client but retained by it by way of payment of a regular fee. *Komon Bengoshi* give legal advice when the client experiences difficulties. Japanese corporations retain *Komon Bengoshi* as a precaution. The market price for such a retainer is said to be from ¥50,000 to ¥200,000 per month.

consultant lawyer by way of a retainer fee (17.1%).[32] As the number of employees per corporation increases, more respondents answered that they retain their own external consultant lawyer by way of a retainer fee. Most of the corporations with more than 300 employees (83.3%) retain their own external consultant lawyer by way of a retainer fee. Accordingly, the size of the corporation is one of the drivers behind engaging lawyers on a retainer basis.[33]

Although corporations are retaining their own external consultant lawyer by way of a retainer fee, there are very few respondents who employ in-house lawyers, only 2.2%. This rate is the same for both large corporations and SMEs.[34] Although seemingly low, 2.2% is actually a high rate considering that the total number of in-house lawyers in Japan was less than 200 as of February 2007.[35] One possible reason for the high percentage is the effect of sampling. We distributed the questionnaire survey to

32. From 2006 to 2007, the JFBA also conducted a questionnaire survey on the legal needs of Japanese SMEs. Its results suggest that only 19.5% of the respondents retain their own external consultant lawyer by way of a retainer fee, and 16.2% of the respondents answered that they do not retain their own consultant lawyer but can get legal advice from a lawyer they know, if required. 61.5% of the respondents (SMEs) answered that they don't get any legal advice from a lawyer even when they have a legal problem. The results of this JFBA questionnaire survey for Japanese SMEs correspond with the results from our Survey (a). The results of the JFBA's questionnaire survey are available at http://www.nichibenren.or.jp/ja/committee/list/data/chusho_chousakekka.pdf (last accessed June 14, 2011).

33. Toshimitsu Kitagawa and Luke Nottage, "Globalization of Japanese Corporations and the Development of Corporate Legal Departments: Problems and Prospects," in William Alford, ed., *Raising the Bar: The Emerging Legal Profession in East Asia* (Cambridge, Mass., 2007), chap. 6, 211–212.

34. To our surprise, while some small sized corporations hire in-house lawyers, no respondent corporations whose staff worker number is over 300 answered that they hire in-house lawyers. We know that super large global corporations hire in-house lawyers. For further information about corporations which hire in-house lawyers, see the Japan In-house Lawyers Association (JILA), "Statistics of the Number of Corporate In-House Lawyers and their Belonging Company in the Second Half of 2009' by the Japan In-house Lawyers Association," available at: http://jila.jimdo.com/資料-統計等/組織内弁護士統計/企業内弁護士の人数と所属企業に関する調査. We guess one reason for this anomalous result is that too few respondents answered that they hire in-house lawyers. Further, large corporations with over 300 employees are more likely to have their own non-lawyer legal departments who satisfy their legal needs.

35. See also the JILA, "Statistics of the Year-to-Year Change of the Number of Corporate In-House Lawyers in the Second Half of 2009" by Japan In-house Lawyers

1000 large and 1000 small corporations as discussed above. There are many more small corporations in Japan than large corporations, however, so the proportion of the larger corporations in our survey is considerably higher than the proportion of larger corporations in Japanese business life generally. This may be one reason for the high rate of respondents indicating that they employ in-house lawyers. Another reason may be that respondents hire outside lawyers as temporary staff on a per-project basis. When we conducted this questionnaire survey, there was a lot of new legislation, including the new codification of the Companies Act (*Kaisha Hō*) and the Financial Products Transaction Act (*Kinyū Shōhin Torihiki Hō*); accordingly, legal specialists would have been in high demand. Further, it may be that corporations with in-house lawyers were more likely to respond to a survey about in-house lawyers and legal needs, as they are generally more aware of the issues surrounding the emerging in-house market in Japan. We also contend that 2.2% is indicative of a change in Japanese corporate legal culture towards hiring more in-house lawyers.[36]

Reasons for Not Utilizing Lawyers

As discussed, many Japanese corporations do not utilize lawyers in their daily business activities because non-lawyer personnel are permitted to deal with legal matters relating to the corporation. We hypothesized, however, that this was not the only reason. We asked the corporations

---

Association, available at: http://jila.jimdo.com/資料-統計等/組織内弁護士統計/弁護士会毎の企業内弁護士数の経年変化.

36. From October to November 2006, the JFBA also conducted a questionnaire survey on the hiring of in-house lawyers in major domestic and foreign corporations in Japan. They sent questionnaires to 3795 domestic and 1457 foreign corporations and collected answers from 1446 corporations. According to this survey, 3.9% of the respondents employ in-house lawyers, and 6.7% of them were accepting applications from lawyers, currently planning or discussing the recruitment of in-house lawyers. We understand from this JFBA survey that the need for lawyers in corporations in Japan is high. The results of this questionnaire survey are available at http://www.nichibenren.or.jp/ja/committee/list/data/soshikinai_Bengoshi_torikumi.pdf (last accessed on 23 July 2010; it has since been removed). Contrary to this, the JFBA's questionnaire survey on the legal needs in Japanese SMEs, conducted from 2006 to 2007, shows that only 1 in 3214 respondents hired a qualified lawyer. As to this questionnaire survey, see the webpage of the JFBA at: http://www.nichibenren.or.jp/library/ja/jfba_info/publication/data/chusho_gaiyou.pdf. The difference between the results of the two questionnaire surveys by the JFBA suggests a gap between a lawyer's role in a major corporation versus in SMEs, which also reflects the results from our Survey (c).

which answered that they do not need to utilize lawyers about the reasons why they so answered.[37] Separately, we asked this question regarding two types of lawyer utilization: first, hiring an external consultant lawyer by way of a retainer fee, and secondly, employing an in-house lawyer. The top reason in both cases was: "There is no work which requires a lawyer's help" (external consultant lawyer: 45.9%; in-house lawyer: 46.2%), followed by the reasons "We are not prepared to utilize lawyers" (28.7% and 30.1%), "Lawyers' fees are too high" (24.8% and 25.1%), and "Difficult to calculate costs and benefits of lawyer's work" (22.3% and 27.4%). The rank order of the answers in the two questions is very similar; in the top five responses only the rankings of "The standards of fees for work are unclear" and "Lawyers' fees are too high" are exchanged. To summarize, most Japanese corporations who do not utilize lawyers say that they have no work which requires a lawyer's help and that they are not prepared to utilize lawyers.

We interpret these results to mean that most Japanese corporations do not know how to utilize lawyers profitably in daily business activities, which may be directly related to the fact that Japanese corporate managers have no fixed role-image of lawyers in daily business activities. Furthermore, because they do not know how to utilize lawyers, they answered that they are not prepared to utilize lawyers. We also extrapolate reluctance on behalf of corporate managers to supervise lawyers because lawyers are regarded as highly independent professionals.

The Relationship Between the Need for Lawyers and Other Law-Related Professionals

In Japan, as discussed above, there are various kinds of law-related, non-lawyer professionals that support corporate business activities. To better understand the divide between lawyer and non-lawyer work, we asked corporations what work they each perform and how they utilize, and want to utilize, law-related professionals and lawyers in their daily business activities. The most often utilized law-related professional, excluding lawyers, is the tax accountant (76.3%), followed by the judicial scrivener

37. Choices were as follows: "There is no work which requires a lawyer's help," "We are not prepared to utilize lawyers," "Lawyers' fees are too high," "Difficult to calculate costs and benefits of lawyer's work," "The standards of fees for work are unclear," "Anxious about lawyer's integrity," "Already utilizing non-lawyer staff workers," "Anxious about lawyer's ability," "Lawyers lack in flexibility," and another reason (free answer).

(57.3%), the public consultant on social and labor insurance (42.8%), and the certified public accountant (42.2%). We sorted the utilization rate of law-related professionals, including lawyers, according to size of corporation. As may be expected, lawyers, certified public accountants, and public consultants on social and labour insurance are utilized in larger corporations, and tax accountants and SME management consultants are utilized in small and middle size corporations.

The utilization of lawyers and other law-related professionals is clearly influenced by the division of work in Japanese corporations generally. In larger corporations, taxation and business diagnosis, which tend to fall into the professional fields of tax accountant and SME management consultant, are dealt with by the corporation's own employees who specialize in those types of work. Court-related matters, business accounting review, and social insurance matters, which belong to the professional field of lawyers, certified public accountants, and public consultants on social and labor insurance, are generally not dealt with in-house. One reason may be that corporations do not maintain this type of professional speciality on an ongoing basis; another may be that these fields are seen as being limited by legally sanctioned service-monopolization.[38] Even larger corporations with ongoing legal matters, however, appear likely to outsource certain legal work to external lawyers, certified public accountants, and public consultants on social and labor insurance.

The Preference to Utilize Law-Related Professionals in Japanese Corporations

We also asked respondents about their preference for utilizing law-related professionals, including lawyers, when it comes to major law-related work. If the law-related work also related to business consulting, corporations first seek advice from a certified public accountant (36.6%), second, a tax accountant (32.2%), third, a lawyer (30.9%), and fourth, a SME management consultant (28.4%).

38. Article 72 of the Attorney Act (*Bengoshi Hō*) prohibits the provision of legal services by non-lawyers for the purpose of obtaining compensation. Lawyers are permitted to monopolize the provision of legal services, in so far as their provision is not permitted for non-lawyers to provide by the Attorney Act itself or by other laws. Other law-related professionals have their own legislation permitting them to provide their own limited, specialized legal services, though lawyers can also provide the services which they provide according to the Attorney Act.

As expected, if the law-related work also relates to human resource management, corporations first turn to public consultants on social and labor insurance (72.2%) and secondly to lawyers (34.4%). As we also expected, the ranking of the law-related professionals whom corporations want to utilize for law-related work involving financial management was: first, tax accountants (63.4%) and second, certified public accountants (52.2%). The ranking of lawyers (11.6%) is lower than that of financial planners (24.1%).

Corporations did not appear to perceive brand value management as a law-related issue, telling us that they did "not want to utilize anyone on this list" for such work (30.3%), although lawyers ranked second (29.1%), followed by certified public accountants (18.8%) and the SME management consultants (17.5%). Once again, tax accountants were the first priority in relation to law-related general assistance for corporate management (49.1%), followed by lawyers (47.8%), certified public accountants (44.1%), public consultants on social and labor insurance (26.6%), and SME management consultants (22.2%).

Comparing these answers to the questions about the relationship between lawyers and other law-related professionals, the perceived need for lawyers in Japanese corporations is relatively high when considered from the perspective of law-related work; however, corporations tend to seek the assistance of law-related professionals other than lawyers in the first instance. One reason may be the perceived specialization required to perform the work, which corporations attribute to law-related professionals who are not lawyers. The more specialized that professionals become, the higher the barriers to entry into their field. Every law-related profession in Japan has constructed its own niche and segregated its own field from the other professions' niches. In light of this entrenched professional segregation, corporations have come to regard lawyers as a special professional with their own niche; that is, court-related legal work.

The Need for Lawyers in Japanese Corporations Under "Ideal Conditions"

We also asked corporations about the need for lawyers under "ideal conditions;" that is, the ability to engage lawyers on suitable occasions for reasonable fees. By asking corporations about their need for lawyers under "ideal conditions," we hoped to clarify the need for lawyers in daily business activities, all other factors being equal. We asked the respondents to rate their level of willingness to utilize lawyers in relation to thirty typical

Figure 2. Corporate Willingness to Use Lawyers Under "Ideal Conditions"

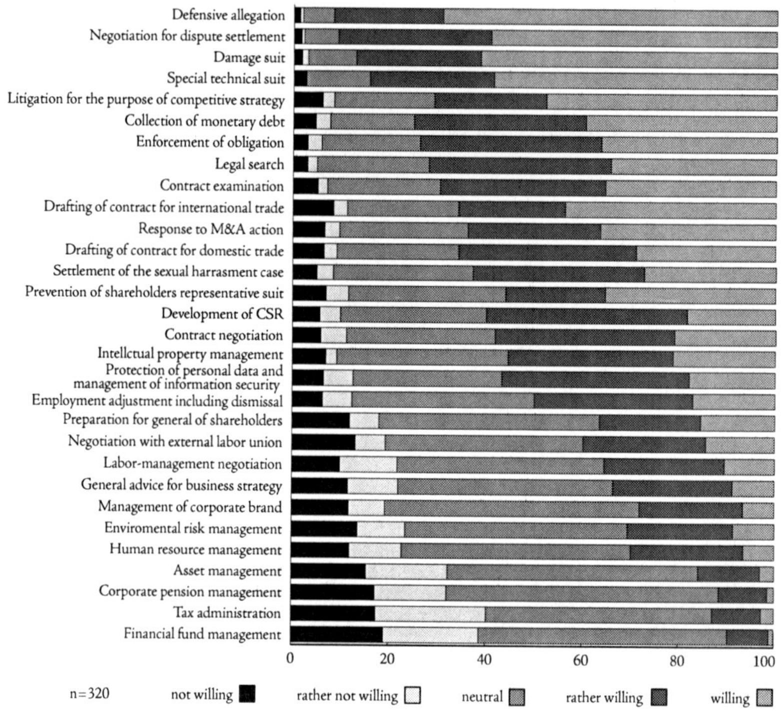

fields of legal work in corporations from No. 1, "not willing to utilize," through No. 2, "rather not willing to utilize," No. 3, "neutral," and No. 4, "rather willing to utilize," to No. 5, "willing to utilize" (see Figure 2).

In "ideal conditions," corporations said that they were most likely to utilize lawyers for the following types of legal work, in order of highest to lowest popularity: "defensive allegation," "negotiation for dispute settlement," "damage suit," "special technical suit," "litigation for the purpose of competitive strategy," "collection of monetary debt," and "enforcement of obligations." All these fields are ex-post, reactive legal practices relating to litigation or disputes. "Special technical suit" and "litigation for the purpose of competitive strategy" are ranked at fourth and fifth, which suggests that corporations are concerned about new types of litigation. After the litigation/dispute work, the second highest type of work is "legal search" and "contract examination," "drafting of contract for international trade," "response to M&A action," "drafting of contract for domestic trade," "settlement of the sexual harassment case," "prevention of the shareholders representative suit," "development of CSR," and "contract negotiation," which mainly reflect preventive legal work. This second highest group is noteworthy because it mostly involves important legal work that is also performed by employees of corporations.

Conversely, the types of work for which corporations are least likely to use lawyers even in "ideal conditions" relate to "human resource management," "asset management," "corporate pension management," "tax administration," and "financial fund management." Corporations simply don't expect lawyers to deal with this type of work because it is traditionally dealt with by non-lawyer sections of the corporation or outsourced to law-related professionals other than lawyers, such as tax accountants or public consultants on social and labor insurance. Accordingly, Japanese corporations still mainly expect lawyers to deal with ex-post reactive legal work concerning disputes, reflecting the traditional barrister-like role-image of lawyers in Japan. The corporations' need for preventive legal work and management support work, however, are fairly high in "ideal conditions," and there is concern about new types of litigation. Finance and accounting-related work is still not expected of lawyers.

The Relationship Between Japanese Corporations and Lawyers: Findings of the Questionnaire Survey on the Legal Work of Private Practice Lawyers, "Survey (b)"

The purpose of questionnaire survey (b) was to find out more about the type of work being performed by private practice lawyers. We asked lawyers from the Osaka Bar Association (OBA)[39] in private practice about

39. Osaka Bar Association (OBA) is the unit bar association in the jurisdiction of the Osaka District Court. The area overlaps with the Osaka Prefecture. The Osaka Prefecture is located in the Middle Western of Japan. Osaka is the largest business area in western Japan. As of May 2011, the population of Osaka Prefecture was 8,862,173, the third largest behind Tokyo Prefecture (13,186,835) and Kanagawa Prefecture (9,058,589). As of 2010, Osaka Prefecture's GDP was the second largest in Japan at about ¥38 trillion (cf. Tokyo prefecture, about ¥92 trillion). The number of the lawyers in Osaka Bar Association is 3712 (as of 1 June 2011). From the point of view of its population, GDP, and number of lawyers, Osaka is a metropolitan area. Almost all large Japanese corporations have their headquarters in Tokyo; most of the corporations which have their headquarters in Osaka are SMEs. From this point of view, Osaka also has the character of a local area. The data of Osaka Prefecture are available at http://www.pref.osaka.jp/en/introduction.

the most common legal work that they performed, using a list of fifty-eight types of legal work. We wanted to contrast the type of legal work being performed by private practice lawyers to those lawyers working in-house. Respondents could choose as many that applied, as set out in Figure 3. The items are sorted according to the number of responses; the items located at the top being the most common type of work performed by private practice lawyers.

Private practice lawyers mainly deal with "divorce," "inheritance," "personal bankruptcy," "adjustment of debts," "restitution claims for undue profit caused by prohibited high interest rates,"[40] "car accidents," "land and building lease disputes," "real estate dealing disputes," "drafting and reviewing contracts," "tort claims," etc, most of which are regarded as typical personal legal issues relating more or less to court procedures. In relation to corporate-related legal work, only "drafting and reviewing contracts" is ranked in the top ten. These results reflect the status of most of the lawyers in the OBA in private practice; that is, solo practitioners or lawyers in small law offices.

We also specifically asked OBA private practice lawyers about the most common legal work performed for corporations, which was the main purpose of Survey (b). We showed them a list of thirty-three types of legal work and asked them about the frequency of their work experiences. Respondents answered the question at five levels of frequency.

The top five most common types of legal work within the field of corporate practice were, from the top, "defensive allegations," "contract examination," "negotiation for dispute settlement," "damage suits," and "the collection of monetary debts." They are mostly ex-post, reactive-type legal work concerning disputes, except for "contract examination," which is important preventive legal work for corporations. The next five most common types of legal work, "the drafting of contracts for domestic trade," "the enforcement of obligations," "legal searches," "legal consultation," and "contract negotiation" are mostly preventive and relate to the daily business activities of a corporation. Conversely, the ranking of le-

40. Restitution claims for undue profit caused by banned high interest rates [*Kabaraikin Henkan Seikyū*] refers to recent amendments to consumer credit law in Japan. See Souichiro Kozuka and Luke Nottage, "Re-regulating Unsecured Consumer Credit in Japan: Over-Indebted Borrowers, the Supreme Court, and New Legislation," *Sydney Law School Research Paper* 07/62 (2007).

Figure 3. Frequent Legal Work of Osaka Lawyers in Private Practice

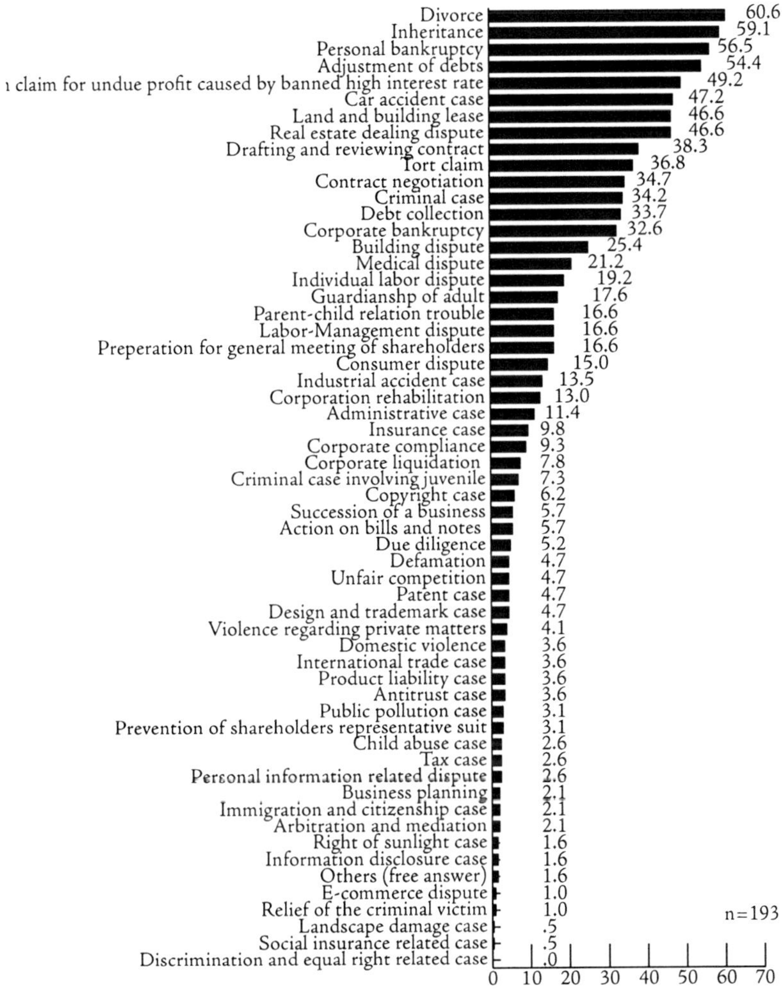

gal work which relates to corporate management is low; financial and tax management work was ranked at the lowest level.

These results correspond to the findings from Survey (a) (see Figure 2). Private practice lawyers are mainly doing ex-post reactive legal work concerning disputes even in the field of corporate practice, but they are also frequently dealing with preventive legal matters. We extrapolate that private practice lawyers themselves also adhere to the traditional role-image of lawyers, and they do not seem willing to deal with corporate legal matters that do not relate to court work or dispute settlement. When pushed by corporate needs, however, they will perform some preventive legal work for corporations.

The Relationship Between Corporations and Lawyers: Findings of the Questionnaire Survey on the Corporate In-House Lawyers, "Survey (c)"

The purpose of questionnaire survey (c) was to find out more about the type of work being performed by in-house lawyers and their required quality and vocational awareness. Using a list of thirty-seven types of typical corporate legal work, we asked corporate in-house lawyers about the most common type of work that they perform. The frequency of work was asked at six levels: 0. "no experience," 1. "less experience," 2. "rather less experience," 3. "rather more experience," 4. "much experience," 5. "routine work". In Figure 5, we set out the types of legal work according to their score.

The five most frequent types of work performed by in-house lawyers, from the top, are "contract examination," "drafting of contract for domestic trade," "legal search," "corporate compliance," and "legal consultation," which are mainly general preventive legal work. The next group, ranked five to ten, is "coordination work of collaboration with external lawyers," "general advice about management strategy," "controlling legal departments," "protection of personal data and management of information security," and "negotiation for dispute settlements," which are management-type work also performed by legal or other departments of corporations (excepting "negotiation for dispute settlement").

The finding that the most common type of legal work performed by private practice lawyers is ex-post reactive work concerning disputes supports the findings in Surveys (a) and Survey (b) (see Figures 2 and 4 respectively); the major legal work of in-house lawyers is mostly preventive legal work or management work for organization. Notably, in-house lawyers are also coordinating the work of outside lawyers (see Figure 5, sixth ranked type of work).

In summary, private practice lawyers are unavoidably reactive because they provide legal services to clients only after accepting a commission. The position of corporate in-house lawyers is obviously different.

Figure 4. Frequency of Legal Work of Osaka Lawyers in Private Practice (%)

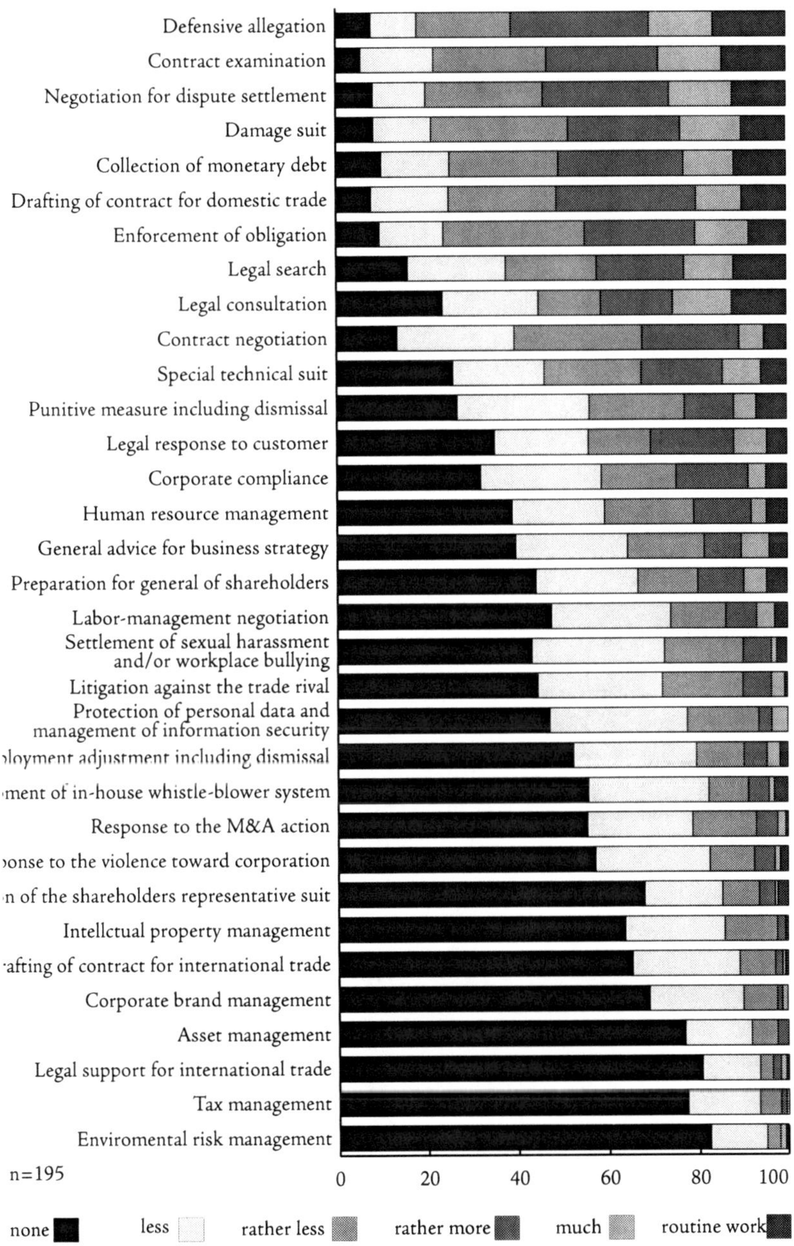

Figure 5. Frequency of Corporate Legal Work of In-House Lawyers in Japan (%)

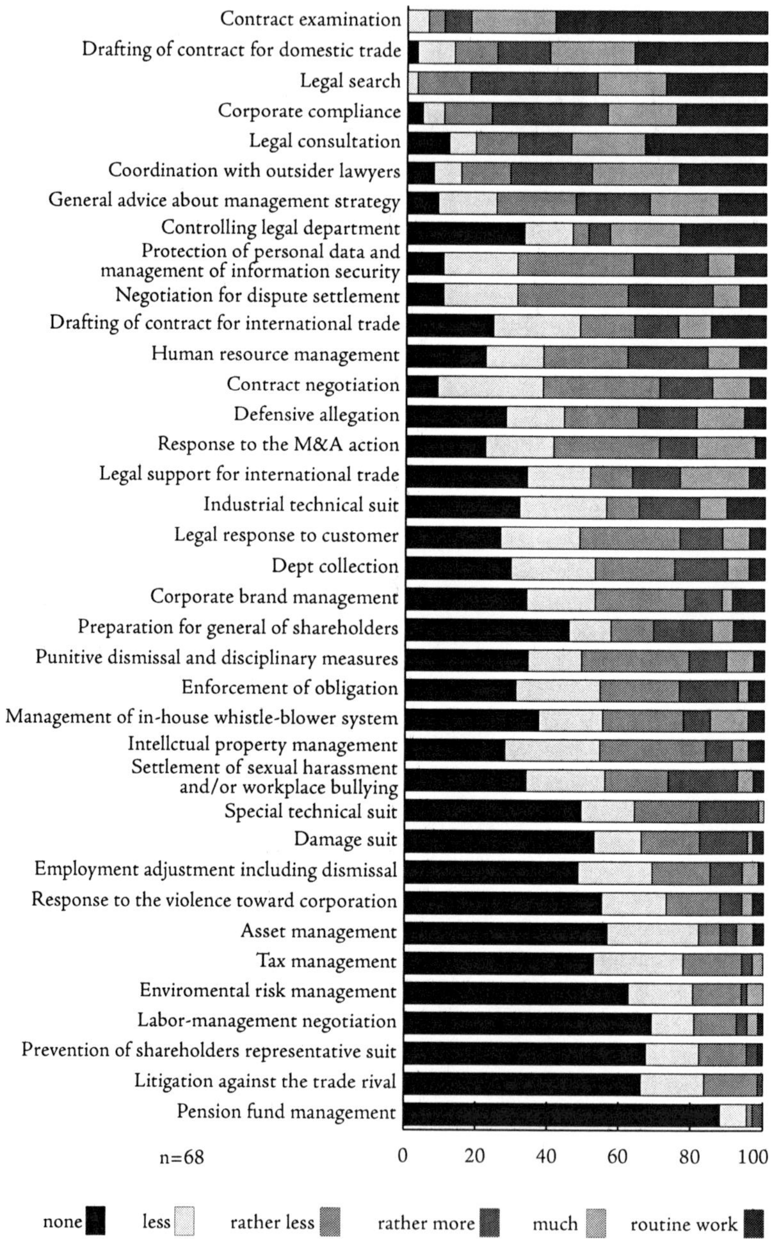

Their work is not only reactive but also sometimes proactive. Further, corporate in-house lawyers are also expected to be able to organize personnel.

Conclusion: Some Thoughts on the "Proper" Population of Lawyers in Japan

The Population of Lawyers Based on the Three Questionnaire Surveys

The results from Survey (a) suggest that the utilization rate of lawyers in Japanese corporations is very low, driven by the traditional barrister-like role-image of lawyers who are independent and only concern themselves in court procedure or dispute settlement. Japanese corporations regard lawyers as one of many specialized, independent professionals who provide law-related professional services; they still have no fixed image to utilize lawyers profitably in daily business activities.

Survey (b) confirms the findings in Survey (a). According to Survey (b), lawyers in private practice still mainly practice old-style, ex-post legal work concerning court procedure or dispute settlement, and the same tendency is also true of their corporate-related work. Private practice lawyers themselves also adhere to the traditional role-image of lawyer, and they do not seem willing to deal with corporate legal matters that do not relate to court work or dispute settlement. Accordingly, the traditional role-image of lawyers held by corporations and lawyers does not leave much room for expanding the population of lawyers in Japan. To change this situation and expand the market for more lawyers, this traditional role-image of lawyers in corporate society in Japan must change.

As indicated in Survey (c), in-house lawyers play a quite different role from the traditional role-image of lawyers in Japanese corporations. In-house lawyers usually perform preventive legal work and support management. They perform preventive legal work efficiently using the wide range of legal knowledge and skills fostered by court related legal training at the Judicial Training and Research Institute and support management by their confidentiality privilege and their network of lawyers belonging to the bar association. According to the results of Survey (a), the potential corporate need for preventive legal work and lawyers who can support management is still high. Accordingly, we expect that the number of in-house lawyers will increase rapidly. If in-house lawyers become popular, the role-image of lawyers in corporations will be dramatically changed,

Figure 6. Number of Lawyers and In-House Lawyers in Japan

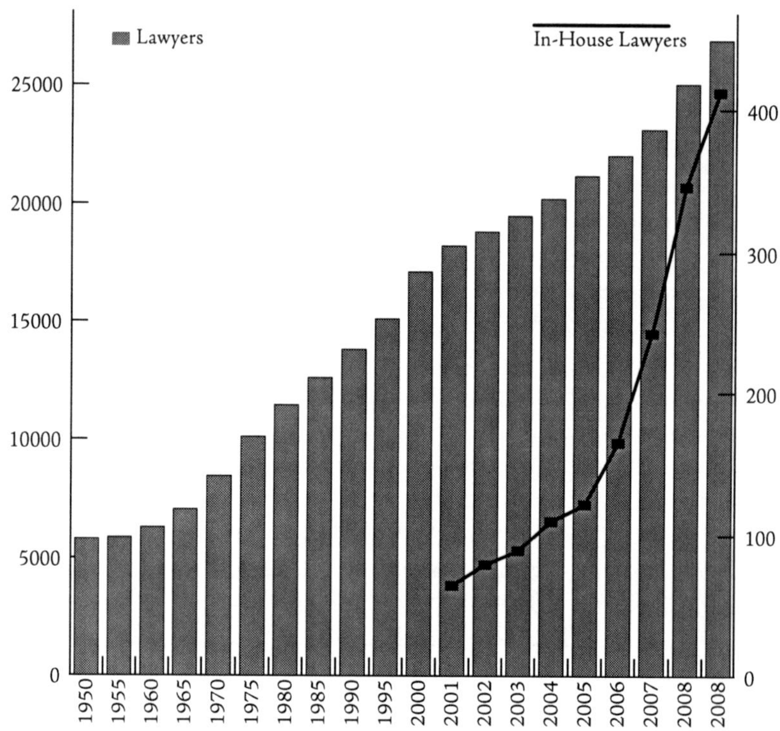

and, in turn, the lawyers themselves may successfully apply their new role-image to Japanese corporate society.

The lawyer's image as an "independent professional" is also an obstacle to increasing the number of in-house lawyers in Japanese corporations. According to the powerful image of the independent professional, corporations are not likely to hire in-house lawyers for daily corporate legal work. According to Survey (c), however, in-house lawyers play an important role as loyal employees in the top corporations in Japan. In smaller corporations, once they begin hiring in-house lawyers, it is likely that corporate managers will recognize that lawyers can play a role as employees, and their population will continue to expand rapidly to a number that better corresponds to their potential needs.

Possibility of Increasing the Number of In-House Lawyers in Japan

The number of Japanese corporate in-house lawyers has been increasing rapidly since 2000 (see Figure 6).[41] Currently, more than 400 lawyers are working as corporate in-house lawyers.[42] Many more lawyers who belong to a private law firm are temporarily working at corporations on a per-project basis, possibly as a result of the current high awareness of corporate compliance and CSR. If the number of corporate in-house lawyers continues to increases and their presence is much enlarged, more Japanese corporations will begin to recognize the usefulness of lawyers for daily business activities. These tendencies are likely to greatly change the role-image of lawyers in Japanese corporate society. In addition, this change in the role-image of lawyers will generate a greater need to utilize external lawyers. This, in turn, will create jobs for the larger population of lawyers generated by the recent legal system reforms in Japan.

In the future, Japanese corporations will be unable to avoid enlarging their legal compliance and CSR. Corporate in-house lawyers are likely to be needed as reliable advisers on these types of legal work. Legal education in Japanese law schools will also need to change to keep up with these trends and a new demand for corporate in-house lawyers.

41. Figure 5-1 reflects the transition of the total number of lawyers in Japan since 1950 and that of corporate in-house lawyers in Japan since 2001 based on JFBA Statistics and the JILA Statistics. See JFBA, "Statistic of the Year-to-Year Number Change of Lawyers from 1950 to 2009;" JILA, "Statistics of the Year-to-Year Change of the Number of Corporate In-House Lawyers in the Second Half of 2009."

42. According to the most recent data on the website of the JILA (as of December in 2009), 412 in-house lawyers are working in corporations in Japan. See JILA, "Statistics of the Number of Corporate In-House Lawyers and Their Belonging Company in the Second Half of 2009."

Saiban-in Trials: An Observation of the Aomori District Court

Takayuki Ii[1]

Introduction

Sixty-six years after the termination of the pre-war jury system, Japan introduced a mixed court system—known as the *saiban-in* system—for serious criminal cases in May 2009.[2] The system was introduced in the early twenty-first-century judicial reform to achieve a firmer popular base in justice.[3] Three judges and six *saiban-in*, who are jurors randomly selected from ordinary citizens, deliberate and make decisions on both the guilt and sentence of the accused.[4]

This chapter considers whether the criminal practice of legal professionals has changed from a model of "prosecutorial justice" toward one of "judicial justice" as proposed elsewhere by Daniel Foote mainly based on two years of observation of *saiban-in* trials at the Aomori district court. Of the twenty cases tried in Aomori as of March 2011, I have observed seventeen cases at least in part.[5] Though a local and limited sample, I hope that my observations might help to examine the actual state of *saiban-in* trials.

1. Associate Professor, Hirosaki University.

2. See Noboru Yanase, *Saiban-in Seido no Rippō Gaku: Tōgi Shugi Minshushugi Riron ni Motozuku Kokumin no Shihō Sanka no Igi no Saikōsei [Research on Legislation of the Saiban-in System: Reconstruction of the Significance of Public Participation in Justice Based on Deliberative Democracy Theory]* (Tokyo, 2009): 14–149.

3. For a general description of the first twenty-first-century judicial reform in Japan see Setsuo Miyazawa, "Law Reform, Lawyers, and Access to Justice", in Gerald P McAlinn, ed., *Japanese Business Law* (Alphen, 2007): 39.

4. See Osamu Ikeda, *Kaisetsu Saiban-in Hō (Dai Ni Han) [Commentary on Saiban-in Law (Second Edition)]* (Tokyo, 2009).

5. The *saiban-in* trials I could not watch were case Nos. 2, 3, and 16. Information about these cases was obtained from articles of a local newspaper, *Toō Nippō*.

I. Overview of *Saiban-in* Trials Nationwide

From August 2009 to the end of March 2011, 1,949 cases and 2,060 accused were tried by *saiban-in* trial, and 16,130 citizens participated as *saiban-in* (11,889) and substitute *saiban-in* (4,241).[6] Their average length of service was 4.4 days. While 2055 defendants were found guilty, only five were found not guilty;[7] the conviction rate was 99.76%. According to the *Jiji Tsushin*,[8] sentences averaged 76.8% of the penalty demanded by prosecutors, while sex crime was 80.9% and murder was 79.6%. Among others, rape causing injury cases were sentenced more severely than before as seen in the court material.[9] There were eight defendants whose sentences were longer than demanded.

The percentage of the convicted who received suspended sentences was 15.9% (326 out of 2,055). Of these, 57.1% (186 out of 326) were put on probation. Five defendants, including one male under the age of twenty, were sentenced to death.

Videotaping of part of the interrogation was conducted in 3,296 cases from April 2009 to March 2011. Among these, DVDs of the recordings were permitted as evidence in 35 cases and the written confessions

6. The Supreme Court of Japan, "Saiban-in Saiban no Jisshi Jyōkyō ni Tsuite (Seido Shikō Heisei 23 Nen 3 Gatsu Matsu・Sokuhō) [On the Implementation Status of *Saiban-in* Trial: From the Introduction of the System to the End of March 2011])" (2011), http://www.saibanin.courts.go.jp/topics/pdf/09_12_05-10jissi_jyoukyou/02.pdf.

7. There were also three cases in which the indicted offender was partly found not guilty.

8. *Mutsu Shinpō* morning edition, May 21, 2011.

9. See The Supreme Court of Japan, "Tokubetsu Shiryō 1 (Ryōkei Shiryō)" [Special Material (Sentence Material)] (a material which was presented to the 12th Saiban-in Seido no Unyō o Kangaeru Yushikisha Kondankai [Meeting of the Learned Persons Contemplating the Administration of *Saiban-in* System]) (2011), http://www.courts.go.jp/saikosai/iinkai/saibanin_kondan/siryo_12/index.html. In the material, the sentence of *saiban-in* trial (from August 2009 to March 2011) is compared with that of professional judge (from April 2008 to March 2011) in eight types of crimes. Both sentences are almost identical in murder, arson of inhabited building and violation of the stimulants control law. On the other hand, the sentence of the *saiban-in* trial seems to be severer in attempted murder, injury resulting in death, rape causing injury, forcible indecency causing injury and robbery causing injury, However, these sentence data should be deemed to be only for reference due to related issues, e.g., limited number of cases, influence by demanded sentence by prosecutor, and "lenient" punishment of sex crime by professional judges.

were deemed to be made voluntarily.[10] The crime victims, the bereaved, and their attorneys participated in 223 defendant cases. This participation came in the form of giving views (189), questioning the defendant (173) and examining the witness (63).[11]

As we have seen, the *saiban-in* system seems to have made little impact on punishment. The former guilty rate of over 99% and the *hachi gake* (80 percent) practice—in which the sentence delivered is around 80% of the prosecutor's demand—remain almost unchanged. The death penalty sentence also remains. On the other hand, the number of suspended sentences on probation in *saiban-in* trial is 1.5 times as high as that in trial by professional judge (36.6 percent).[12] This seems to be a sign of *saiban-ins* so as not to permit a second offence by putting offenders under probation.

In order to make the trial easier to understand by *saiban-ins* and to reduce their burden, criminal procedure was reformed in some points. Concentrated and high speed trials have been put into practice by pre-trial arrangement and intensive hearings, though in some cases it takes time between indictment and opening of the *saiban-in* trial. Interrogation has also been made a bit transparent by partial video recording. Other reforms include crime victim participation in trial system, which coincided with the *saiban-in* system.

Public perception of the *saiban-in* trial is ambiguous. Japanese people have had trust in criminal justice to some extent. According to the public opinion poll conducted by *Asahi Shimbun* in December 2008, over 70% of respondents answered that they had trust in criminal trial (74%) and legal professionals (judge: 80%, prosecutor: 75% and attorney: 70% each).[13] The

10. *Mainichi Shimbun* morning edition, May 21, 2011.

11. Ibid.

12. There is an inscription in the material of the question No.10 of the public opinion poll conducted by the Supreme Court in January 2011 that "the proportion of suspended cases put on probation is 56.6% in *saiban-in* trial and 36.6% in trial only by professional judge so far". See the Supreme Court of Japan, "Saiban in Seido no Unyō ni kansuru Ishiki Tyōsa [Consciousness Research on the Operation of *Saiban-in* System]" (2011): 59, http://www.saibanin.courts.go.jp/topics/pdf/09_12_05-10jissi_jyoukyou/h22_isiki_5.pdf.

13. See Asahi Simbun Public Opinion Poll Center, "Interview Survey in December 2008" in *Journalism* 225 (2009): 124 and 128.

NHK survey in the same period, however, revealed that views on criminal justice were divided into two; proper (43.4%) and problematic (43.6%).[14]

Around two thirds of respondents (66.6%) had a high opinion of the actual *saiban-in* trial according to the NHK survey as of May 2010.[15] The Supreme Court's public opinion poll in January 2011 shows that half of citizens (50.4%) got more interested in the trial and judiciary after the start of *saiban-in* system, while 1.6% decreased their interests and 48.0% answered no change in particular.[16] Generally, the *saiban-in* system seems to be viewed favorably by the public in terms of fairness, reliability and convincingness.[17] It should also be noted that not a few people think sentencing by judges is lenient and expected *saiban-in* trials to deliver severe punishment, which did not necessarily happen.[18] This expectation of *saiban-in* has a lot to do with people's recent rootless feeling that Japan is no longer a crime-free country,[19] which led to the movement of

14. See NHK Research Office for Broadcasting and Culture,"Saiban-in Seido ni Kansuru Yoron Tyōsa Tanjun Shukeihyō (Dai 1-3 Kai)[Tables of the Count of Results of Public Opinion Polls on *Saiban-in* System (the First to the Third)]"(2010): 3, http://www.nhk.or.jp/bunken/summary/yoron/social/pdf/100524.pdf.

15. Ibid.

16. See the Supreme Court of Japan, "*Saiban-in* Seido no Unyō ni kansuru Ishiki Tyōsa": 56.

17. Ibid., 58.

18. In the Asahi Shimbun's public opinion poll research, respondents answer that Japan's sentence is "severe"(1%), proper (30%), "lenient"(30%) and "others/no response" (10%). In the same survey, respondents expect severe sentence will "increase"(27%), "decrease"(13%), "not change"(49%) and "others/no response" (11%) after the introduction of the *saiban-in* system . See Asahi Simbun Public Opinion Poll Center, "Interview Survey in December 2008": 119 and 123.

19. The above cited Asahi Shimbun survey shows that people's views on security in Japan in these five years has "got better" (3%), "worsened" (76%), "unchanged" (20%) and "others/ no response" (1%). See ibid.: 129. The result of another public opinion poll by the Cabinet Office (December 2006) was almost the same; the respondents answered that security in these ten years of Japan has "got better" (11.3%), "worsened" (84.3%) and "others"(4.4%). Source of their feeling on security was largely based on mass communication; the respondents relied on "TV and radio" (95.5%), "newspaper" (81.1%), and less on mini communication; "conversation with family, friends and others" (38.4%) and "local publicity" (25.8%). See the Cabinet Office Minister's Secretariat Government Publicity Room, "Chian ni Kansuru Yoron Tyōsa [Public Opinion Poll on Public Safety]" (2006), http://www8.cao.go.jp/survey/h18/h18-chian/index.html.

severe punishment from the victim's perspective, called penal populism in Japan.[20]

On the other hand, citizens are largely reluctant to serve themselves as *saiban-in*. The situation has not changed even after the enforcement of the *saiban-in* system; when asked "Do you think you want to participate in criminal justice?" positive answer was only 15.0% ("want to participate" (4.6%) and "may participate" (10.4%), while "do not want to but cannot help because it is a duty" was 42.6%, negative one ("do not want to even though it is a duty") was 41.4% and "do not know" was 1.0% as of January 2011.[21] Uncertainty to of judgement judge and psychological burden are the major deterrence.[22] However, it is known that many citizens change their views on *saiban-in* once they have experienced it. According to the Supreme Court survey, most former *saiban-ins* (95.2%) view their experience as good (very good (55.5%) and good (39.7%)), while 3.5% felt not good (not so good (2.5%) and not good (1.0%)), though only around one third of the respondents (31.1%) had wanted to serve as *saiban-ins* before being selected.[23]

While the experience of *saiban-ins* is relatively "good," in another survey, two thirds (67%) of former *saiban-ins* answer that they felt a psychological burden by participating in criminal justice and 15% retain the burden after the trial.[24] These answers of former *saiban-ins* seem to be contradictory. It might be related to *saiban-ins'* tendency to commit deep-

20. See Koichi Hamai and Tom Ellis, "*Genbatsuka*: Growing Penal Populism and the Changing Role of Public Prosecutors in Japan?" *Hanzai Shakai Gaku Kenkyu [Japanese Journal of Sociological Criminology]* 33 (2008), 67.

21. Ibid, 60.

22. Ibid, 59. Reasons of anxiety and trouble to participate as *saiban-ins* are as follows; "feel heavy responsibility to decide defendant's fate" (78.7%), "uncertain to make judgment rightly, which is difficult for lay persons" (63.4%), "uncertain to make judgment calmly" (53.6%), "uncertain to express my view on equal terms with professional judges" (52.6%), "uncertain to be threatened by defendant and the party concerned"(49.3%), "bring trouble to job" (38.6%), "uncertain to keep secret in relation to *saiban-in* work" (33.1%), "bring trouble to bringing-up and nursing care" (18.2%), "nothing in particular" (3.7%), "others" (2.0%) and "do not know" (0.3%).

23. See the Supreme Court of Japan, *Saiban-in Keikenn Sha tō ni Taisuru Anketo Kekka Hōkokusho [Report on the Result of Questionnaire Research Survey on Former Saiban-ins etc.]* (2011): 6.

24. NHK broadcast news of May 21, 2010. The target of the survey was 330 former *saiban-ins*.

ly to cases and remain concerned with defendants' situations after the trial.[25]

II. *Saiban-in* Trial Cases at the Aomori District Court

Aomori prefecture is a northern part of the main island of Japan with a population of 1,373,164 as of October 1, 2010; however, it has only one courtroom for the *saiban-in* trial. At the Aomori District Court, which is situated in Aomori city and opens *saiban-in* trial, twenty *saiban-in* cases were tried by the end of March 2011 as shown in the table.

Table 1. Saiban-in Trials at the Aomori District Court (2009 to March 2011)

No.	Calendar	Indicted offence	Demanded sentence by prosecutor	Judgment	Note
1	2-4/9/2009	Two robberies and rapes and others	15 years	15 years (100%)	Young defendant, appealed but dismissed
2	17-19/11	Robbery causing injury and others	8 years	6 years 6 months (81.3%)	Repeater
3	23-26/3/2010	Robbery and injury	7 years	4 years 6 months (64.3%)	Joint offence with No.7
4	19-22/4	Dangerous driving resulting in death and injury	7 years	5 years 6 months (78.6%)	Young defendant
5	18-20/5	Attempted arson of inhabited building	3 years	3 years (suspended under probation)	Defendant with mental disorder

25. According to the survey by *Asahi Shimbun*, 62.9% of the 140 former *saiban-ins* replied that they are interested in the present stuation of the defendant they decided the sentence (*Asahi Shimbun* morning edition, May 17, 2010). *Yomiuri Shimbun* asked 334 former *saiban-ins* what they often recall after the trial, the result of which was "reformation of the defendant" (60%), "rights and wrongs of their own judgment"(35%), "feelings of the victim and bereaved" (30%), "whether the defendant will appeal or not and prospect of the appellate court's judgment" (25%) (*Yomiuri Shimbun* morning edition, May 17, 2010).

6	15-17/6	Attempted rape and others	5 years	3 years 6 months (70%)	
7	22-24/6	Robbery and injury	5 years	3 years (60%)	Young defendant, joint offence with No. 3, reversed (3 years, suspended under probation))
8	13-15/7	Arson of inhabited building	4 years	1 year 6 months (37.5%)	Defendant with mental disorder,
9	25-27/8	Robbery causing injury and others	6 years	4 years 6 months (75%)	
10	31/8-2/9	Attempted rape causing injury	10 years	10 years (100%)	
11	5-8/10	Robbery causing injury and others	5 years	3 years (suspended under probation)	The name of an offence was contested
12	13-15/10	Arson of inhabited building	4 years	3 years (suspended under probation)	Defendant with mental disorder
13	25-27/10	Counterfeiting	6 years, 6 years	4 years (66.7%)	Joint offence with No. 15
14	17-19,22/11	Robbery and murder and others	Life Imprisonment	Life Imprisonment (100%)	The name of an offence was contested
15	24-26/11	Counterfeiting	8 years	6 years (75%)	Joint offence with No. 13
16	6-9/12	Murder	13 years	7 years 6 months (57.7%)	Murder by son weary of nursing his father, appealed
17	13-16/12	Robbery and injury and others	8 years, 8 years	8 years, 8 years (100%)	Joint offence with No. 18, one of the defendant appealed

18	25-27/1/2011	Accessory to robbery and injury	3 years	2 years 8 months (88.9%)	Joint offence with No. 17
19	21-24/2	Arson of inhabited building	4 years	3 years (75%)	Defendant with mental disorder
20	7-11/3	Murder	18 years	16 years (88.9%)	The name of an offence was contested

The *saiban-in* trial of September 2009 was filled with an unusual kind of excitement. More than one thousand people and many media reporters rushed to watch the trial every day,[26] because it was not only the first *saiban-in* trial in Aomori prefecture and the third one nationwide, but also a sexual offense was tried for the first time in the *saiban-in* court.

There were four things I was struck by watching the first *saiban-in* trial in Aomori. The first was the manner of criminal proceedings. Evidence and points of issue were focused beforehand in pretrial arrangement and the trial was concentrated in three days. The second thing was a strong presence of *saiban-ins*. They were eagerly engaged in the trial and five of them asked sharp questions of the defendant. Some of them asked with honest reaction to the offence and local accent. It was curious that the defendant seemed to be relatively relaxed in answering questions by *saiban-ins*. The third thing was that prosecutors and defense counsels applied seriously to their work. They tried to prove the offence and defend the defendant orally and visually using power point slides. The fourth thing was that, as a result, the trial was rich in content and felt humanistic.

Among twenty cases, nos. 3 and 7, nos. 13 and 15, and nos. 17 and 18[27] were joint offences. All of the accused were found guilty. The name of an offence was contested in three cases (nos. 11, 14 and 20); however, these contestations were in vain. Confession cases usually end within a few days. Defendants in three cases were put on probation under suspended

26. The courtroom for the *saiban-in* trial of the Aomori district court has 72 seats, 34 of which were allocated to the media. Therefore, there was keen competition to get into the courtroom. In fact, most citizens stood in line for admission tickets to the gallery were part-time workers employed by the media. I got the tickets in exchange for making comments to a television station.

27. Nos. 21, 22, 23, and 25, which were tried after March 2011, were also joint offences with nos. 17 and 18.

sentence. In addition, two cases were reversed at the Sendai High Court and the defendants were also put on probation under suspended sentence. The reason for these reversals is said to be the defendant's deep regret and compensation to the victim after the *saiban-in* trials.

The sentences of *saiban-in* trials averaged around 80% of those demanded by the prosecutor in Aomori, which endorse *hachi-gake* practice. In some cases, the sentence was the same as the prosecutor's demand (nos. 1, 10, 14, and 17). Cases nos. 1 and 10 were sex crime cases, and in the former case two victims delivered their sufferings to the courtroom. In case No. 14, the damage of the bereaved was so great they demanded capital punishment in the courtroom. The defendants in case No. 17 had a history of criminal convictions and had gang connections. It seems that offences which leave little room for compassion such as sex crime and gang-related cases tend to be punished more severely, while offences *saiban-in* can sympathize with or cases in which defendants' family or relatives, are expected to support their reformation do not.

Surprisingly, except for gang-related cases (nos. 13, 15, 17, and 18) and a repeater case (no. 2), more than half the cases that went to *saiban-in* trial in Aomori were committed by general citizens: amateurish robberies (nos. 3, 7, 11, and 14), impetuous sex crimes perpetrated by young men (nos. 1 and 10), sex crimes between acquaintances (nos. 6 and 9), murder by relatives weary of nursing (no. 16), negligence (no. 4), and mental disorder (nos. 5, 8, 12, and 19). Most cases seem to have been caused in a vicious circle of the defendants' family and economic problems.

In the Aomori District Court, *saiban-in* trials are carried out in one collegiate body comprised of three judges. They have been the same judges since April 2010, although there is a possibility of transfers every three years. As of the end of March 2011, 36 defendants had been indicted to the Aomori District Court for *saiban-in* trial, and 22 have been judged. Therefore, 14 defendants were waiting for their turns for a decision. In 2010, the court could dispose of only half the cases (17 of 35) to be decided by *saiban-in* trial.[28] The three judges in charge of *saiban-in* trials have other work to do, so they must be overloaded. The same problem applies to prosecutors and attorneys who reside in regional areas like Aomori. As of March 2011,

28. See The Supreme Court of Japan, "Heisei 22 Nen ni okeru Saiban-in Saiban no Jisshi Jyōkyō to ni Kansuru Siryō [Material on the Implementation Status *etc.* of *Saiban-in* Trial in 2010])" (2011): 5 and 7, http://www.saibanin.courts.go.jp/topics/pdf/09_12_05-10jissi_jyoukyou/h22_siryo1.pdf.

there are nine prosecutors and 82 attorneys, among which 49 (59.8%) sign a contract as court-appointed counsel for *saiban-in* cases. In almost all *saiban-in* cases, three prosecutors and two defense counsels appear at the trial.[29] Legal professionals in Aomori must have become busier after the introduction of the *saiban-in* system.

Sometimes *saiban-in* trials in Aomori are watched by university students. They are regularly surprised that judges would voice their negative opinions to the defendant in front of the *saiban-in*, e.g., "I do not believe what you are saying," or "I suspect you kicked the victim." My students frequently comment that, contrary to their classroom preconceptions, the judges do not seem to be neutral. Similarly, they often say that prosecutors were well-prepared in comparison to opposing counsel. In fact, while some defense counsels are eloquent and zealous, many are not so committed. This traditional stance of legal professionals has virtually not changed even now, especially in cases tried only by professional judges without *saiban-ins*.

Most citizens in Hirosaki, a city in Aomori, are reluctant to become *saiban-in*;[30] however, once selected, they seem to perform their role very well. They often raise questions to the defendant and witnesses, and judges question further after that. Depending on the case, *saiban-in* seem to feel for or even encourage the defendant. The defendant in case no. 2, for example, actually expressed his gratitude to the *saiban-in*.[31]

29. In Aomori, prosecutors are so few that there is virtually no distinction between investigative prosecutors and trial prosecutors. The Aomori district public prosecutor office seems to have keen interest in *saiban-in* trials and the deputy chief prosecutor and around ten staffs watch every *saiban-in* trial. Aomori prefecture has been infamous for its shortage and improper regional balance of attorneys and legal services. When a crime occurs in the region, defense counsel near the region is usually paired with the veteran one in Aomori city. As a result, some attorneys assume court-appointed defense counsel for *saiban-in* cases several times a year.

30. In April 2010, my postal survey of 1,000 citizens conducted in Hirosaki city showed that while 4.4% would like to participate in justice as *saiban-in* and 15.9% may do so, around 60% were reluctant to become *saiban-in* (42% response rate).

31. *Toō Nippō* morning edition, November 19, 2009. Concerning the defendants' response to *saiban-in* trials, see Takayuki Ii, "Saiban-in Saiban no Kōsei, Chiyu Kōka ni Kansuru Shiron [Reformative and Therapeutic Effects of *Saiban-in* Trial: Preliminary Study]," *Studies in Humanities Social Sciences* (Faculty of Humanities, Hirosaki University) 24 (2010): 133.

How do former *saiban-ins* feel about crime and their experience? Three former *saiban-ins* in Aomori talked about a change in their view of offenders. Crime was distant from them, but they came to think it in connection to their lives after having served as *saiban-ins*. They said that "my view of an offender has changed. The defendant I tried was a seemingly ordinary young man. I came to observe background of persons and think about problems in regions we live in." "Criminal cases were distant from me before serving as *saiban-in*. However, I came to realize that crime is an extension of our daily lives and negative feelings. My life is commonplace, but I tried to think about the defendant's crime mobilizing all my past feeling and experience. That task also led me to look into myself. I felt weight and warmth in judging person by person." "My way of thinking and feeling toward an offender has certainly changed. I have watched a series of trial, made judgment and realized that an offender was put on that route. I take it to heart not to commit crime, as an offender is not quite a stranger to me."[32]

As we have seen, most *saiban-ins* answer that their experience was "good." They seem to consider carefully crime and themselves in judging the trial, all the better for its burden. Former *saiban-ins* in Aomori told, "I felt a burden on my heart after the *saiban-in* trial. I often dreamt the trial. It was an unforgettable event in my life. The burden might seem to be negative, however, I do not think it is a minus. I can think deeply and look back one more time due to the burden. I feel a burden and think what I can do at the same time." "I feel a burden, but it is not unpleasant. A 'good' experience of *saiban-in* does not imply 'happy' or 'beneficial.' I came eye to eye to the defendant, talked in questioning and communicated something to him. These seem to relate to be 'good.'"[33]

III. *Saiban-in* Trial No. 20

Among the *saiban-in* trials in Aomori, the final case, which was held from March 7 to 11 in 2011, seemed to be the most difficult for *saiban-in* to find

32. Remarks of three former *saiban-ins* in Aomori at the round-table discussion of the symposium titled "Experience of *Saiban-in* Trial", which was held at Hirosaki University, October 23, 2010. Its manuscript is viewable at: http://www.saibanhou.com/seminar2010report_4_2b.pdf.

33. Ibid.

the facts and make a judgment. Actually, when the East Japan Disaster occurred, I was at the Aomori District Court awaiting *saiban-in* trial no. 20's verdict. We had a blackout and the judgment was delivered under emergency lighting.

The *saiban-in* trial was a murder case in which the defendant knifed his acquaintance to death. The defendant was drunk and could not remember the crime, but the victim was stabbed in the heart with the defendant's knife. One of the main issues of the case was how the defendant knifed the victim. Although the defendant had lost his memory, there was a written confession in the investigation document which read, "I hung over the victim and knifed him, who was flat on his back."

The defendant did not have a good grasp of the written or spoken word, as he did not fully attend elementary school classes in order to care for his sickly mother. In fact, he could not read or write Chinese characters and seemed to have a hard time understanding the spoken words and questions of prosecutors, counsel, *saiban-in*, or judges in the courtroom. He asked questions again and again and did not make a proper response.

The defendant's confession in the document was well written. It is hard to believe that he could make such a detailed confession. According to his written confession, he hung over the victim, who was lying on his back, and knifed him face-to-face. The defendant, however, said in the courtroom that he did not remember the scene of the crime. According to him, the investigator told him during the interrogation, "You must know how you behaved as you have killed one person." The confession seemed to have been elicited from the defendant by giving him "hints" such as, "Didn't you hang over the victim and knife him, who was flat on his back?"—"I do not remember... but you may be right." This must have been the way the defendant's written confession was prepared.

In order to place confidence on the defendant's written confession, the prosecutor submitted to the court a DVD in which the investigation process was documented. The DVD was played back for the first time in the *saiban-in* trial in Aomori. The prosecutor demanded that the video of the DVD should be not be openly played back in the courtroom on the grounds that the human rights of the accused should be protected and that future accused might refuse the video recording for fear that the video would be played in the courtroom. Defense counsel raised objection to the prosecutor's demand, but the judges did not sustain the objection on the ground that the court should consider the prosecutor's concern for future interrogations.

The video could be watched only by *saiban-in* and judges, while the audience, including myself, could only hear the audio of the DVD. Although the DVD was around forty minutes long, most of it was the voice of the prosecutor reading the written confession and confirming with the defendant that the written confession was correct. According to defense counsel, the defendant in the video denied what the prosecutor said several times with a shake of his head, which could not be confirmed by the audience.

Strangely, there was a conflicting witness. A female witness testified that "the defendant attacked the victim in the rear and knifed him over his shoulder." Therefore, the *saiban-in* and judges were forced to decide which was more reliable, a defendant's confession in the investigation document, *chōsho*, or a third-party witness who was at the scene of the crime. The testimony included many points which were different from that of the defendant. For instance, concerning the defendant's encounter with the witness, the defendant claimed that she told him, "Let's get married," but the witness would not admit to this. Also, in terms of where they were sitting immediately before the crime, there was a discrepancy between the defendant and the witness. The judges did not seem to have trust in her testimony.

A doctor who carried out an autopsy on the victim testified that the knife must have been stuck at a right angle and revolved at least four times inside the victim's body. He said it was so unusual that he had never seen such an injury.

The victim's son appeared and gave his opinion. He said that he was distraught and the defendant should be punished severely. The prosecutor spoke for the victim's sister and parents; they desired capital punishment.

The defendant received a sixteen-year prison sentence. It was 88.9 percent of the sentence demanded by the prosecutor, an eighteen-year prison sentence. I was interested in how the *saiban-in* court would judge the way the defendant knifed the victim. Do they rely on a written confession or a witness's testimony? The *saiban-in* court decided that "the defendant attacked the victim in the rear and knifed him over his shoulder. After that, the defendant hung over the victim and knifed him, who was flat on his back," as insisted by the prosecutor. Hearing this, the defense counsel exclaimed, "It is inconceivable." The court relied on both the written confession and the witness's testimony, which were in conflict. The judgment seems to be a last-resort attempt to reconcile a fictitious investigation document with the testimony of a dubious witness.

This case might have been hard for *saiban-in* so they relied on professional judges who, as always, relied on prosecutors. The stance of prosecutors and judges seems to be almost unchanged even under the *saiban-in* court system and in partly video-recorded investigations. Among the judges, although the youngest one was relatively neutral in questioning the defendant other two elder ones seemed to have a biased confidence in the written confession.

The accused and the two defense counsel insisted on a charge of lethal injury instead of murder, which, again, was a vain effort. When a long knife is stabbed into a heart, an intent to commit murder is presumed in Japan's criminal courts.[34] In this case, professional judges must have followed this precedent. Regardless, the sentence seems to be more severe if the defendant excuses himself and does not feel any regret for what he has done. Therefore, the sentence in this case might have been lower if the defendant had simply maintained his confession to murder and issued a heartfelt apology, even though he could not remember his crime. The sentence of sixteen years in prison must have been severe for the defendant, whose only previous violation was a traffic accident in his youth.

Furthermore, the defendant admitted that he was guilty, but he did not remember his crime at all. He testified that he had no memory of what occurred from the time he restarted to drink alcohol prepared by the witness to the time the witness shook him on his shoulders to wake him up. After coming around, the defendant said that he saw the witness lying on and crying over the victim, but the witness testified that she had only touched the victim. The prosecutor could not prove who pulled out the knife from victim's body. There were many suspicious things around this case, including that the defendant, who was photographed a few hours after the murder, did not seem to be stained with blood. In showing the picture as evidence, the prosecutor went out of his way to explain, "The defendant was stained with blood, though it may be hard to see from this photograph." Although it would have been hard to prove his innocence, the defendant should have pled not guilty to the crime.

34. This way of ascertaining the fact is taught at the Legal Research and Training Institute to the passers of bar exam, which is often under criticism.

IV. The Stance of Legal Professionals

The stance of judges seems to be hard to change. Judges have normally made judgments in reference to sentences demanded by prosecutors. As is widely known, the conviction rate in Japan has long been over 99 percent and sentences have been around 80 percent of the prosecutor's demand. This is caricatured as though judges and prosecutors play the same song in different keys, each dancing in step with the other.[35] When a verdict of not guilty is returned or the term is less than half of that demanded, prosecutors normally appeal to a higher court. In a sense, judges have relied on prosecutors and taken a "safety-first" maxim to heart. As a result, they unconsciously follow the stance of prosecutors themselves when they question the defendants. While judges can behave more freely and think more fairly about individual cases with *saiban-in* at trial, their traditional way of thinking seems to persist. The stance of judges might not change by the time younger generations become presiding judges.

Likewise, although the prosecutors' approach to proof was changed to be to the point and visualized, the interrogation documents have retained an unparalleled importance. In fact, prosecutors often stand and read the document in court for hours on end. In May 2011, Chief Justice Takesaki of the Japanese Supreme Court specifically voiced some concern about a reversion to document based criminal proceedings.[36]

According to a survey of prosecutors in 2011,[37] 27% of prosecutors surveyed have been instructed by their superiors to prepare untrue interrogation confession documents, and 28% answered that he or she has heard or seen problematic interrogations. This situation is the result of articles 321 and 322 of the law of criminal procedure, which permits interrogation documents prepared by a prosecutor with conditions to be admitted as evidence as an exception of hearsay rule, and the documents'

35. David T. Johnson, *The Japanese Way of Justice: Prosecuting Crime in Japan* (New York, 2002): 66.

36. Takesaki Hiromitsu, "A Remark on the Constitution Memorial Day", May 2, 2011.

37. The survey was conducted anonymously for all prosecutors in February 2011 on the internet web site. The response rate was 90.4%. See "Haifu Shiryō 3 Ishiki Chōsa (Survey) no Gaiyō [Distribution Material No. 3: Summary of the Survey on Consciousness]" (2011), which was presented to the 12th Kensatsu no Arikata Kento Kaigi [Examination Council to Contemplate What Prosecutors Should Be]: 21 and 24, http://www.moj.go.jp/content/000071328.pdf.

tolerant acceptance by judges. Against this practice, a former judge Akira Kitani insists that when the defendant's testimony from the courtroom and the interrogation document are in conflict, the former should be attached greater importance and the investigator should lose.[38] According to him, judges need to change their way of thinking to reform the practice of proving interrogation. His view, however, does not seem to be supported by most judges.

On the other hand, defense counsels seem to have historically relied heavily on judges. They have had a tendency to provide judges with every material they can think of to receive "generous judgments." In a sense, defense counsel have deferred to judges to judge. In *saiban-in* trials, however, *saiban-in* would like to know a punishment the counsel deems to be proper as opposed to the sentence demanded by the prosecutor. A new stance of legal professionals, in which prosecutors and defense counsel exchange their views and a neutral judge decides which is more reasonable, might lead to a genuine adversarial system of justice.

According to the abovementioned prosecutor survey, 31% answered that a not guilty verdict would have a negative impact on the future career of the prosecutor who was in charge of the case.[39] The personnel evaluation system should also be reformed.

Citizens seem to be accustomed to Japan's conventional form of criminal justice and might, therefore, expect judges' and prosecutors' authoritative manner. This pattern of popular thinking is difficult to change immediately, but such change will follow the actual stance of legal professionals.

Conclusion

This chapter has considered the impact of a *saiban-in* trial system based mainly on its first two years operation in the Aomori District Court.

As a result, the *saiban-in* system has made little impact on punishment, albeit small changes that suspended sentence on probation has been increased, and some types of crime including sex crime seem to be punished severer for the moment.

38. Akira Kitani, *Keiji Saiban no Kokoro [The Mind of Criminal Trial]* (Tokyo, 2004): 59.

39. See "Haifu Shiryō 3 Ishiki Chōsa (Survey) no Gaiyō": 14.

On the other hand, the introduction of the *saiban-in* system seems to have an effect on Japanese people. As the recent survey shows, almost half of the citizens have become more interested in trials and judiciary. Most people are reluctant to serve themselves as *saiban-ins*, while most former *saiban-ins* answer that their experience as *saiban-ins* to be "good". They must come to consider carefully crime and themselves in judging, all the better for its burden.

Throughout this chapter, it was recognized anew that the *saiban-in* trial is formed by humans, namely, defendants, witnesses, victims, judges, prosecutors, defense counsel, *saiban-in*, the audience, and the public. Japan's criminal procedure has been changed to go with the *saiban-in* trial, however, the stance of legal professionals does not seem to have changed so much. Will the criminal practice of legal professionals also change from "prosecutorial justice" to "judicial justice" as proposed by Foote? This question cannot be answered at present, but it may be a steep hill to negotiate.

Ryuichi Hirano, a famous scholar of criminal procedure, predicted that we could considerably get rid of *chōsho saiban* (an interrogation document centered trial) by introducing lay participation in justice. He thought that lay participation would have an impact on investigation documents, interrogation, and the length of custody and transform "precise justice" to "core justice," not "rough justice."[40] His prediction seems to have come true in part;[41] however, it will take time for legal professionals to change their practices.

A former judge Hiroshi Yasuhara has praised the *saiban-in* system for turning judges' experience into an advantage, for getting rid of the risk that judges will become "accustomed to guilty," which has been the biggest problem of Japanese criminal justice, and for injecting a fresh way

40. Ryuichi Hirano, "Sanshinsei no Saiyō ni yoru "Kakushin Shihō" wo: Keiji Shihō Kaikaku no Ugoki to Hōhō" ["Core Justice" by Introducing Mixed Court: Movement and Method of Criminal Justice Reform], *Jurist* 1148 (1999): 5.

41. The percentage of detention requests that were denied had been around 0.2% in the 1990s; however, it began to slightly rise in the middle of the 2000s and reached 0.9% in 2009. See *Hanzai Hakusho [White Paper on Crime] 2009*. The rate of granting bail is also increasing. The rate was 13.8% in 2005, but it rose to 17.4% in 2009. See *Shihō Tōkei Nenpō Keiji Hen [Judicial Statistics Yearbook Criminal Edition] 2009*. As for the crimes to be decided by *saiban-in* trial, the rate rose from 4.5% in 2005 to 8.3% after the introduction of the *saiban-in* system. See The Supreme Court of Japan, "Tokubetsu Shiryō 1": 1.

of thinking *saiban-in* into the courts.[42] Judges and prosecutors, as a result, might need to learn this "freshness" from the *saiban-in* and remember their original intentions for serving in the justice system.

The principle of trial including presumption of innocence and the hearsay rule must be adhered to. Sentencing should be scrutinized in light of its effect on defendant's reformation, aside from precedents which had been produced in the interplay between judges and prosecutors with no legitimate reason. Community correction and continuous social care for the defender are pending issues to prevent second offence, about which most *saiban-ins* worry. The situation of public safety in Japan should also be judged accurately based on criminal statistics, which show a recent decrease of offence. *Saiban-ins'* direct experience of seeing and judging defendants in the courtroom is precious and their findings should be made known to the public, instead of being at the mercy of sensational information supplied by the mass media. It is expected that lay participation in the justice system will have an impact on criminal justice as well as Japanese society as a whole in the long run.

42. Hiroshi Yasuhara, "Saiban-in Seido Dōnyū no Igi ni Tsuite Kangaeru [Taking the Significance of the *Saiban-in* System Seriously]", in Tōru Motobayashi et al., eds., *Shimin no Shihō wo Mezashite [Searching for the Judiciary for the People]* (Tokyo, 2006): 448–452.

Lay Prosecution of U.S. Military Crimes in Japan by Prosecutorial Review Commissions and the *Saiban-in* Trial

Hiroshi Fukurai[1]

Introduction

On January 12, 2011, nineteen-year-old Koki Yogi returned from Tokai City of the Aichi Prefecture to his hometown of Kitanaka Gusuku in Okinawa to attend the official adulthood ceremony of his twentieth birthday organized by the local government.[2] A few days before the ceremony, at 9:43 p.m., a vehicle driven by a twenty-three-year-old American military serviceman from the Army and Air Force Exchange Service (AAFES) suddenly swerved into the oncoming lane, striking the compact car driven by Koki Yogi.[3] The AAFES employee was taken to U.S. Naval Hospital Okinawa on Camp Lester but soon released, while Yogi was taken to Chubu Tokushukai Hospital and died the next morning.[4]

AAFES spokesperson Sergeant First Class Jon Cupp gave an official statement on the incident, stating that because the driver was a civil-

1. Professor of Sociology and Legal Studies, University of California, Santa Cruz. This research was supported by the 2009 Toyota Foundation Grant (D9-R-0081). Appreciation is extended to Tom Ginsburg at the University of Chicago, William Qiu at the University of California, Berkeley and Wendy Martyna at the University of California, Santa Cruz for their valuable suggestions and comments on the original manuscript. Finally, English translations are my own unless otherwise provided.

2. "Beiheihanzai Fukiso ni Kogi [Protest against Non-Prosecutorial Decision]," *Akahata Shinbun*, April 19, 2011, http://www.jcp.or.jp/akahata/aik11/2011-04-19/2011041904_01_1.html; "Japanese Man Died After Vehicle Collision with AAFES Employee on Okinawa" *Stars & Stripes*, January 13, 2011, http://www.stripes.com/news/pacific/okinawa/japanese-man-dies-after-vehicle-collision-with-aafes-employee-on-okinawa-1.131710 (hereinafter AAFES).

3. AAFES.

4. Ibid.

ian employee of the U.S. military, he would remain in U.S. custody and not be handed over to the Japanese authorities.[5] Sergeant Cupp refused to disclose additional information regarding the driver's name, background, or the probable cause of the accident –including the possibility of drunk driving.[6]

As Yoki's mother Manami Kamiya prepared for her son's funeral in Kitanaka Gusuku, she was informed on March 24th by the Okinawa Prosecutor's Office that it had decided not to indict the American soldier, explaining that the traffic collision took place while the soldier was on official duty. The Japanese prosecutor cited Article 17 of the U.S.-Japan Status of Forces Agreement (SOFA), which gives the the American military the primary right to exercise jurisdiction over all accidents or crimes committed by its service members on official duty, thereby legally precluding the Japanese authorities from prosecuting the soldier.[7] Meanwhile, the U.S. military announced that it had decided to punish the American military employee by suspending his driving privileges in Japan for the next five years.[8]

On April 25, nearly a month after the Japanese prosecution's non-indictment, Kamiya filed a complaint with the local Prosecutorial Review Commission (PRC)—Japan's grand jury system—in Naha, requesting a citizens' panel to review the Japanese prosecutors' non-indictment decision.[9] The PRC Law specifically allows victims' families or their proxy to file a petition with an eleven-member civic panel to examine whether or

5. Ibid.

6. Ibid.

7. The term, SOFA (or U.S.-Japan SOFA in this article), refers to the Agreement under Article VI of Mutual Cooperation and Security between Japan and the United States of America, Regarding Facilities and Areas and the Status of United States Armed Forces in Japan; Article 17(3)(a)(ii), http://www.mofa.go.jp/mofaj/area/usa/sfa/pdfs/fulltext.pdf; See also Keiko Itokazu, "Shitsumon Shuisho [Main Question Document]," House of Councilors, the National Diet of Japan, April 1, 2011.

8. "Beigunzoku, Kisosoto Chiikyotei ga Hikokusekini ["Indictment is Proper" for Military Employee: SOFA is on Defendant's Seat]," *Okinawa Times*, May 29, 2011, http://www.okinawatimes.co.jp/article/2011-05-29_18467. See also "Beihei Hanzai: Gunzoku Meitei: Izoku "Karui" Okinawa-shi Jiko Fukiso Beigawa Shobun ni Ikidori [American Soldier Crime: Driving Suspension is "Too Light" Victim's Family Upset on Non-Indictment in Okinawa City Auto Accident]," D-Navi, May 18, 2011, http://d-navi.org/node/2087.

9. "Beigunzoku Fukiso Izoku, Kenshin ni Fufuku Mositate [Victim's Family File Complaint to the PRC Against the Non-Indictment of American Military Employee],"

not this decision was legitimate or appropriate on the basis of evidence and investigative materials submitted to, and gathered by, the civic panel. During this investigation, it came to light that the American driver consumed alcohol at an official party prior to the accident.[10]

The next day, on April 26, the Okinawa Prefectural Assembly voiced support for the local prosecution of the serviceman by issuing a statement, condemning both the driver's actions and the subsequent non-indictment by the Japanese prosecutors.[11] The assembly also demanded equitable revisions of the U.S.-Japan SOFA and a significant reduction of American military bases in Okinawa.[12] The victim's mother announced that she also planned to meet local women's groups, as well as members of the Japanese Diet, local assemblies, and local grassroots organizations to demand the revision of the SOFA, stating that "the courts dropped the case in a one-side[d] decision, and I'm not going to accept that in silence."[13]

On May 25, after long deliberation, the Naha PRC reversed the Japanese prosecutors' non-indictment decision and determined that the indictment is proper for the given case.[14] The PRC specifically cited a 1960 U.S. Supreme Court decision which found that in military-related crimes and incidents overseas, civilian employees and contractors of U.S. military bases, as well as dependents of military service-members were not subject to military rules and regulations governed by the Uniform Code of Military Justice (UCMJ), thereby excluding them from the privileges granted under the SOFA.[15]

The PRC also reasoned that in the NATO SOFA signed with European countries, the U.S. military had accepted a similar limited juris-

---

Ryukyu Shinpo, April 25, 2011, http://ryukyushimpo.jp/news/storyid-176467-storytopic-111.html.

10. "Drinking at U.S.F 'Official Event' is Regarded as Party of 'Official Duty,'" *Japan Press Weekly*, April 24 and 26, 2011, http://www.japan-press.co.jp/modules/news/index.php?id=1784.

11. "Beikugunzoku no Otokofukiso: Kengikai ga Kengikai ga Kogiketsugi Sibo Jikode [Non-indictment of Air Force Soldier in Deadly Accident: Protest by the Prefectural Assembly]," Asahi.com, April 26, 2011, http://mytown.asahi.com/areanews/okinawa/SEB201104250017.html.

12. Ibid.

13. "Traffic Fatality Victim's Mother Angry at Court," *Weekly Japan Update*, April 14, 2011, http://www.japanupdate.com/?id=11075.

14. "Beigunzoku Kisosoto," *Okinawa Times*.

15. Ibid.

diction over its civilian components, such as family members, civilian employees, and contractors during peacetime. [16] The PRC also cited a case in the South Korean Supreme Court which stipulated that the U.S. military has no right to exercise its jurisdiction over civilian employees of American military bases during peacetime, a decision similar to the 1960 U.S. Supreme Court ruling.[17]

Political Pressure to Modify the U.S.-Japan SOFA

In August, a group of Japanese governors representing fourteen U.S. military-occupied prefectures urged Cabinet ministers to establish a new system of tracking U.S. military crimes.[18] On November 21, Japan's new Prime Minister Yoshihiko Noda announced during a Diet session that the SOFA policy "needs to be reviewed immediately and... to speed up the talks."[19] On November 23, under tremendous pressure from the Japanese government, politicians, Okinawan communities, and the victim's mother and her large group of supporters, the Japanese and U.S. governments then reached a new agreement that allowed Japanese courts to try American civilian employees of U.S. military bases even if they were on duty at the time of the crime or accident.[20] Specifically, the new agreement first allowed U.S. authorities to determine whether or not they will bring criminal prosecution over a case and notify the Japanese side of their decision. If they decide not to prosecute, the Japanese authorities can request a trial within 30 days after the U.S. notification.[21] Two days later on November 25, the Naha District Public Prosecutor's Office indicted the American military civilian who worked at a supermarket inside Camp Foster.[22]

16. Ibid.

17. Ibid.

18. "Local Officials Seek More Information on U.S. Military Crimes in Japan," *Stars & Stripes*, August 1, 2011, http://www.stripes.com/news/pacific/local-officials-seek-more-information-on-u-s-military-crimes-in-japan-1.150806.

19. Travis Tritten, "U.S., Japan Review SOFA Rules on How DOD Civilians are Tried for Crimes," *Stars & Stripes*, November 22, 2011, http://www.stripes.com/news/u-s-japan-review-sofa-rules-on-how-dod-civilians-are-tried-for-crimes-1.161421.

20. "Okinawa Prosec Indict U.S. Base Employee," *House of Japan*, November 25, 2011, http://www.houseofjapan.com/local/okinawa-prosec-indict-us-base-employee.

21. "U.S. Civilian Worker in Okinawa Indicted for Fatality," *Asahi Shimbun*, November 25, 2011, http://ajw.asahi.com/article/behind_news/politics/AJ201111250057.

22. Ibid.

It is important to note that the new agreement only applies to the crime or accident caused by the civilian component of American military personnel, and is not applicable to members of U.S. Armed Forces. Furthermore, U.S. authorities must still give their consent for such cases to move to Japanese courts. Additionally, for accidents or crimes committed by on-duty military personnel, the Naha District Public Prosecutor's Office still faced a difficult decision on whether or not to issue the indictment against the soldier.[23] If the Japanese side chooses not to indict, it was most likely that someone like Yogi's mother would have to file another complaint to the local PRC, asking the civic panel to review the appropriateness of the prosecutors' reluctance to prosecute. If the PRC decides for the second time that the indictment is appropriate in the given case, the PRC Act mandates that the Japanese prosecutors be forced to initiate the prosecutorial action against the American defendant. Such a decision would then possibly provoke an even greater legal controversy whereby the U.S. side insists on its legal right to exercise primary jurisdiction over its own personnel against the PRC's binding authority to continue with the prosecution of the American soldier in Japanese court.

Indeed, this impasse will certainly create new legal disputes with regard to litigation, possibly challenging different jurisdictional conditions specified by the SOFA and the PRC Act. There is, however, some ambivalence on this issue. While the U.S. military considers official duty in cases where a person is driving directly home from work or a military function, it has—at least in public—suggested that such jurisdictional conditions contained in the SOFA may be open for review.[24]

This paper examines the political roles of Japan's new twin systems of lay adjudication in the prosecution of military crimes in Japan. The structure of this paper is as follows. Part I provides the historical development of Japan's twin systems of lay adjudication, i.e., a *Saiban-in Seido* (a quasi-jury system) and a new Prosecutorial Review Commission (PRC or Japan's grand jury system). The Japanese government introduced both systems in 2004 and implemented them in 2009.

Part II reviews the broader investigative application of the PRC's authority to review and examine non-indictment decisions rendered by

23. Chiyomi Sumida, "Okinawans Protest U.S.-Japan Status of Forces Agreement," *Stars & Stripes*, June 29, 2011, available at http://www.stripes.com/news/pacific/okinawa/okinawans-protest-u-s-japan-status-of-forces-agreement-1.147755.

24. Ibid.

Japanese prosecutors on incidents/crimes committed by U.S. Armed Forces personnel regardless of their official duty status. The PRC Act does not discriminate the investigation of criminal cases based on duty status. If the PRC decides twice that the indictment is imminent in a given case, the PRC decision becomes legally binding, thereby initiating the forced prosecution of military personnel. This section examines how the legal status of military personnel possibly influences the PRC's power to engage in the forced prosecution of American military personnel.

Part III examines SOFA modifications needed in order to bring about proper accountability for American soldiers' actions and behaviors in Japan, as well as to restore the primary right to exercise jurisdiction over their crimes, regardless of the classification of their official duty status. And lastly, Part IV summarizes the potential modification of the SOFA in an attempt to bring equitable legal recourse to the victims of U.S. military crimes in Japan.

I. Historical Evolution of Japan's Twin Systems of Lay Adjudication: *Saiban-in Seido* and *Kensatsu Shinsakai*

The Japanese government first introduced the lay adjudicatory legislation in 2004 and established two new systems of lay participation in legal institutions: (1) a *Saiban-in Seido* (a quasi-jury system)[25] and (2) a new *Kensatsu Shinsakai* (new Prosecutorial Review Commission (PRC) or a Japanese-style grand jury system).[26] Those two systems were then implemented in 2009.

The Saiban-in Seido (the Quasi-Jury System) and Kensatsu Shinsakai (the PRC)

On May 28, 2004, the Japanese Diet passed the Act Concerning Participation of Quasi-Jurors in Criminal Trials ("Quasi-Jury Act").[27] This law created a new system of lay adjudication in Japan. While Japan had once adopted the American-style jury system in 1923, which operated briefly from 1928 to 1943, the Japanese government abolished such classic all-citizen jury trials before the end of WWII, and professional judges were

25. See Hiroshi Fukurai, "The Rebirth of Japan's Petit Quasi-Jury and Grand Jury Systems: A Cross-National Analysis of Legal Consciousness and the Lay Participatory Experience in Japan and the U.S.," *Cornell International Law Journal* 40 (2007): 315.

26. Ibid.

27. "*Saiban-in* no sanka suru keiji siban ni kansuru horitsu," Law No. 63 of 2004, http://law.e-gov.go.jp/announce/H16HO063.html.

then asked to adjudicate all criminal cases.[28] The return to the system of lay adjudication in 2004 to determine the culpability of the criminally accused is thus a significant departure from the exclusive reliance on the professional judge trial in Japan since 1943.

This quasi-jury system consists of two different panels of professional and lay participants to adjudicate the most serious and violent crimes. In a trial where there is no dispute on evidence, a group of one professional and three lay judges are asked to determine both the conviction and sentence phases of the trial.[29] In a trial with disputed evidence and testimony, a group of three professional and six lay judges are empaneled to determine both the conviction and sentence of criminal defendants. All lay participants are to be chosen at random from the list of registered rolls in local communities.[30]

Since its introduction in May 2009, the quasi-jury trial has drawn nationwide attention.[31] In 2010, a total of 1,506 defendants received sentences by quasi-jury panels.[32] Nearly nine thousands (n=8,673) participated as lay judges in *saiban-in* trials. The majority of them were male (54.6%), middle-aged (23.0%, 21.5%, and 20.2% for those in 30s, 40s, and 50s, respectively), and full-time employees (54.8%).[33] Nearly 70% of trials ended in less than four days (70.3%) and two-thirds of lay participants said that they had no problem in understanding the trial proceeding (63.1%).[34] Almost all of lay participants also felt that the experience of lay adjudication was very positive (95.2%).[35] All available statistical indications suggested that the collaborative panel of both lay and professional judges has seemed to function rather smoothly in Japan since its first introduction in 2009.

28. Fukurai, "Rebirth" (reviewing historical and current roles for lay participation in Japanese justice including the former all-citizen jury system).

29. Ibid.

30. Ibid.

31. See Makoto Ibusuki, "'Quo Vadis?' First Year Inspection to Japanese Mixed Jury Trial," *Asian-Pacific Law & Policy Journal* 12 (2010): 25 (reviewing the first year operation of the *saiban-in* trial in Japan).

32. Supreme Court of Japan, "Saiban-in Seido no Jisshi Jokyo ni Tsuite [Actual Implementation of a *Saiban-in Seido*]," April, 2011.

33. Ibid.

34. Ibid.

35. Ibid.

In addition to the *saiban-in* system, the Japanese government also revised its criminal procedure and introduced a new grand jury system (Prosecutorial Review Commissions or PRC) in 2004. On the day that the Japanese Diet enacted the Quasi-Jury Act, it also passed the Act to Revise the Code of Criminal Procedure (hereinafter "PRC Act").[36] A total of 165 commissions were created with at least one in each of Japan's fifty district court jurisdictions.[37] Prior to the PRC Act, a total of 201 commissions functioned as civic review panels; the new law streamlined the function of grand jury participation. As with the quasi-jury panel, commission members are selected at random from voter rolls.[38] However, unlike the quasi-jury trial, its deliberation is conducted exclusively by lay judges themselves without professional judges' participation. Furthermore, in order to take advantage of full citizen participation, each commission member is asked to serve for six months.

A case comes to the PRC when a victim, his/her proxy, or a commission itself brings a complaint against the Japanese prosecutor's office for their failure to issue an indictment to pursue the prosecution of an alleged offense.[39] The lay oversight of the Japanese prosecution system originally evolved as a response to the post-war American occupation reformers who had advocated the necessity of establishing the American-style grand jury system in order to restrict what they perceived as the excessive power and overreaching influence of Japanese prosecutors in criminal affairs prior to the end of WWII.[40] The PRC was first introduced in 1948, representing the hybrid of both an American-style grand jury proceeding and lay elements of a Japanese criminal jury trial first introduced in 1928.[41]

36. "Keiji soshohoto no ichibu o kaiseisuru horitsu," Law No. 62 of 2004, http://law.e-gov.go.jp/htmldata/S23/S23HO147.html.

37. See Supreme Court of Japan, http://www.courts.go.jp/kensin/q_a/q3/index.html (providing general overviews of the PRC system, including a total number of PRCs in Japan).

38. PRC Act, Arts 4, 14, 21.

39. PRC Act, Art. 2(3), 30.

40. Mark West, "Prosecution Review Commissions: Japan's Answer to the Problem of Prosecutorial Discretion," *Columbia Law Review* 92 (1992): 695–96. See also David T. Johnson, *The Japanese Way of Justice: Prosecuting Crime in Japan* (New York, 2002) (examining the enormous power imbedded in Japan's prosecutors and their influence in criminal matters).

41. See generally Fukurai, "Rebirth."

Much like America's civil grand juries, the all-citizen panel has the right to review and investigate the proper functioning of a local government, including local jails, educational boards, police units, prosecutors' offices, and other offices in a local county government, as well as civic complaints against government offices or civil servants filed by local residents in the community. The Japanese prosecutors are legally required to respond to criminal complaints filed by citizens against government officials and business establishments. The prosecutor's failure to issue an indictment against the accused allows concerned citizens to file another complaint to the local PRC to pursue prosecution. Much like the U.S. grand jury, the PRC has the authority to indict criminal alleged criminal offenders. Since 1948, more than a half-million Japanese citizens have participated in the PRC and reviewed the non-indictment decisions made by the Japanese prosecution.

Based on the evaluation of evidence, the PRC then issues prosecutors one of the following three non-binding recommendations: (1) non-indictment is proper (i.e., the prosecutor's decision was appropriate); (2) non-indictment is improper (i.e., the prosecutor should reconsider the non-charge decision); and (3) indictment is proper (i.e., the prosecutor should have prosecuted the accused).[42] Prior to 2009, however, the commission's recommendations were regarded as merely advisory and the Japanese prosecution rarely acted on them. In response to the public demand to modify the adjudicatory power of the PRC decision, the new PRC Act was put into effect in 2009 to establish the second PRC prosecutorial decision as legally binding.

The most distinct feature of Japan's grand jury system is its ability to extend the investigative jurisdiction beyond criminal cases to potentially civil or even administrative matters. With the PRC's new ability to issue a legally binding resolution, the PRC thus became the important institution of civic oversight in examining the allegation of corporate predation and governmental abuse of power.

As of December 31, 2010, the PRC had deliberated a total of 156,419 cases, including 142,967 petitions filed by proxies or families of victims and 13,452 cases in which the PRC initiated its own investigation.[43] The

42. PRC Act, Art 39(5).

43. Supreme Court of Japan, "Kensatsu Shinsakai no Juri Kensu Giketsu Kensuto [Petitions and Deliberations of the Prosecutorial Review Commission]" (2011).

PRC made the indictment decisions in 2,366 cases (1.5% of all non-indictment reviews). In 2009, the year when the new PRC Law was put into effect, the PRC deliberated 2,613 cases and recommended the forceful prosecution in a total of 11 cases (0.4% of all non-indictment cases).[44]

In 2010, the commission also deliberated a total of 2,663 cases (2,613 requested and 50 self-initiated reviews)[45] and issued eleven forced prosecution decisions, including the following three prominent indictment decisions, involving: (1) the Deputy Police Chief of the Akashi Police Station in Hyogo Prefecture in January; (2) three past presidents of the West Japan Railway Company (JR-West) in March; and (3) Ichiro Ozawa, the former secretary of the Liberal Democratic Party and currently a prominent member of the ruling Democratic Party of Japan (DPJ) in October.[46]

Despite numerous calls for the prosecution of the Akashi Deputy Police Chief for his failure to institute effective police oversight to prevent a deadly stampede incident in Akashi City in 2001, the Japanese prosecution refused to prosecute him on numerous occasions.[47] This particular incident resulted in the injuries of 274 people and deaths of nine children, ranging from five months to nine years of age, who were crushed to death in a crowded pedestrian bridge in Hyogo Prefecture.[48] The PRC had deliberated on the same case on numerous occasions, each time deciding that the officer should be indicted for prosecution, but local prosecutors continued to ignore the PRC recommendations. Their indifferent reaction to the PRC decision continued until 2009, when victims' families resubmitted their complaint to the PRC which, followed by another indictment decision, finally forced the local prosecutors to indict and prosecute the chief police officer.[49]

44. Ibid.

45. Ibid.

46. "Akashi Hodokyo Jiko: Naze Koredake Jikanga Kakattanoka—Izoku Kaiken [Akashi Pedestrian Incidents: Why Did It Take This Long?—Testimony of Victims' Families] (hereinafter Akashi)," *Sankei News*, Jan. 27, 2010.

47. See Hiroshi Fukurai, "Japan's Prosecutorial Review Commissions: Lay Oversight of the Government's Discretion of Prosecution," *East Asia Law Review* 6 (2011): 15–18 (reviewing the 2001 Akashi stampede incident, including the chronology of prosecutorial non-indictment decisions and PRCs' repeated recommendations to indict the officer).

48. Ibid.

49. "Akashi," *Sankei News*.

The PRC also issued a forced indictment to three former presidents of the JR-West in 2010, one of Japan's largest and most powerful corporations.[50] After setting a new precedent with the indictment of the deputy police chief, the PRC in the same prefecture went on to deliberate on the corporate malfeasance case involving a train derailment incident that killed 107 and injured 555 others.[51] As expected, after the brief investigation on the case, the Japanese prosecutors decided not to indict the three former presidents of JR West, indicating that they were not directly responsible for failing to institute the Automatic Train Stop (ATP) system which could have prevented the speeding train from slamming into a multi-story parking garage in the ground floor of a nearby apartment building.[52] But the PRC determined that the major factor contributing to the deadly accident was the company's disregard for customer safety in its official management policy.[53] In March of that year, it decided for the second time that the three former JR-West presidents should be indicted for professional negligence resulting in injuries and deaths.[54]

The last of the three significant PRC decisions was a forced prosecution of Ichiro Ozawa in October 2010. Ozawa previously served as a powerful chief Secretary of the Liberal Democratic Party (LDP) and has been dubbed as a "shadow shogun" of the Japanese polity, in which the political stature of Ozawa was often equated to that of former U.S. Vice President Dick Cheney. The PRC returned an indictment against him in a case involving illegal financial records of his organization called Rikuzankai.[55] Three of his staff members had already been indicted for the violation of the Political Fund Control Law for failing to report a ¥400 million (US$4 million) loan from Ozawa to Rikuzankai in its final report.[56] In October, the Tokyo High Court appointed three attorneys to prosecute

50. "JR Nishi Rekidai 3 Shacho, Kyoseikiso-e: Kobe Daiichi Kensatsuga Kiso Giketsu [Kobe PRC Decides on Indictment Against Three JR-West Presidents] (hereinafter JR Nishi)," *Sankei News*, Mar. 26, 2010.

51. "JR West, Victims' Relatives Mark Amagasaki Crash," *Japan Times*, Oct. 26, 2005, http://search.japantimes.co.jp/cgi-bin/nn20051026a4.html.

52. Ibid.

53. "JR West's Actions Show Lack of Remorse," Resolve, *Daily Yomiuri*, Oct. 24, 2009, at 4.

54. "JR Nishi," *Sankei News*.

55. Takano Takahashi, "Ozawa Sues Government Over Indictment Process," *Japan Times Online*, Oct. 16, 2010.

56. Ibid.

Ozawa.[57] The continued PRC investigation of non-indictment decisions by the Japanese prosecution thus represents a significant step towards establishing the effective civic oversight of Japanese criminal justice system in the prosecution of Japan's power elites.

II. The Prosecutorial Review Commission and Its Ability to Examine the Prosecutor's Non-Indictment Decisions on Alleged Military Crimes in Japan

Saiban-in Trials of Military Personnel in Okinawa

The first-ever trial of American military personnel in a lay-judge court in Japan took place on May 24, 2010 in the Naha District Court in Okinawa.[58] After three days of trial, Jonathan Kim, a Korean American and nineteen-year-old Marine, was sentenced to three to four years in a Japanese prison for robbing and injuring a fifty-eight-year-old taxi driver.[59] After the sentencing, the Japanese lay judges asked a chief judge to read a statement directed at Kim: "[W]e want you to reflect and think why you committed such a crime… We know you can rehabilitate. You have strength to become a good, law-abiding citizen. We believe in you."[60] His Korean-born mother also traveled from their home in Philadelphia to observe the quasi-jury trial of her son in Okinawa.[61]

Three months after this first ever lay judge trial, Phillip Edward Sawyerr became the second American soldier to be tried in lay court in Okinawa. He also became the first American soldier to be adjudicated by

57. Yuka Hayashi, "Japan's Ozawa Indicted Over Political Funds Law," *Wall Street Journal*, Jan. 31, 2011, http://online.wsj.com/article/SB10001424052748703833204576115181733628572.html (noting that Ozawa was formerly indicted on the basis of the PRC's recommendation on January 31, 2011).

58. Hiroshi Fukurai, "Japan's Quasi-Jury and Grand Jury Systems as Deliberate Agents of Social Change: De-Colonial Strategies and Deliberate Participatory Democracy," *Chicago-Kent Law Review* 86 (2011): 789. See also Hiroshi Fukurai, "People's Panel vs. Imperial Hegemony: Japan's Twin Lay Justice Systems and the Future of American Military Base in Japan," *Asian-Pacific Law & Policy Journal* 12 (2010): 95 (reviewing the 1995 rape of a twelve-year-old girl by three American soldiers in Okinawa).

59. David Allen and Chiyomi Sumida, "Kinser Marine Gets Jail Time for Robbing Cabbie," *Stars & Stripes*, May 29, 2010, http://www.stripes.com/news/kinser-marine-gets-jail-time-for-robbing-cabbie-1.104603.

60. Ibid.

61. Ibid.

the lay judges for an alleged sexual assault in Japan.[62] From an immigrant family like Kim, Sawyerr was born in the United Kingdom, immigrated to the United States with his parents when he was thirteen, and later gained U.S. citizenship.[63] After his father left the family, Sawyerr lived with his mother and two brothers. While in college, he was physically assaulted and suffered serious injuries.[64] In order to pay for his medical expense, he decided to join the Marines in 2004, soon to become a sergeant and dispatched to a military base in Okinawa where he met and wed his Japanese wife.

On August 3, 2010, Sawyerr—who would later be assigned to the Marine Corps Air Station at Iwakuni in Yamaguchi, a prefecture thirty miles west of Hiroshima—arrived in Okinawa for vacation at the Kadena Air Base.[65] He made an arrangement for sleeping accommodations on the base, where he met a new friend named "Dee." That night, Dee invited Sawyerr for a drink in Naha City, and they visited two nightclubs late at night, both of which were already closed. Sawyerr later testified that that he did not drink that night, but he smoked a "cigarette" given to him by Dee; Sawyerr himself suspected that there was a strong possibility that this was in fact an illicit drug of sorts. They both then drove back to the base whereupon Sawyerr saw a woman walking home. He parked the car and followed the woman to her apartment stairs.[66]

At 3:43 am on August 4, he sneaked up on the twenty-six-year-old woman from behind, as she tried to enter her second floor apartment.[67] Sawyerr then forced his way into her apartment, pushed her into a room, covered her mouth with his hand, and inappropriately touched her as she struggled to escape.[68] Her neighbor heard screams coming from the apart-

62. David Allen and Chiyomi Sumida, "Marine Indicted on Sexual Assault and Trespassing charges on Okinawa," *Stars & Stripes*, August 25, 2010, http://www.stripes.com/news/pacific/okinawa/marine-indicted-on-sexual-assault-and-trespassing-charges-on-okinawa-1.115882.

63. Naha District Court, "Hanketsu Shushi [Summary Judgments]," Dec. 2, 2010 (file with the author).

64. Ibid.

65. Ibid.

66. Ibid.

67. Ibid.

68. David Allen, "Police Recommend Sexual Assault Charges against Iwakuni-based Marine," *Stars & Stripes*, August 5, 2010, http://www.stripes.com/news/pacific/okinawa/police-recommend-sexual-assault-charges-against-iwakuni-based-marine-1.113506.

ment and immediately called the police. Once the police arrived, they spotted Sawyerr jumping from the second-story entryway into a parking lot and attempting to run away. Sawyerr ran a short distance before he was apprehended. The victim stated that she did not know Sawyerr and was treated for minor injuries, which required a week of recovery.[69]

Sawyerr was taken into custody but denied the accusations against him. Since his crime was committed while off-duty, the Naha Police Department claimed the primary right to exercise jurisdiction over his alleged offense, and Phillip Sawyerr was held in the Naha Detention Center.[70] After twenty-one days, prosecutors faced the decision to indict or release him, and on August 24, Sawyerr was formally charged with illegal entry and sexual assault.[71]

On November 30, 2010, Phillip Sawyerr was tried in the lay court in Naha, and he appointed a Japanese public defender to represent him. In the trial, lay judges asked Sawyerr why he attacked the woman, but he remained silent and failed to respond to the question.[72] Jurors also asked Sawyerr to describe the situation in full detail and Sawyerr responded by saying that he could not remember the details of the whole event. Nonetheless, Sawyerr told the court that he remembered climbing the stairs, the woman striking him and the police handcuffing him. He testified that he could not remember much and denied that he physically attacked and assaulted the victim. Sawyerr told jurors that he believes that the cigarette given to him by Dee affected his behavior and was the main reason for his irrational action.

The jurors also asked Sawyerr how he thought the victim felt after this incident, and he responded in remorse.[73] Finally, jurors asked Sawyerr if he could assure the jury that he would never commit any such crime again, and he said yes.[74] After three days of trial, on December 2, 2010, the lay court found Phillip Sawyerr guilty, and he was sentenced to three years and six months in a Japanese prison.[75] Sawyerr also paid the victim ¥80,000 (US$800) in compensatory damages for the injuries

69. Allen and Sumida, "Marine Indicted."
70. Ibid.
71. Ibid.
72. Naha District Court, "Hanketsu."
73. Ibid.
74. Allen, *supra* note 68.
75. Ibid.

she suffered.[76] Sawyerr did not have sufficient funds in his savings, so the majority of the money came from his mother, and the rest came from his Marine Corps salary. Sawyerr appealed the guilty decision, but the appeal was denied by the Naha Branch of the Fukushima High Court in May 2011.[77]

Aside from the significant installation of American military bases, the island of Okinawa already houses thirty-five Japanese self-defense forces bases and military installations.[78] Japanese military personnel have also committed many crimes, victimizing the residents of Okinawa.[79] The second-ever quasi-jury trial in Okinawa involved a twenty-four-year-old member of the Japanese Maritime Self-Defense Force (JMSDF) who sexually assaulted an Okinawan woman in June 2009.[80] This case became the first ever quasi-jury trial on the allegation of sexual assault in Okinawa.[81] The mixed panel consisted of three women and three men lay judges. In January of 2010, the lay court found the Japanese soldier guilty of rape resulting in bodily injuries and gave him a three-year prison sentence, suspended for five years.[82] A close observer of the case disclosed that, in order to create the most favorable impression with professional and lay judges, the defendant's two male defense attorneys had to persuade him to ex-

76. Ibid.

77. "Kyosei Waisetu Chisho Beihei no Koso Kikyaku [Denial of Appeal Made by American Soldier Convicted of Sexual Assault]," *Okinawa Times*, May 11, 2011, http://www.okinawatimes.co.jp/article/2011-05-11_17637/.

78. "Kichi no Gaikyo: Okinawa no Beigun Kichi Oyobi Jieitai Kichi (Tokeishiryo) [Military Base Conditions: U.S. Military Bases and Japanese Self-Defense Forces Bases in the Prefecture of Okinawa: Statistical Data]," Military Base Affairs Division, in the Prefectural Office of Okinawa, March 2009, 4, http://www3.pref.okinawa.jp/site/view/contview.jsp?cateid=14&id=19687&page=1.

79. "Recent Incidents Involving Japanese Self Defense Forces," Okinawa Peace Network of Los Angeles (OPNLA), March 18, 2001, http://www.uchinanchu.org/history/sdf_incident.htm.

80. "JMSDF Sailor Nabbed for Attempted Rape," *Weekly Japan Update*, June 18, 2009, http://www.japanupdate.com/?id=9573.

81. "Seihanzai to *Saiban-in*: Higaisha no Hogo ni Banzen'o [Sexual Crime and Quasi-jurors: Absolute Protection to Crime Victim]," *Okinawa Times*, January 16, 2010, http://www.okinawatimes.co.jp/article/20100116_1699/.

82. "Motojieikan ni Yuyokei: *Saiban-in* Saiban [Suspended Sentence for Former Self-Defense Force Personnel: The Quasi-Jury Trial]," *Okinawa Times*, January 16, 2010.

press his remorse and sympathy towards the victim in court.[83] The same Japanese soldier had previously committed a similar crime in Hawaii.[84]

Other Japanese Self-Defense military personnel who have also engaged in predatory crimes in other regions include a fifty-two-year-old Sergeant Major Sadao Sakai, who was convicted on February 8, 2011 of grand larceny for stealing ¥13.2 million worth of valuables in Akita Prefecture;[85] a twenty-two-year-old, former Ground Self-Defense officer Jun'ichi Kojima, who was convicted of indecent assaults involving a fourteen-year-old, middle-school female student in Ohita Prefecture on May 11, 2011;[86] and a twenty-two-year-old, former Self-Defense Officer Akihiro Okumoto, who was sentenced to death by a quasi-jury panel for killing three members of his family on December 7, 2010 in Miyazaki Prefecture.[87] While the media's attention was more prominently focused on serious and violent crimes committed by American military personnel, Japanese self-defense personnel have been equally, if not more prominently, culpable of violent and serious criminal offenses in Okinawa and other regions with heavy military presence.

The PRC and the U.S.-Japan Status of Forces Agreement (SOFA)

Once a military personnel is indicted for a serious and violent offense, the quasi-jury panel is asked to adjudicate his or her crimes and determine both the conviction and the severity of sentence. Yet, successful crimi-

83. Ryota Ishikawa, June 10, 2010 (the author's person-to-person interview with Ryota Ishikawa, a reporter for Okinawa Times who followed the trial). The interview was conducted in Naha, Okinawa, on July 10, 2010.

84. Ibid.

85. "Jieikan ni Choeki 3nen 6gatu: Renzoku Setto de Akita Chisai Hanketsu [3 years and 6 months Imprisonment to Japanese Self-defense soldier: Akita District Court Decision on Successive Larcenies]," 47 News, February 8, 2011, http://www.47news.jp/localnews/akita/2011/02/post_20110208094524.html (this case did not involve a quasi-jury proceeding).

86. "Kyosei Waisetu nadono Moto Jieikan ni Yuzai Hanketsu [Conviction to Former Self-Defense Officer on Indecent Assault Charges]," Oita Broadcasting System, May 11, 2011, http://genkichanz.blog.fc2.com/blog-entry-110.html; See also "Jieitai-in: 14sai Odoshite Hadaka no Shashin Okuraseru [Self-Defense Officer: Forced the 14 Year Old to Send a Naked Picture]," *Sponichi Annex*, October 6, 2010, http://www.sponichi.co.jp/society/news/2010/10/06/kiji/K20101006Z00002270.html.

87. "Miyazaki, Kazoku 3 nin Satsugai: Bengogawa Sikeikaihi Shucho Kososhin Hajimaru [Miyazaki: Murder of Three Family Members: Defense Arguments to Avoid Death Penalty: Appeal Process Begins]," *Mainichi Shinbun*, May 20, 2011.

nal prosecution initially depends on the ability of the Japanese police and prosecutors to engage in competent investigations of alleged criminal offenses, and the panel must issue an indictment on the basis of investigative materials, testimony, and other evidence.

As stated earlier, when the Japanese prosecution decides not to indict the suspect, the PRC can begin its investigation of the non-prosecution decision by recourse to one of two methods. First, victims (or their families or proxies) can submit a complaint to the review commission which then determines whether or not to proceed with their own investigation of the complaint behind the closed doors.[88] Second, the PRC can also carry out an investigation on its own initiative, upon a majority vote of its eleven members.[89]

There are, however, three potential problems with respect to the PRC's ability to review prosecutor's non-indictment of American military personnel. First, according to the SOFA, the U.S. military is the primary judge in determining whether or not military accidents or crimes took place while the offender was on-duty or off-duty. The SOFA also stipulates that the U.S. military has the primary right to exercise jurisdiction over incidents that occur during on-official duty, while off-duty crimes and accidents are adjudicated by the Japanese authority. Many Japanese grassroots organizations and civic groups rightfully complain about the ostensible abuse of this particular power, given that while many accidents and crimes take place outside of military compounds—before or after they completed their daily official duties at the base—military authorities have classified virtually all of them as on-duty incidents.[90]

Second, even in instances where U.S. authorities do classify an incident as off-duty whereupon the Japanese authority then holds the primary right to exercise jurisdiction, it often fails to exercise its jurisdiction to investigate these alleged offenses when either the suspects flee to and hide behind military bases or witnesses simply refuse to cooperate. When

88. PRC Act, Art 30.

89. PRC Act, Arts 2(3).

90. "Beiheihanzai ni Tachimukatte [Stand Up Against American Military Crimes]," *Okinawa Times*, May 1, 2010; see also the activities of a grassroots organization called Beigunhanzai Higaisha Kyusai Senta [The Support Center for the Victims of American Military Crimes], http://reliefcenter.blog101.fc2.com/ (providing information on military related crimes, including activities of grassroots organizations and civic activists in Japan).

these external exigencies force the Japanese prosecution to issue a non-indictment decision, the U.S. military swiftly considers this as the Japanese government's official forfeiture of its right to prosecute the case in its own criminal justice system. Under these circumstances, any subsequent PRC review carries no legally binding authority in the future prosecution of that particular crime.

Lastly, some criminal offenses involving U.S. military servicemen simply cannot be pursued further due to their furtive nature; inter-governmental agreements have effectively excluded a class of offense and incident from prosecution, preventing the PRC from exercising its civic oversight, particularly in areas like Okinawa. At least one such governmental agreement revealed that a certain class of criminal offenses had already been excluded from prosecution in Japan since the 1950s.[91]

III. Suggested Modifications of SOFA Legal Provisions in the Adjudication of Military Crimes in Japan

SOFA Modifications for the Possible Adjudication of On-Duty Accidents/Crimes

Modifications to the U.S.-Japanese SOFA have been extremely difficult, as it requires extensive bilateral negotiations and the willingness on both sides to alter the agreement. Oftentimes, the request to review and modify the SOFA provision comes from the side of host countries. The U.S. government has signed a SOFA with more than a hundred countries in the world, each of which was devised to take into the consideration unique socio-political circumstances, special requirements, and strategic missions of U.S. armed forces of the host countries and their strategic importance to the U.S. geopolitical agenda.[92]

Nonetheless, an analysis of the SOFA provisions helps to identify two key elements that have historically impeded host countries' ability to pursue the prosecution of crimes committed by American soldiers, civilian military employees, and their families. The host countries' incapacity to extend proper jurisdiction over foreign soldiers and their dependents

91. "Priority Given to Military Operations Over Any Sense of Justice," *Japan Press Weekly*, April 7, 2010, http://www.japan-press.co.jp/modules/feature_articles/index.php?id=170.

92. Condoleezza Rice and Robert Gates, "What We Need in Iraq," *Washington Post*, Feb. 13, 2008, http://www.washingtonpost.com/wp-dyn/content/article/2008/02/12/AR2008021202001.html.

has led to the loss of sovereignty and geopolitical autonomy. The recourse to the following key elements may thus extend host nations' rights for proper adjudication of crimes committed by American military personnel: (1) official duty certificates and jurisdictional waivers and (2) special custody provisions applied to U.S. service members in host countries. The following section examines each of these special provisions and addresses possible political and legal strategies in relation to them.

The Certificate of Official Duty and the SOFA's Jurisdictional Waivers. Standard within every bilateral SOFA is the allocation of the right to criminal jurisdiction between the U.S. and the government of the respective host country—a feature commonly known as concurrent jurisdiction. When a soldier commits a crime, which violates the law of both countries, concurrent criminal jurisdiction provisions establish a system of priorities delineating which country holds the primary right to prosecute. As mentioned earlier, the current U.S.-Japan SOFA gives the U.S. primary criminal jurisdiction over inter se crimes and acts or omission done during the performance of official duty. In all other cases, Japan can exercise its jurisdiction. The U.S. has adhered to the position that only the U.S. government as a sending state may make the determination of whether or not a criminal offense arises out of performance of official duty.[93] Thus, under the U.S.-Japan SOFA, the U.S. military is given priority to determine what constitutes official duty by issuing a so-called "certificate of official duty." [94] Specifically, the provision states that

> [I]mmediately after receipt of information concerning an offense committed by a member of the U.S. armed forces subject to the concurrent jurisdiction of the U.S. and Japan, the unit commander... will make a determination as to the official duty status of the accused. If the unit commander determines the alleged offense arose out of an act, or omis-

93. Major Mark R. Ruppert, U.S.AF, "Criminal Jurisdiction Over Environmental Offenses Committed Overseas: How to Maximize and When to Say 'No,'" *Air Force Law Review* 40 (1996): 28.

94. Criminal and Disciplinary Jurisdiction Under the Status of Forces Agreement, Art 13(2)(1), http://www.af.mil/shared/media/epubs/5AFI51-102.pdf (explaining the way in which the U.S. Air Force must respond to the Japanese authority in case AF service members violate the law in Japan).

> sion of an act, in the performance of official duty, he will complete and forward the certificate as to official duty."[95]

It also states that the official duty certificate "will be delivered to the chief prosecutor of the district... within ten calendar days after the official written notification of the offense was received."[96] Thus the release of the official duty certificate by the U.S. authority confirms whether or not the American service member was on official duty at the time of the incident.

A recently released internal document on the minutes to the U.S.-Japan SOFA sheds new light and detail on the authenticity of this certification process. Specifically, it states that "[w]here a member of the U.S. military personnel is charged with an offense, a certificate issued by his commanding officer stating that the alleged offense, if committed by him, arose out of an act or omission done in the performance of official duty, shall, in any judicial proceedings, be sufficient evidence of the fact unless the contrary is proved."[97] In other words, the document assumes from the outset that any acts committed by the accused took place while the individual was on-duty—without justification—and thereby relegating the burden of proof on the part of the plaintiff and prosecution to reveal evidence that claims the contrary. Based on this bilateral agreement, the Japanese government faithfully followed this protocol in the certification of official duties involving American military personnel.[98]

Furthermore, the U.S.-Japan joint committee's 1953 secret "agreed official minutes" regarding Article 17 of the SOFA also indicates that if the Japanese government fails to advise the U.S. forces within a set period of time—regardless of whether it will in fact exercise its jurisdiction over the military crimes—the U.S. can exercise such right. The periodic condition imposed on the Japanese government was very short: (1) five days (revised to ten days in 1960) for crimes "punishable under Japanese law by confinement for 6 months or less," including trespassing, assault, and driving under the influence; and (2) twenty days for alleged offenses "pun-

95. Ibid.

96. Ibid.

97. "Japanese Government's Submission to U.S. Revealed in Dealing with U.S. Soldiers' Crimes," *Japan Press Weekly*, May 19, 2008, http://www.japan-press.co.jp/2008/2574/usforces_3.html.

98. Ibid.

ishable under Japanese law by confinement for more than 6 months."[99] Such an arrangement was made by the insistence of American military officials that any delay in determining the proper steps regarding a service member would interfere with military affairs. At the same time, this arrangement was also created in order to impose the forced implementation of the 1953 secret agreement that propels the Japanese side to renounce its rights to exercise jurisdiction over certain classes of crimes committed by U.S. servicemen.[100]

In order to maximize the projection of the U.S. jurisdiction in SOFAs, the U.S. government has also been reluctant to define what truly constitutes as an offense arising in the performance of official duty for the purposes of favorably constructing any act or omission to have occurred under the performance of official duty. [101] In cases where the U.S. holds the right to exercise its jurisdiction, the Japanese government still has the right to request a waiver of the U.S. jurisdiction over on-duty accidents or crimes. Nonetheless, the U.S. military has consistently refused such requests. According to Managing Director Hiroshi Oohashi of the Criminal Justice Division in the Ministry of Justice, who testified in response to Communist Party Member Seiken Akamine's question, "Japan has never requested a waiver of the U.S. jurisdiction over on-duty incidents."[102] In actuality, the U.S. has only given in to Japanese demands in a very limited number of cases as described below.

One major obstacle for the Japanese government has been the presence of the dominant legal culture of the U.S. military and its rigid procedures for examining and assessing the merits for granting such requests. The standard protocol is to first "promptly notify the base SJA

99. "Priority Given to Military Operations." *Japan Press Weekly.*

100. Ibid.

101. There is an exception in the Korea SOFA, in which Agreed minutes to Art XXII, specifying that the term official duty "is meant to apply only to acts which are required to be done as functions of those duties which the individuals are performing." See Agreement Under Article IV of the Mutual Defense Treaty Between the United States of America and the Republic of Korea, Regarding Facilities and Areas and the Status of United States Armed Forces in Republic of Korea with Agreed Minutes, Agreed Understandings, Exchange of Letters and Other Implementing Agreements, Jul. 9, 1966, 17 U.S.T 1677, UNTS 163, Art XXII.

102. "Zainichi Beigun: Jiken, Jiko 20mankencho [American Military in Japan: More Than 200,000 Crimes and Accidents]," *Shinbun Akahata*, July 2, 2005, http://www.jcp.or.jp/akahata/aik4/2005-07-02/2005070201_02_1.html.

[staff judge advocates] [which] ... in turn will notify the accused's unit commander. The commander will forward his recommendations for approval or disapproval of the requested waiver ... within 5 calendar days after receipt of such notification."[103] The instruction further requires that "trial by courts-marshal ... will not be initiated until authorization has been received from HQ 5 AF/JAI [Headquarter of the Fifth Air Force International Law Division in Yokota Air Base in Japan]."[104]

In the past, there have only been a few cases in which the U.S. military waived its jurisdiction to Japan.[105] Conversely, the U.S. military seemed to consider Japan's waiver of jurisdiction as a matter of course and inserted a provision to the SOFA in order to expedite such a process, stating that "signatories should give sympathetic consideration to requests for waivers", encouraging the Japanese authorities to give up the right of jurisdiction. The U.S. further inserted the following phrase for the same end, claiming that it itself claims the right of jurisdiction "in all cases except those they [Japan] consider of particular importance."

The substantive evidence of successful U.S. pressure on the Japanese authority was shown in the report, "United States Overseas Military Bases," complied in December by Frank C. Nash who served as the Special Assistant to the President for National Security in 1957. Nash was commissioned to do an in-depth study of U.S. bases overseas in the light of Cold War developments. His report stated that "during the three and a half years ending in May 31, 1957, out of 38,315 cases which might have been tried in foreign courts, only 11,320 servicemen have been actually tried in

103. Ibid., Art 18.

104. Ibid. The Fifth Air Forces (5 AF) is the United States Air Force Pacific Air Forces (PACAF) which headquarters is located at Yokota Air Base in the City of Fussa, Tokyo Japan. The largest combat wing of the PACAF is located in Kadena Air Base in Okinawa, Japan.

105. The U.S. first granted waivers to Japan in 1957. See Wilson v. Girard, 354 U.S. 524, 529 (1957) (granting Japan's request for waiver). In this case, the U.S. forces voluntarily relinquished the right to jurisdiction to allow Japan to try Girard. In return, the Japanese government secretly promised to give a light sentence to Girard. In the aftermath of a twelve-year old Okinawan girl being raped by three American soldiers in Okinawa, the U.S. government also decided to offer a "sympathetic consideration (*koiteki koryo*)," to Japanese requests to waive the U.S. jurisdiction and hand over military personnel prior to an indictment." See Fukurai, "People's Panel" (examining several heinous crimes committed by American soldiers whose custody has been handed down to the Japanese authority after 1996) (cited in n. 58).

such courts."[106] Regarding the U.S. forces in Japan, Nash reported, "Japan agrees that it will renounce its primary jurisdiction unless the case holds materially great significance to Japan."[107]

The army statistics recently unearthed by Shoji Niihara indicate that the Japanese government has waived its jurisdiction in ninety-six percent of all cases between 1954 and 1958.[108] This high waiver rate was an anomaly in comparison to other SOFA nations like Great Britain that have waived only nineteen percent of its cases during the same period.[109] This pattern of waiving jurisdiction rights continues to remain extremely high in Japan; the Japan Peace Committee reported that eighty-three percent of accidents or crimes for which Japan held the primary jurisdiction were exempted from prosecution from 2001 and 2008.[110]

Prosecutorial Review Commissions and the Forced Prosecution of Military Suspects. U.S. military protocol, the SOFA, and secret Japanese-U.S. bilateral agreements have all hindered Japanese prosecutors' ability to criminally prosecute and try military personnel in Japan. Japanese prosecutors have in most cases chosen not to issue an indictment against criminal offenses committed by U.S. soldiers. Hence, the PRC becomes an important tool to rectify this particular failure on the part of the state itself. Civic complaints filed by victims of military crimes, their families or proxies, or PRC's own investigative initiative can lead to the critical assessment of this particular shortcoming. The PRC as a vehicle for determining whether the indictment of American soldiers is imminent in the given case can reverse the original non-indictment decision by the Japanese prosecutors.

Since the implementation of the PRC Act in 2009, at least two victims of alleged military crimes have filed a complaint with the local PRC. These cases involved: (1) vehicular manslaughter of sixty-six-year-old Yoshio Onda on a civilian road by Jamie M. Wallace, a civilian employee

106. "DoD Presses Japan to Waive Jurisdiction," *Japan Press Weekly*, April 6, 2010, http://www.japan-press.co.jp/modules/feature_articles/index.php?id=169.

107. "Japanese Government's Submission to U.S. Revealed in Dealing with U.S. Soldiers' Crimes," *Japan Press Weekly*, May 19, 2008, http://www.japan-press.co.jp/2008/2574/usforces_3.html.

108. "DoD," *Japan Press Weekly*.

109. Ibid.

110. Ibid.

of the American military base in Iwakuni, Yamaguchi Prefecture in the early morning of September 7, 2010;[111] and (2) the Koki Yogi case on January 12, 2011 in Okinawa as already mentioned.

In the first case, the deceased was a key member of the grassroots organization called "Atagoyama o Mamoru Kai [The Protection Group of Mount Atago or PGMA]." The PGMA has been protesting the construction of 1,060 new housing units on Mount Atago and inside the existing U.S. Marine Iwakuni Base. The construction of new residential units for additional American military personnel and their families was needed to accommodate the planned transfer of fifty-nine carrier-borne aircraft currently stationed at the U.S. Navy Atsugi Base in Kanagawa Prefecture to the Iwakuni Base in Yamaguchi Prefecture. Of the fifty-nine aircraft, forty-eight are FA18 Super Hornets, the most advanced, state-of-the-art combat aircraft in the U.S. military.[112]

The PGMA insisted that the increased presence of military personnel and their dependents likely leads to the greater instances of military-related accidents and crimes in the nearby residential communities. Despite these protests, the Japanese government in 2010 decided to expedite $817 million for the housing construction for a planned expansion of Marine Corps Air Station Iwakuni.[113]

In September 2010, the PGMA submitted a petition to Iwakuni City, demanding that Wallace be punished under Japanese law, along with a revision to the SOFA, granting Japan the primary right to exercise jurisdiction over crimes and accidents committed by U.S. military personnel and civilian employees in the base.[114] Nonetheless, on October 7, the Japanese prosecutor's office decided not to indict Wallace.[115]

111. "U.S. Base Employee Must be Tried in Japanese Court: Iwakuni Residents," *Japan Press Weekly*, September 15, 2010, http://www.japan-press.co.jp/2010/2687/U.S.F1.html.

112. "No to U.S. Military Beef-Up in Post-Disaster Mess," *Japan Press Weekly*, May 17–18, 2011, http://www.japan-press.co.jp/modules/news/index.php?id=1854.

113. "Japanese Cost for Iwakuni Housing Expansion Estimated at $817 Million," *Stars & Stripes*, September 20, 2010, http://www.stripes.com/news/japanese-cost-for-iwakuni-housing-expansion-estimated-at-817-million-1.118836.

114. "Iwakuni Residents Demand U.S. Base Employee be Tried in Japanese Court," *Japan Press Weekly*, September 15, 2010, http://www.japan-press.co.jp/modules/news/index.php?id=1304.

115. Tsutomu Niigaki, "Yamaguchi-ken Iwakuni Deno Doshu Jijitsu [The Same Incident in Iwakuni, Yamaguchi], Nichibei Chiikyotei Kaisei o Jitsugensuru NGO

Yoshio Onda was no ordinary Japanese citizen. His life had been deeply affected by the war, including Japan's colonial war in the 1940s, an atomic bomb, and the presence of American military bases near his home throughout his life. His father was killed in the Philippines during WWII, and when he was one-year-old, one of his sisters and his cousins were also killed by the nuclear blast in Hiroshima. His mother had to take care of her entire family by working at a nearby U.S. military base. While supporting her family, his mother died when she was only fifty-one years of age.[116]

After the auto accident, his remaining family members filed the complaint to the local PRC on October 29, 2010.[117] On March 11, 2011, the civic panel deliberated on the case and determined that the non-indictment was a proper decision, stating that "the soldier's accident took place while on-duty. As indicated in the U.S.-Japan SOFA, the duty status properly gives the U.S. government the primary right to exercise jurisdiction over the accident [thereby, the non-indictment by the Japanese prosecutors was a proper decision]."[118] The U.S. military then announced that Wallace would be punished for causing the deadly accident by having her driving privileges suspended for four months.[119]

The conditions surrounding the death of Yoshio Onda in Iwakuni are nearly identical to those of Koki Yogi's death in Okinawa. Both cases involved an auto accident that resulted in the death of a Japanese civilian; both drivers were civilian employees of military bases, not U.S. Armed Forces service-members. The U.S. military determined that the accidents occurred in the performance of official duty, and the Japanese prosecutors decided not to indict the American drivers because of their perceived lack of the primary right to exercise jurisdiction over the accidents.

The PRC's investigation into these nearly identical conditions and subsequent deliberations, however, produced different outcomes. The Iwakuni PRC agreed with the Japanese prosecutors' original decision

---

[NGO for the Revision of the U.S.-Japan SOFA]," June 13, 2011, http://kaiteingo.ti-da.net/e3594968.html.

116. "Beigun Hazai: Beigungunzokujiko Fukiso Izoku Kenshin Moshitate-e [Military Crimes: Victim's Family Filed Complaint to the PRC]," D-Navi, April 10, 2011, http://d-navi.org/node/1960.

117. Ibid.

118. Ibid.

119. Niigaki, "Yamaguchi-ken."

that the non-indictment against the American driver was a proper ruling, while the Naha PRC reversed the Japanese prosecutors' original decision, recommending that the American military employee be indicted for the death of a Japanese citizen.

The indictment decision of the Naha PRC was based on their critical investigations of legal rulings on crimes and accidents caused by military personnel in the U.S. and host countries that signed the SOFA with the U.S. government. Japan's civic panel was able to unearth court decisions differentiated on the basis of status distinctions between American armed forces service members and civilian personnel of the U.S. military. The Naha PRC specifically cited the ruling of the U.S. Supreme Court in *McElroy v. Guagliardo* in 1960, which determined that during peacetime, the Uniform Code of Military Justice (UCML) could not be applied to civilian employees of U.S. Armed Forces overseas in non-capital offenses, recognizing that different jurisdictional applications exist between U.S. Armed Forces service-members and civilian components of armed forces personnel.[120] The Supreme Court in *Grisham v. Hagan* in 1960 further ruled that the different jurisdictional principle be applied to civilian employees in capital cases as well.[121]

The U.S.-Japan Security Treaty in 1953 stipulated that there was no clear discernible distinction between members of the armed forces and civilian components of the armed forces in the American military exercise of jurisdiction in Japan. The U.S.-Japan SOFA also incorporated a similar understanding with respect to rights of exercising Japanese jurisdiction over the members of the armed forces and their civilian components. The U.S. Supreme Court in 1960 first recognized this bifurcated system of U.S. military rule and regulation in criminal matters on the basis of employment status in the U.S. military, eliminating the peacetime court-marshal jurisdiction over dependents of military personnel and civilian employees in foreign countries. The Naha PRC further cited the recent Korean Supreme Court's decision that also recognized a similar bifurcated system of jurisdiction. The PRC decision is to likely influence subsequent dispensation of justice involving serious crimes and deadly accidents caused by civilian employees of armed forces in Okinawa and other regions in Japan. The PRC's citation of these court cases also served to expose the

120. *McElroy v. United States ex rel.* Guagliardo, 361 U.S. 281 (1960).
121. *Grisham v. Hagan*, 361 U.S. 278 (1960).

limitation of U.S. military juridical rule over its civilian components, such as family members, civilians under its employed and civilian contractors who provide services pursuant to a specific contractual agreement with the military.[122] Both nation-wide and Okinawa community surveys conducted in 2010 indicated that the great majority of Japanese citizens support the idea that crimes or accidents committed by military personnel, regardless of their official status, should be adjudicated by representative civic panels selected from the local communities.[123]

In addition to playing an important conscionable role in exposing the U.S. military's jurisdictional limitations, the Naha PRC also serves as a conduit for channeling local concerns and sentiments of ordinary citizens living in Okinawa into the deliberation process, as it challenged non-indictment decisions made by the government. In the Yogi case, the PRC was able to investigate and examine all relevant military crimes and their judicial reviews, not only in Japan, but also in the U.S., Korea, and NATO countries in Europe. Their examinations shed a new critical light on the varying interpretive dispositions of crimes and accidents caused by civilian components of the U.S. military. Subsequently, both the Japanese and U.S. government have agreed to establish the bifurcated system for the prosecution of crimes and accidents on the basis of the employment status of American military personnel in Japan.

Lay Adjudication of Military Crimes in Host Countries. Prosecuting foreign military personnel for crimes committed in Japan has several advantages for the Japanese citizenry. First, the entire process ensures victims' families that justice was achieved in their local jurisdiction by members of the local community, not behind the closed doors of a foreign military tribunal. The local prosecution also facilitates the processes of gathering evidence and identifying witnesses to testify in court. In Japan, for example, new victim participation programs introduced in 2008 allow victims of heinous crimes and their family members to directly partici-

122. See generally Susan S. Gibson, "Lack of Extraterritorial Jurisdiction Over Civilians: A New Look at an Old Problem," *Military Law Review* 148 (1995): 114.

123. Hiroshi Fukurai, "Lay Prosecution of U.S. Military Crimes in Okinawa," presented at the Sho Sato International Conference on Japanese Legal Reforms, the University of California, Berkeley, March 11–13, 2011, conference paper.

pate in court proceedings.[124] While some critics argue that active participation of victims and their families as witnesses or advocates for the prosecution may create an undesirable imbalance of power in the courtroom, their participation may act as a preventive and deterrent force against future crimes committed by foreign soldiers and their dependents in local communities.[125]

Second, Japan's PRC is uniquely situated to help rectify the Japanese government's inability to prosecute accused military personnel. In the U.S. and other common law countries, the prosecutorial role played by the civic panel such as the institution of a grand jury in the U.S. may principally determine the indictment of the accused. Since evidential and investigative materials usually come from the side of prosecution, the grand jury has often been criticized as a mere rubber-stamp institution for local prosecutors to maintain the governmental authority by indicting anyone that the government cares to bring before it. Japan's PRC, however, operates on a different prosecutorial principle; it reviews and challenges the government's final decision to prosecute. Similarly to what the Naha PRC achieved in Okinawa, the commission's decision squarely challenged the Japanese governmental decision, reversed the original non-indictment case, and recommended the forced prosecution of a military employee. Japan's PRC also establishes an important public space for local residents to inject their sentiments and equitable sense of justice into the deliberation process, thereby overriding the conservative approach taken by the Japanese government in the adjudication of military crimes. Furthermore, the PRC may help remove the adjudicative role of the U.S. military by putting it directly in the hands of local residents who have long been victimized by protracted foreign military presence.

Lastly, the PRC is presented with a unique opportunity to preside over other criminal matters involving other foreign nationals. Recently the Naha PRC decided to indict forty-two-year-old Chinese fisherman Zhan Qixiong whose trawler hit Japan Coast Guard ships in September of 2010.[126] The powerful collision took place near the disputed East China Sea Islands, called Senkaku in Japan and Diaoyu in China, escalating

124. Masami Ito, "Victim Participation in Trials Risky, Experts Say," *Japan Times*, March 30, 2007, http://search.japantimes.co.jp/cgi-bin/nn20070330a3.html.

125. Ibid.

126. "Call for Indictment of Chinese Skipper Illegal: Spokesperson (Call for Indictment)," Jiji Press Ticker Service, April 19, 2011.

Sino-Japanese tensions. Zhan was arrested on charges of obstructing the duties of the Japanese Coast Guard, but the Japanese government soon released him, fearing further deterioration of bilaterals relation with the Chinese government. In October, a group of five Japanese citizens, including a journalist, filed a criminal complaint against Zhan with the prosecutors' office in Naha.[127]

When the Naha prosecutors' office decided not to indict him on January 24, 2011,[128] the same group filed another complaint with the Naha PRC to review the prosecutors' non-indictment decision.[129] The civic review panel then voted on April 18 to seek the indictment of the captain who returned to China last September.[130] In response to the PRC's recommendation, the Naha prosecutors' office once again investigated the matter and decided again not to indict the Chinese fisherman on June 28.[131] On July 21, the Naha PRC decided for the second time that Zhan face charges for obstructing justice, violating fishing rights, and causing criminal damages to Japanese ships.[132]

IV. Conclusions

The death of Koki Yogi became an important symbol that highlighted the politics of the U.S.-Japan SOFA and its inequitable prosecutorial process. Yogi's best friend, Shoji Arakaki, summarizes Japanese sentiments toward the document perfectly: "[N]ever did I dream that there were such rules like the SOFA that make light of our human rights. Our grandparents and parents have suffered from the burden of heavy military presence and unfair treatment. How much longer do we need to suffer?"[133]

Foreign governments and alien soldiers have dominated the history of Okinawa. There have been few means by which the indigenous peo-

127. "Probe Sought on Decision Not to Indict Chinese Skipper," Jiji Press Ticker Service, January 24, 2011.

128. Ibid.

129. "Call for Indictment," Jiji Press Ticker Service.

130. Ibid.

131. "Japanese Prosecutors Again Drop Charges Against China Skipper," Jiji Press Ticker Service, June 28, 2011.

132. "Chugokujin Sencho "Kisosubeki" Naha Kensatsushinsakai ga Giketsu [Indictment is Proper for Chinese Captain, According to the Naha PRC]," *Ryukyu Shinpo*, July 21, 2011.

133. Sumida, "Okinawans Protest" (cited in n. 23).

ple could assert their sovereignty or political independence, as both the Japanese and U.S. governments thoroughly control the political and economic sectors of the island. The introduction of twin systems of both the *Saiban-in Seido* and the PRC in Okinawa, nonetheless, began to change the mindset of the colonized subjects in the island. The lay adjudication of American and Japanese military personnel in 2010 and 2011 helped express indigenous voices and create a possible path for indigenous independence and de-colonization of people in the island. There will be more American and Japanese military defendants subject to these judicial processes, as lay adjudication begins to play a prominent role in placing the burden of responsibility squarely on the shoulders of military personnel, thereby functioning as an effective judicial oversight of the activities of military personnel in Okinawa. Whether or not the quasi-jury trial and PRC continue to create an important public space in which to articulate effective decolonial voices and an equitable future of the island is something to be examined in coming years.

Environmental and Worker Safety Law in Japan: Recent Changes, the Impact of Reform Laws and Movements, and the Prospects for the Future

Eri Osaka[1]

I. Introduction

In Japan, asbestos disasters are seen not only as occupational accidents but also as environmental pollution caused by a failure of regulation. Compared with other developed countries, asbestos regulations in Japan have been too slow. Even after the establishment of an administrative compensation scheme for asbestos-related diseases, a substantial number of asbestos victims have chosen to go to court. These lawsuits are of a public interest nature. With help from experienced lawyers through environmental litigation in the past, plaintiffs are pursuing the State's liability for promoting the use of asbestos and not preventing asbestos-related injuries as well as demanding the expansion of the administrative compensation scheme.

This article consists of three parts. In the first part, I will briefly overview the development of environmental and worker safety laws in Japan. In the second part, I will examine the ongoing asbestos disaster, possibly the biggest negative legacy of industrial pollution in Japan and will look into the regulations, legislation, and litigation dealing with asbestos. In the final part, I will make some observations about the possible reasons for belated asbestos regulations and the future of asbestos disasters.

1. Associate Professor of Law, Toyo University Faculty of Law (Japan). The research work for this article was supported by Grant-in-Aid for Young Scientists (B) (19730077) of the Japan Society for the Promotion of Science. The author would like to thank Professors Harry N. Scheiber and Tom Ginsburg for their help in publishing this article.

II. Brief Overview of Environmental and Worker Safety Laws in Japan

Industrial Pollution in the Early Days

In the early twentieth century, the government of Japan strongly encouraged industrial development. People in rural areas were affected by copper mining and the refining industry, resulting in significant harm to their health and agricultural resources. People in urban areas suffered from air pollution caused by factories, thermal power stations, and an increasing number of automobiles. Nevertheless, with only a few exceptions,[2] neither central nor local governments made efforts to control environmental pollution. Regarding workers safety, the Factory Act[3] was enacted in 1911, and went into effect in 1916; however, people generally worked in poor conditions.[4] In 1931, the Workers' Accident Aid Act[5] for factory and mining workers and the Workers' Accident Aid Liability Insurance Act[6] for other workers were enacted.

Development of Environmental and Worker Safety Laws

Reconstruction Period after the Second World War

After the Second World War, Japan made economic reconstruction the first priority. The Government redeveloped old industrial areas and started to construct petrochemical complexes in several coastal zones. From 1954 to 1973, Japan experienced an era of high economic growth. Japan reached its pre-war economic level by 1955 and came to have the world's second largest GNP in 1968.

Development of Environmental Law

In the 1960s, serious environmental pollution became a growing concern in Japan. The four major pollution issues were the Minamata Disease

2. Osaka enacted its air pollution control ordinance in 1932. It was the first environmental regulation in Japan.

3. Kōjōhō, Law No. 46 of 1911.

4. See Wakizo Hosoi, *Jokō Aishi [A Tragic History of Factory Women]* (Tokyo, 1927) (describing how young girls were forced to work under harsh conditions at spinning mills).

5. Rōdōsha Saigai Fujo Hō, Law No. 54 of 1931.

6. Rōdōsha Saigai Fujo Sekinin Hoken Hō, Law No. 55 of 1931.

caused by methyl-mercury poisoning from industrial wastewater in Kumamoto and Niigata, the Itai-itai Disease caused by mining pollution in Toyama, and the Yokkaichi Asthma caused by air pollution in Mie. These pollution cases went to court in the late 1960s and early 1970s (the Four Big Pollution Cases).[7] In response to this increase in pollution victims, the Law Concerning Special Measures for the Relief of Pollution Related Health Damage[8] was enacted in 1969, which was superseded by the Pollution-Related Health Damage Compensation Law[9] in 1973.

In response to serious environmental pollution, a total of fourteen environmental statutes were amended or newly enacted during the extraordinary Diet session in November and December 1970, which was later called the "Pollution Diet." Such statutes included the Basic Act for Environmental Pollution Control,[10] the Air Pollution Control Act,[11] the Water Pollution Control Act,[12] and the Wastes Disposal and Public Cleansing Act.[13] On July 1, 1971, the Environmental Agency was established. Since then, environmental laws and regulations have been developed dramatically. With some exceptions, however, these laws have been designed to prevent environmental problems from occurring rather than to redress the environmental problems which have already occurred. From past to present, civil liability rules have been playing a significant role in environmental pollution cases.

Development of Worker Safety Law

The Constitution of Japan declares that the right of workers to organize as well as to bargain and act collectively is guaranteed (Art. 28), and standards for wages, hours, rest, and other working conditions shall be fixed by law (Art. 27(2)). Shortly before the promulgation of the Constitution, the Labor Relation Adjustment Act[14] was enacted. In 1947, the Labor

7. For more details, see Julian Gresser, Fujikura Koichiro, and Akio Morishima, *Environmental Law in Japan* (Cambridge, Mass., 1981).

8. Kōgai ni kakaru Kenkō Higai no Kyūsai ni kansuru Tokubetsu Sochi Hō, Law No. 90 of 1969.

9. Kōgai Kenkō Higai no Hoshōtō ni kansuru Hōritsu, Law No. 111 of 1973.

10. Kōgai Taisaku Kihon Hō, Law No. 132 of 1967. It was later replaced by Kankyō Kihon Hō [the Basic Environmental Law], Law No. 91 of 1993.

11. Taiki Osen Bōshi Hō, Law No. 97 of 1968.

12. Suishitsu Odaku Bōshi Hō, Law No. 138 of 1970.

13. Haikibutsu no Shori oyobi Seisō ni kansuru Hōritsu, No. 137 of 1970.

14. Rōdō Kankei Chōsei Hō, Law No. 25 of 1946.

Standards Act[15] and the Workers Accident Compensation Insurance Act[16] were enacted. In 1949, the new Labor Union Act[17] was also enacted. Thus, the laws involving fundamental rights for workers were quickly developed in this earlier stage; however, the safety of workers was put off. For instance, soon after the Second World War, the Government began enhancing coal production for ensuring a stable energy supply. In 1960, the Pneumoconiosis Act[18] was enacted for the purpose of requiring employers to conduct medical examinations for pneumoconiosis on workers regularly engaged in dusty work (Art. 8). It was only enacted, however, after the Government shifted the focus of its energy policy from coal to oil.

In 1972, the Industrial Safety and Health Act[19] was finally enacted with the aim to secure workers' safety and health in their workplaces as well as to facilitate the establishment of a comfortable working environment (Art. 1).

Development of a Compensation System

Pollution-Related Health Damage Compensation System. People suffering from pollution-related health issues can receive compensation if s/he is certified as a "pollution disease patient." Under the Pollution-Related Health Damage Compensation Law, two types of areas are designated: the Class I areas where severe air pollution occurs and many people suffer from respiratory disease and the Class II areas where many people are poisoned by mercury, cadmium, and arsenic causally related to industrial or mining waste.

Prefectural governments with one or more designated areas are required to administer the compensation system including certificating pollution victims. Because the certification is a highly technical task, prefectural governors establish municipal health damage certification councils for their consultation. Regarding the Minamata Disease, the Environmental Agency (currently the Ministry of the Environment) set the

15. Rōdō Kijun Hō, Law No. 49 of 1947.
16. Rōdōsha Saigai Hoshō Hoken Hō, Law No. 50 of 1947.
17. Rōdō Kumiai Hō, Law No. 174 of 1949.
18. Jinpai Hō, Law No. 30 of 1960.
19. Rōdō Anzen Eisei Hō, Law No. 57 of 1972.

certification criteria in 1971,[20] which was replaced by narrower criteria in 1977.[21]

a) The compensation for certified patients includes:
  i) medical care itself or medical expenses,
  ii) disability compensation for certified patients over 15 years old,
  iii) compensation allowance for certified patients under 15 years old, and
  iv) treatment allowance.

b) The compensation for the bereaved family of certified patient includes:
  i) survivors compensation pension or lump-sum benefit, and
  ii) expenses for funeral rites.

The funding complies with the polluter-pays principle because the law was intended to provide prompt and just compensation for pollution victims. Regarding the fund for non-specific disease in Class I areas, 80 percent is raised from industrial levies and 20 percent is raised from an automobile tonnage tax. Regarding the fund for specific poisoning in Class II areas, responsible companies are required to pay in full. For instance, the compensation of certified patients of the Kumamoto Minamata Disease is paid by the offending company, the Chisso Corporation.

The Law was amended in 1978[22] and went into effect on March 1, 1988, which led to the removal of the entire Class I designation. While then-certified patients continue to receive compensation, no more victims are certified as Class I patients.

The Pollution-Related Health Damage Compensation System certainly helped many pollution victims. It is also true, however, that the certification criteria of Minamata Disease set by the Environmental Agency and the removal of the Class I designation left the grievances of a huge number of pollution victims unredressed, which has resulted in a large number of lawsuits.[23]

20. Environmental Agency, *Kōtensei Minamata Byō no Handan Jōken ni tsuite [In re the Criteria for Judging Post-Natal Minamata Disease]* (1977).

21. Environmental Agency, Kōgai *ni kakaru Kenkō Higai no Kyūsai ni kansuru Tokubetsu Sochiho no Nintei ni tsuite [In re the Certification under the Law Concerning Special Measures for the Relief of Pollution-Related Health Damage]* (1971).

22. Kōgai Kenkō Higai Hoshō Hō no Ichibu wo Kaisei suru Hōritsu, Law No. 97 of 1987.

23. For more details, see Eri Osaka, "Re-evaluating the Role of the Tort Liability System in Japan," *Arizona Journal of International and Comparative Law* 26 (2009): 393.

Workers' Compensation System. When a worker accident occurs on the job or in or around the workplace, s/he can receive compensation under the Worker's Accident Compensation Insurance System, conditional on the approval by the head of relevant labor standards supervision office. Under the Pneumoconiosis Act, those whose classification for supervision of pneumoconiosis (including asbestosis) has been decided as No. IV, and those deemed to be suffering from complications are able to receive compensation.

a) If an employee is absent from work due to medical treatment, s/he is entitled to receive:
  i) the medical care compensation benefit (all medical care expenses),
  ii) the temporary disability compensation expenses (60% of basic daily benefit per day after an absence of four days), and
  iii) the injury and diseases pension, in case s/he does not recover from injury or disease after 18 months from the beginning of treatment.

b) If an employee sustains a permanent disability, s/he is entitled to receive the physical sickness compensation pension or lump-sum based on the severity of the injury.

c) If an injured worker needs 24-hour care or care as needed, s/he is entitled to receive the care compensation benefit.

d) If an injured worker dies, s/he is entitled to receive:
  i) the survivors compensation pension or lump-sum benefit, and
  ii) the expenses for funeral rites (funeral rites benefit).

Even if s/he receives compensation under the Worker's Accident Compensation Insurance System, s/he can still pursue employer's liability for her/his damages not covered under the System.

Development of Civil Liability Rules

Tort Liability

General Tort Rule. Article 709 of the Civil Code[24] provides the general rule of tort liability. Under this provision, the plaintiff/victim bears the burden of proof that (a) a defendant/tortfeasor acted intentionally or negligently; (b) the defendant infringed any right or legally protected interest of the plaintiff, in other words, the defendant's act was wrongful; (c) the plaintiff sustained any damage; and (d) there was a causal relationship between the defendant's act and the plaintiff's damage.

24. Minpō, Law No. 89 of 1896.

Courts have found that the defendant acted negligently if s/he had breached the duty to avoid the foreseeable harm to the plaintiff.[25] The foreseeability and avoidability are decided based on a reasonable person standard; however, courts have set a high standard for the duty to foresee the harm and the duty to avoid the foreseeable harm in some complex cases, such as environmental pollution cases.[26] In complex cases, proving a causal relationship is difficult. The Supreme Court held that the standard of proof is "not a scientific standard that leaves no doubt, but a case of strong probability that a specific event caused a specific loss by considering all the evidences based on the rules of thumb."[27] The standard is important in toxic tort cases involving non-specific diseases, such as asthma, where the causation issue presents a major barrier for plaintiffs. Courts have admitted epidemiological evidence in such cases.[28]

The primary remedy in tort is monetary damages (Art. 722). The main purpose of tort liability is to compensate a victim for his/her losses caused by the tortfeasor's act. Therefore, courts have awarded plaintiffs with compensatory damages only. It is generally agreed that the tort liability has some deterrent effect on wrongful act, and some commentators even affirm that it functions as a sanction.[29] The Japanese Supreme Court, however, has denied the concept of punitive damages.[30]

In case law, the losses claimed by a plaintiff can be compensated if they had a relationship of "adequate causation" with the tortfeasor's act.[31] The plaintiff has the burden of proof for the amount of damages, both pecuniary and non-pecuniary. In cases involving many victims, courts have allowed plaintiffs to demand their damages as an inclusive "pain and suf-

25. *Ōsaka Alkali Co., Ltd. v. Sotomura, 22 Daihan Minroku* 2474, (Great Ct. Judicature, 1916).

26. See, for example, *Ōno v. Showa Denko Co.*, 642 *Hanrei Jihō* 96 (Niigata D. Ct., 1971); *Watanabe v. Chisso Corp.*, 696 *Hanrei Jihō* 15 (Kumamoto D. Ct., 1973).

27. *Miura v. State, 29 Minshū* 1417 (Sup. Ct., 1975).

28. See, for example, *Komatsu v. Mitsui Mining & Smelting Co., Ltd.*, 635 *Hanrei Jihō* 17 (Toyama D. Ct., 1971); *Shiono v. Shōwa Yokkaichi Sekiyu Co., Ltd.*, 672 *Hanrei Jihō* 30 (Tsu D. Ct., Yokkaichi Branch, 1972).

29. See, for example, Kazuo Shinomiya, *Jimukanri, Futōritoku, Fuhōkōi (Chu-kan) [Mandate, Unjust Enrichment, and Torts Vol. 2]* (Tokyo, 1983), 265–266.

30. *Northcon I v. Mansei Kōgyō Co.*, 51 *Minshū* 2573 (Sup. Ct., 1997).

31. *Ōsaka Shōsen Corp. v. Murakane Shōten Corp.*, 5 *Daihan Minshū* 386 (Great Ct. Judicature, 1926).

fering damages."[32] Such a calculation method is justified by the difficulty for victims in providing their itemized losses and the difference of each victim's anticipated losses.

In case law again, when a victim dies, his/her bereaved family inherits his/her right to demand compensation for damages.[33] The parents, spouse, and children of the deceased victim may demand their own nonpecuniary damages (Art. 710).

Special Tort Rules. An employer can be vicariously liable for his/her employee's tortious conduct (Art. 715). When multiple tortfeasors are involved, they owe joint and several liability (Art. 719).

An operator of a defectively constructed or maintained structure on land may be liable for causing loss to another (Art. 717(1)). If the operator can prove that he took reasonable care to prevent such loss, the owner of the defective structure must accept strict liability (Art. 717(2)).

Statute of Limitations. Under tort liability, s/he must bring his/her case into court within three years from the time when s/he comes to know of his/her damage and the identity of the tortfeasor (the former clause of Art. 724). A victim's tort claim is automatically precluded after twenty years have elapsed from the time when the tort was committed (the latter clause of Art. 724). Courts amended this twenty years rule for toxic tort cases. When a victim's injury is of an accumulative and latent nature, courts have set the starting point of the period of prescription on the date when s/he develops his/her injury.[34] Similarly, the Product Liability Act[35] sets the starting point of its 10-year period of prescription on the date when the victim's damage occurs (Art. 5(2)).

Product Liability

Before the enactment of the Product Liability Act in 1994, product liability claims were brought under breach of contract, breach of warranty, or tort liability rules.

Under the Act, a manufacturer shall be liable for damages arising from infringement of the life, body, or property of others that is caused

32. See, for example, *Watanabe*, 696 *Hanrei Jihō*.

33. *State v. Iwasaki*, 5 *Daihan Minshū* 150 (Great Ct. Judicature, 1926).

34. See, for example, *State v. Yamamoto (Chikuho Pneumoconiosis Case)*, 58 *Minshū* 1032 (Sup. Ct., 2004).

35. Seizōbutsu Sekinin Hō, Law No. 85 of 1994.

by a "defect" in the delivered, manufactured product (the main clause of Art. 3). The same holds for a processor, importer, or person who is considered to be a manufacturer (Art. 2(3)(ii)–(iii) and 3). The "defect" means a lack of safety that the product ordinarily should provide, taking into account the nature of the product, the ordinarily foreseeable manner of use of the product, the time when the manufacturer delivered the product, and other circumstances concerning the product (Art. 2(2)). The Act did not adopt any inference rule on defects; therefore, a burden of proving a defect is on the victim. If the manufacturer can prove the defect in such a product could not have been discovered given the state of the scientific or technical knowledge at the time when the manufacturer delivered the product, s/he can be exempt from liability (Art.4(1)).

Employer's Obligation to Pay Attention to His/Her Worker's Safety
Courts recognize that an employer has an obligation to pay attention to his/her worker's[36] safety based on a principle of faith and trust (Art. 1(2) of the Civil Code).[37] In 2007, the Labor Contract Act[38] put this obligation into statutory form (Art. 5). Therefore, for instance, when an worker becomes ill through toxic exposure on the job or around his/her workplace, s/he can sue his/her employer based on his/her breach of this obligation. In such cases, s/he may be able to sue his/her employer under tort liability, but its three-year statute of limitations may preclude his/her claim. If s/he sues his/her employer under the breach of this obligation, however, s/he is able to bring his/her case into court within ten years from the time when s/he can exercise his/her right (Art. 166 of the Civil Code).

State Liability
State Liability in General. Sovereign immunity is not accepted under the Constitution of Japan (Art. 17). Under the State Compensation Law,[39] when a public official who is in a position to exercise public power has, in course of performing his/her duties, illegally inflicted losses on another person intentionally or negligently, the State or a public entity is liable to compensate such losses (Art. 1(1)). When a defect in the construction or

36. Direct contractual relationship is not necessarily required. *Saiki v. Mitsubishi Heavy Industries Case,* 1931 *Hanrei Jihō* 3 (Sup. Ct., 1991).
37. *Kudō v. State,* 29 *Minshū* 143 (Sup. Ct., 1975).
38. Rōdō Keiyaku Hō, Law No. 128 of 2007.
39. Kokka Baishō Hō, Law No. 125 of 1947.

maintenance of public property has inflicted losses on another person, the State or a public entity is also liable to compensate such losses (Art. 2 (1)).

State Liability for Occupational Disease. As the energy revolution in 1960's moved ahead, coal mines around the country closed one after another.[40] Meanwhile, the number of black lung disease victims increased.

From 1985 to 1987, a total of 480 former coal miners and their bereaved families in Chikuho area, Fukuoka, sued the State and six coal mining companies for damages. In 1995, the Iizuka Branch of the Fukuoka District Court found that all defendant companies were liable for breach of employers' obligation but denied State liability.[41] Both plaintiffs and defendants appealed. During the appeal hearing, three companies settled with a part of the miners and their bereaved families. In 2001, the Fukuoka High Court found that not only three companies but also the State was liable for the damage suffered by workers and their bereaved families.[42] Even after the enactment of the Pneumoconiosis Act in 1960, the court held that the State failed to take appropriate measures to prevent mining workers from contracting disease until 1986. The court ordered the State to pay solely ¥320 million as well as to pay jointly and severally an additional ¥420 million with the three companies, while the companies were to pay ¥1.17 billion. Two more companies entered the settlement before the Supreme Court decision.

On April 24, 2004, the Supreme Court upheld the high court order.[43] It was the first Supreme Court decision which recognized State liability in pneumoconiosis/black lung disease cases.

State Liability for Pollution-Related Disease. One of the worst incidences of pollution in Japan is undoubtedly the methylmercury poisoning that occurred in Minamata area, Kumamoto. The Kumamoto Minamata Disease is caused by the consumption of a lot of fish and shellfish contaminated by methylmercury compounds discharged into seas and rivers by the Chisso Corporation. The disease was officially discovered in 1956. The victims targeted Chisso, the one and only offending company. Eventually

40. All coal mines and fields have been closed in Japan, except for the Kushiro Coalfield in Hokkaido.

41. *Takemoto v. State*, 1543 *Hanrei Jihō* 3 (Fukuoka D. Ct., Iizuka Branch, 1995).

42. *Takemoto v. Mitsui Mining Co.*, 1785 *Hanrei Jihō* 89 (Fukuoka H. Ct., 2001).

43. *Yamamoto*, 58 *Minshū*.

they started to pursue the liability of the State and Kumamoto Prefecture for not preventing the Kumamoto Minamata Disease. One of the collective lawsuits was called the "Minamata Kansai Lawsuit," because they were brought by the Minamata disease victims living in Kansai region. They left Minamata area due to the harsh economic and social environment. In 1994, the Osaka District Court found that Chisso was liable, but it denied the liability of the State and Kumamoto Prefecture.[44] In 2001, the Osaka High Court found that the State failed to exercise its power to order Chisso to take appropriate measures to improve its wastewater treatment process or to stop its operation under the then-water pollution control laws as late as the end of 1959 and that Kumamoto Prefecture failed to exercise its power to order Chisso to install or improve the equipment for removing hazardous substances from its wastewater under the then-ordinance adjusting fisheries as late as the end of 1959.[45] Therefore, the high court held that all the defendants were liable for those afflicted with the Minamata Disease. Only the State and Kumamoto Prefecture appealed.

On October 15, 2004, the Supreme Court basically upheld the high court decision.[46] It ordered the State and Kumamoto Prefecture to pay damages totaling ¥17.5 million for thirty-seven victims who were uncertified under the Pollution-Related Health Damage Compensation System.

Relationship Between Environmental Pollution and Workers' Accident

Both traditional environmental pollution and worker accidents are caused by the dangerous activities of industry. While the former is a harmful act to residents and the latter is a harmful act to workers, they have a lot in common. For instance, both the people living near dangerous facilities and the people working at such facilities have difficulty avoiding the danger even if they were aware of some risk beforehand. This is because they must move to another area and/or quit their job to avoid the danger. Moreover, the group with the highest risk of environmental pollution or worker accidents is, in most cases, the most vulnerable members of the community. It is difficult for them to settle their problems through dialogue without community-wide assistance or the strong help of a sup-

44. *Araki v. Chisso Corp.*, 1506 *Hanrei Jihō* 5 (Osaka D. Ct., 1994).
45. *Araki v. Chisso Corp.*, 1761 *Hanrei Jihō* 3 (Osaka H. Ct., 2001).
46. *State v. Araki*, 58 *Minshū* 1802 (Sup. Ct., 2004).

port organization or labor union. The vulnerable can, however, easily be isolated when the majority of the community or workers are voluntarily or involuntarily supportive of industrial activity. Another example can be seen in many toxic tort cases. When local residents suffer a pollution-related disease caused by hazardous substances emitted by an offending company, the workers at the offending company often also suffer the occupational disease caused by the same substances either prior to or concurrently with local residents.

In the next chapter, I will focus on the typical negative legacy of industrial pollution: the asbestos disaster. Kenichi Miyamoto, one of the leading environmental economists, says, "The asbestos disaster is a complex, accumulative disaster all over the economic process: workers' accidents in the production process, environmental pollution for workers' families and neighborhood residents, pollution caused by consumer products (the injuries involved from the consumption of more than 3,000 kinds of consumer product, especially the pollution caused by demolishing them), and the pollution caused by waste."[47]

III. Asbestos Regulation, Legislation, and Litigation in Japan

Regulating Asbestos

History of Asbestos in Japan

As in other advanced industrial countries, Japan had valued asbestos highly as a "magic mineral" for a long time. Asbestos was even mentioned in *Taketori Monogatari (Tale of the Bamboo Cutter)*, the old Japanese folktale, dating back well over a millennium, as *Hinezumi no Kawaginu (Fire-Rat Robe)*. In 1764, Hiraga Gennai, a famous inventor in the Edo period, discovered asbestos minerals for the first time in Japan and made asbestos cloth called "*Kakanpu*" (Fire-Resistant Blanket).[48]

Advancing modern industrialization was accompanied by an increased use of asbestos. In total, over ten million tons of asbestos had been

47. Kenichi Miyamoto, *Kankyō Keizaigaku [Environmental Economics]*, 2nd ed. (Tokyo, 2007), 127–28. Kenichi Miyamoto recently published the comprehensive work on the asbestos disaster in Japan. Kenichi Miyamoto, Kenji Morinaga, and Hiroyuki Mori, *Asbestos Disaster: Lessons from Japan's Experience* (Tokyo, 2011).

48. Gennai Hiraga, *Kakanpu Ryakusetsu [Brief Description of the Fire-Resistant Blanket]* (Osaka, 1765).

imported into Japan by 2005.[49] Though more than three-thousand kinds of asbestos products have been manufactured, supplied, and used, most of them were asbestos-containing construction materials. Data shows that a total of 5.4 million tons of asbestos were used for construction materials from 1971 to 2001.[50]

Asbestos Problems as an Occupational Injury

Asbestosis as Pneumoconiosis. As later discussed, in 1937, the Government conducted a study on the occupational safety of some asbestos spinning factories and found that 80 out of 650 workers acquired asbestosis; however, no legal measures were taken at that time.

Regulating Asbestos at a Snail's Pace. In 1971, the Ordinance on Prevention of Hazards Due to Specified Chemical Substances[51] listed asbestos as a specified chemical substances and required ventilators to be installed at asbestos-related workplaces. This was the first regulation placed on asbestos in Japan.

In 1975, asbestos was placed on the carcinogens list under the Ordinance on Prevention of Hazards Due to Specified Chemical Substances, and spraying asbestos was generally banned. In 1976, the Ministry of Labor issued its notification "Promotion of Measure to Prevent Health Problems Caused by Asbestos Dust,"[52] which promoted employers to instruct their workers to remove asbestos from their working clothes by washing and not to take them home.

In 1978, the Ministry of Labor set up the Certification Standards for Workers' Compensation of Asbestos-Related Diseases.[53]

49. See Japan Asbestos Association, "Nihon ni okeru Asubesuto no Yunyū Ryō [Asbestos Import Statistics]" (March 16, 2007), http://www.jati.or.jp/data/toukei_07.pdf.

50. Japan Asbestos Association's Environmental Safety and Health Committee, "Ishiwata Ganyū Kenchiku Zairyō Haikibutsuryō no Yosokuryō Chōsa Kekka Hōkokusho [The Report of Survey Results of Predictive Quantity of Asbestos-containing Construction Waste]" (Dec. 1, 2003).

51. Tokutei Kagaku Busshitsu Shōgai Yobō Kisoku, Ordinance of Ministry of Labor No. 39 of 1971.

52. Ministry of Labor, Ishiwata Funjin ni yoru Kenkō Shōgai Yobō Taisaku no Suishin ni tuite (1976).

53. Ministry of Labor, Ishiwata ni yoru Shippei no Rōsai Nintei Kijun (1987).

In 1988, the Working Environment Evaluation Standards[54] was enacted to set up the control concentration level for asbestos.

Partial Ban on Asbestos. In 1995, the Enforcement Order of the Industrial Safety and Health Law[55] was revised to ban the manufacture, import, supply, and use of crocidolite and amosite.

In 2004, the Enforcement Order of the Industrial Safety and Health Law banned the manufacture, import, supply, and use of ten selected materials (e.g., building materials) containing more than one wt% asbestos. This partial ban on asbestos made the shift from regulation on manufacturing asbestos-containing materials to regulation on demolishing asbestos-containing materials. Therefore, in 2005, under the Industry Safety and Health Law, the Ordinance on the Prevention of Asbestos Hazards[56] was separately established from the Ordinance on Prevention of Hazards Due to Specified Chemical Substances. This Asbestos Ordinance reinforced the prevention measures for asbestos exposure during demolition work.

"Kubota Shock." On June 29, 2005, a newspaper disclosed that seventy-nine workers died from asbestos-related diseases at the former Kanzaki plant of Kubota Corporation, one of the leading machinery makers in Japan.[57] What is called the "Kubota Shock" was just the beginning of asbestos problems in Japan. Other asbestos-related companies made similar announcements as Kubota did, and the media covered the asbestos prob-

54. Ministry of Labor, Sagyō Kankyō Hyōka Kijun (1988).

55. Rōdō Anzen Eisei Hō Shikōrei, Cabinet Order No. 318 of 1972.

56. Ishiwata Shōgai Yobō Kisoku, Ministry of Health, Labor and Welfare Ordinance No. 21 of 2005.

57. *Mainichi Shinbun*, (Osaka), evening edition,, June 29, 2005, 1. Kubota Corporation later paid relief money to its former workers and neighbors who contracted asbestos related disease or their believed families. The amount of relief money for each victim is from as little as ¥25 million to as much as ¥46 million, which is roughly equivalent to the benefit under the workers' compensation system. Kubota Corporation, "Kyū Kanzaki Kōjō Shūhen no Ishiwata Shippei Kanja narabini Gokazoku no Minasama ni taisuru Kyūsaikin Shiharai Kitei [Rules concerning Paying Relief Money to Patients with Asbestos Related Disease and Their Family Around the Former Kanzaki Plant]" (Apr. 16, 2006). By March 31, 2011, Kubota Corporation had paid this relief money to 212 victims in total. Kubota Corporation, Sekimen Mondai he no Taiō Jōkyō ni tsuite [In re the State of Response to Asbestos Problems], http://www.kubota.co.jp/kanren/index15.html.

lems extensively every day. This "Kubota Shock" finally pushed the Government and the legislature to adopt a serious stance against asbestos.

Total Ban on Asbestos (with Some Exceptions). On July 1, 2005, the Regulation for the Prevention of Asbestos Hazards came into force. On August 2, 2006, the Enforcement Order of the Industrial Safety and Health Law was revised to ban the manufacture, import, supply, and use of all materials containing more than 0.1 wt% asbestos, except certain unsubstitutable materials.

Asbestos Problems as Environmental Pollution

In 1986, repair of the USS Midway was carried out at the US Naval Base at Yokosuka. A large amount of asbestos waste from this operation was sneakily taken off Base, and it was soon found out that it was treated with other municipal waste in Chiba. This incident raised concerns about environmental pollution caused by asbestos. In 1987, sprayed asbestos from educational facilities became a larger social concern. Asbestos had been used as sound-absorbing or fireproof materials, especially at gathering places such as elementary schools. In 1988, the Environment Agency, the Ministry of Health and Welfare, and the Ministry of Education issued notifications to local governments to prevent air pollution caused by the demolition and repair work of buildings.[58] In 1989, the Air Pollution Control Law was revised to classify asbestos as "special dust" and to set up its concentration standard at the boundary of the asbestos dust generation facilities (Art. 2 (9)). In 1992, the Waste Disposal and Cleanup Law was revised to classify airborne asbestos as "special control industrial waste" and to set up the disposal standard (Art. 2 (5)). In general, however, asbestos has been inappropriately removed and disposed even after these revisions.

The Great Hanshin Awaji earthquake disaster occurred on January 17, 1995. In addition to the collapse of the Hanshin Expressway, the earthquake completely or partially destroyed many roads, bridges, railroads, quays, and other public facilities as well as individual houses. As the recovery efforts continued, workers' risk of exposure to asbestos became the

58. Ministry of Education, Asubesuto (Sekimen) ni yoru Taiki Osen no Mizen Bōshitō to ni tsuite [In re Prevention of Air Pollution by Asbestos] (1987); and Environmental Agency and Ministry of Health and Welfare, Kenchikubutsu Nai ni Shiyō sareteiru Asubesuto ni kakaru Tōmen no Taisaku ni tsuite [In re Temporary Measure on Asbestos Used for Building] (1988).

subject of concern.[59] In 1996, the Air Pollution Control Act was amended to require notification of the governor when demolishing a building that utilized spraying asbestos (Art. 18-15).

Legislation against Asbestos Disaster

Toward Legislation

On July 29, 2005, in the middle of the Kubota Shock, the Council of Ministers on Asbestos Problems was established to develop an immediate response. On December 27, the Council issued the "Comprehensive Measure for Asbestos Problems," which focused on (i) providing redress for asbestos victims, (ii) preventing further damages caused by asbestos, and (iii) calming public fears about asbestos.[60]

On January 20, 2006, the Cabinet approved the Bill on the Relief of Health Problems Caused by Asbestos and the Bill for Partial Amendments to the Air Pollution Control Act, etc., for Preventing Health Damages, etc., Caused by Asbestos and submitted both of them to the Diet. On January 31, both bills were passed by a vote in the Lower House plenary session. On February 3, they were passed by a vote in the Upper House plenary session and were promulgated on February 10.

Law on the Relief of Health Problems Caused by Asbestos

Not "Compensation" but "Relief." During the Upper House plenary session, whether the State was liable for the delayed regulation on asbestos, among others, was discussed. In responding to this question, the Government said that they have been taking measures against asbestos based on the best scientific knowledge available, while admitting that the collabo-

59. A demolition worker who had been exposed to asbestos from the rubble of the Great Hanshin Awaji Earthquake and contracted mesothelioma became a beneficiary from the workers' compensation in February 2008. *Kobe Shinbun*, "Hanshin Awaji Daishinsai Fukkyū de Sekimenka, Rōsai Nintei: Takarazuka no Dansei [Workers' Compensation for Asbestos Disaster through the Restoration of the Great Hanshin Awaji Earthquake: A Man in Takarazuka]," Aug. 24, 2012, http://www.kobe-np.co.jp/news/shakai/0005325301.shtml. After the Great East Japan Earthquake on March 11, 2011, the Ministry of the Environment and the Ministry of Health, Labor, and Welfare jointly established the "Joint Meeting on Countermeasure against Asbestos in the Great East Japan Earthquake" to discuss the validity of current measures to prevent asbestos exposure and how to monitor airborne asbestos.

60. Council of Ministers on Asbestos Problems, Asubesuto Mondai ni kakaru Sōgō Taisaku (2005).

Table 1. Total Number of Certified Sufferers Under the Relief System as of May 31, 2011

	Mesothe-lioma	Lung Cancer	Asbestosis	DPT	Others	Total
Certified	2,788	653	5	9	—	3,455
Uncertified	343	444	20	9	111	927
Withdrawn	478	271	4	1	69	823
Withheld*	108	75	6	3	—	192
Pending	48	5	2	7	—	62
Total	3,765	1,448	37	29	180	5,459
Bereaved family of the sufferer who died before the implementation of law						
Certified	2,971	139	26	7	—	3,143
Uncertified	51	359	4	4	10	427
Withdrawn	204	114	3	0	15	336
Withheld*	2	4	0	0	—	6
Pending	0	1	0	0	—	1
Total	3,228	617	33	10	25	3,913
Bereaved family of the sufferer who died before applying certification						
Certified	194	55	0	0	—	229
Uncertified	79	46	0	2	3	130
Withdrawn	17	11	1	0	1	30
Withheld*	27	10	0	0	—	37
Pending	15	5	0	0	—	20
Total	332	127	1	2	4	466

*Additional information is required for medical judgment.

Source: Environmental Restoration and Conservation Agency http://www.erca.go.jp/win_news/files/020631.pdf

ration among ministries was not sufficient. Moreover, the Government explained the reason why they used the term "relief" instead of "compensation." According to them, the "relief" system to be established under the law would be based on neither civil nor State liability but a part of the social security system.

Designated Disease under the Law. The Law on the Relief of Health Problems Caused by Asbestos[61] established the Asbestos Victims Relief

61. Ishiwata ni yoru Kenkō Higai no Kyūsai ni kansuru Hōritsu, Law No. 4 of 2006.

Fund for the certified sufferer who contracts (i) mesothelioma or (ii) lung cancer caused by asbestos and her/his bereaved family who are not subject to workers' compensation. Since July 1, 2010, (iii) asbestosis and (iv) diffuse pleural thickening (DPT) have also been covered if such sufferer has a substantial impairment of their respiratory function under the Cabinet Order for Partial Amendments to the Order for Enforcement of the Law on the Relief of Health Problems Caused by Asbestos.[62]

Benefits under the Law. Compared with the benefits under the Worker's Accident Compensation Insurance System, the benefits under the relief program are small. The benefits for certified sufferers are:

(a) Medical care expenses born by the sufferers,

(b) Medical care allowances: ¥103,870/month,

(c) Funeral expenses: ¥199,000 (paid to the person who held the funeral), and

(d) Relief benefit adjustment money (paid to the bereaved of the certified sufferers up to ¥2.8 million including the medical care expenses and medical care allowances that have already been paid).

The bereaved families of former workers who died from asbestos diseases before the implementation of the Law on the Relief of Health Problems Caused by Asbestos can receive benefits under the workers' compensation system. The bereaved families of former workers who died from asbestos diseases before applying for certification under the Law can also receive benefits under the workers' compensation system. These benefits are:

(a) Special condolence for the bereaved family: ¥2,800,000, and

(b) Special funeral expenses: ¥199,000.

Procedure. The relief program is administered by the Environmental Restoration and Conservation Agency (ERCA). The certification procedure is as follows: (i) a sufferer or a bereaved family member applies to the ERCA for a certification claim for relief benefit; (ii) the ERCA requests the Ministry of the Environment's medical judgment concerning the sufferer; (iii) the Ministry of the Environment consults with the Central Environmental Council[63] and announces their medical judgment; (iv)

62. Ishiwata ni yoru Kenkō Higai no Kyūsai ni kansuru Hōritsu Shikōrei no Ichibu wo Kaisei suru Seirei, Cabinet Order No. 142 of 2010.

63. The Central Environmental Council is the advisory body of the Minister of the Environment established under Article 41 of the Environmental Basic Act.

and the ERCA makes its decision on certification. The sufferers whose certification claim is rejected can appeal to the Review Committee of the Pollution-Related Health Damage Compensation.

Fund. The fund is raised from the contributions from business operators, the State, and local governments. All business operators and ship owners contribute 0.00005% of their annual income through the workers' insurance system.[64] In addition, the business operators that have substantial connections with asbestos offer extra contributions.[65] In 2005, the State contributed ¥38.76 billion.[66] Though the State contribution decreased to ¥105 million in 2006, it has been gradually increasing since 2007: ¥7.69 billion in 2007, ¥7.73 billion in 2008, and ¥9.70 billion in 2009.[67]

Amendments to Environmental Laws

By the Law for Partial Amendments to the Air Pollution Control Act, etc. for Preventing Health Damages, etc. Caused by Asbestos,[68] the Air Pollution Act was amended to require the person to notify the governor if she/he demolished the structure using asbestos materials (Art. 18-15). The Waste Disposal and Cleanup Law was also amended to promote the treatment rendering asbestos waste harmless (Art. 9-10).

Asbestos Litigation

Asbestos Litigation before the Kubota Shock

The First Asbestos Lawsuit in Japan. In the United States, 730,000 individuals had brought asbestos lawsuits against 8,000 defendants by the end

64. Ishiwata ni yoru Kenkō Higai no Kyūsai ni Kansuru Hōritsu Dai 37 Jō Dai 1 Kō oyobi Dai 2 Kō no Ippan Kyoshutsu Kin Ritsu, Ministry of the Environment Announcement No. 150, Dec. 20, 2006.

65. In 2010, Kubota Corporation paid ¥181.61 million, Nichias Corporation paid ¥114.58 million, Taiheiyo Cement Corporation paid ¥25.71 million, and Resort Solution Co. Ltd. paid ¥10.24 million. Record of the Proceedings of the Diet, No. 11 of the Committee on the Environment of the House of Councilors, the 177th Diet Session (Aug. 25, 2011).

66. This information is available at http://www.erca.go.jp/koukai/pdf/h17zishiwata.pdf.

67. This data is available at http://www.erca.go.jp/koukai/low22.html#mark3.

68. Ishiwata ni yoru Kenkōtō ni kakaru Higai no Bōshi no tame no Taiki Osen Bōshi Hōtō no Ichibu wo Kaisei suru Hōritsu, Law No. 5 of 2006.

of 2002.[69] In Japan, however, less than twenty asbestos cases went to court before the Kubota Shock.[70] The first asbestos lawsuit was brought by a former worker with the bereaved family of a deceased worker. The workers had been exposed by asbestos spraying at various building sites and later suffered asbestosis or bronchopneumonia caused by asbestosis. The defendants were Nihon Asbesto (one of the top asbestos makers in Japan) and its subsidiary construction company. The plaintiffs argued that the defendants were liable for their damages because they had breached their duty to pay attention to workers' safety. While pending at the Tokyo District Court, the case reached a settlement in 1980 (*Nihon Asbestos Case*).[71]

Asbestosis Lawsuits. In 1977, three former asbestos spinning workers, with the bereaved families of seven deceased workers, brought lawsuits against their employer Heiwa Asbestos, its de facto parent company Asahi Asbestos (one of the top asbestos makers in Japan), and the State. This was the first asbestos lawsuit pursing State liability. The plaintiffs argued that the Ministry of Labor and the Nagano Labor Standards Supervision Office failed to exercise their authorities to prevent pneumoconiosis, including Asbestosis, among workers. On June 27, 1986, the Nagano District Court held that Heiwa Asbestos and Asahi Asbestos were jointly and severally liable to nine former workers for more than ¥190 million in damages because they had breached their duty to pay attention to workers' safety, while it denied State liability. One former worker was barred because of the statute of limitations.[72] On July 11, Asahi Asbestos and Heiwa Asbestos entered a settlement with all the plaintiffs for approximately ¥180 million.[73]

Lawsuits Brought by Shipyard Workers. In 1988, eight former shipyard workers with asbestosis sued Sumitomo Heavy Industries Ltd., who con-

69. Stephen J. Carol et al., *Asbestos Litigation* (2005), xxiv, http://www.rand.org/pubs/monographs/2005/RAND_MG162.pdf.

70. Ikeda Naoki, "Nihon ni okeru Asubesuto Soshō: Genjō to Kongo no Kadai [Asbestos Litigations in Japan: Current and Future Problems]," *NBL* 827 (2006): 40–47.

71. Ban Asbestos Network Japan, Ishiwata Taisaku Zenkoku Renraku Kaigi Dai 12 Kai Sōkai Gian [Proposal for the Twelfth General Meeting of BANJAN] (Nov. 6, 1998), http://park3.wakwak.com/~banjan/main/taisaku/pdf/taisaku-25-1.pdf.

72. *Takeda v. Heiwa Asbestos Co., Ltd.*, 1198 *Hanrei Jihō* 3 (Nagano D. Ct., 1986).

73. Ban Asbestos Network Japan, Proposal for the Twelfth General Meeting of BANJAN.

ducted the repair work of the USS Midway mentioned above. In 1995, the bereaved family of a shipyard worker who died from asbestos-related lung cancer also sued the same company. While pending at the Yokosuka Branch of the Yokohama District Court, the case reached a settlement in 1997 for a total amount of ¥104 million (*Yokosuka Asbestosis Case*). In 1998, lawsuits were brought to the Yokosuka Branch of the Yokohama District Court by twelve former shipyard workers at the United States Naval shipyard repair facility with the bereaved families of four deceased shipyard workers. Because of the U.S.-Japan Status of Forces Agreement, the defendant was not the United States but the Japanese Government.[74] The plaintiffs argued that they were exposed to asbestos on their job and contracted asbestosis. On October 7, 2002, the district court held that the defendant had breached its duty to pay attention to workers' safety and was liable for the plaintiff's damages; however, two plaintiffs were barred because of the statute of limitations.[75] The defendant appealed to the Tokyo High Court. On May 27, 2003, the high court held that the defendant was liable; however, three more plaintiffs-appellees were barred because of the statute of limitations. Each succeeding plaintiff received from ¥14 to ¥25 million.[76] Other former workers and bereaved families also sued the Government for the same reason, and those cases reached a settlement (*The US Naval Base at Yokosuka Asbestosis Case*).[77]

Kansai Hoon Kogyo Case: New Approach to Foreseeability. A bereaved wife of a worker who died from mesothelioma brought a lawsuit against his former employers. Regarding Kansai Hoon Kogyo Co., Ltd.,

74. Article 12 (4) of the Agreement under Article VI of the Treaty of Mutual Cooperation and Security between Japan and the United States of America, Regarding Facilities and Areas and the Status of United States Armed Forces in Japan provides: "Local labor requirements of the United States Armed Forces and of the organizations provided for in Article XV shall be satisfied with the assistance of the Japanese authorities." Under this provision, the Japanese Government is the employer for Japanese workers on the U.S. base and can be subject to liability under the State Compensation Law.

75. *The US Naval Base at Yokosuka Asbestosis Case*, 1821 *Hanrei Jihō* 65 (Yokohama D. Ct., 2002).

76. *The US Naval Base at Yokosuka Asbestosis Case*, 50 *Shōmu Geppō* 1971 (Tokyo H. Ct., 2003).

77. Asbestos-Lawsuit Attorneys League, Kantō Bengodan no Katsudō [Activity of the Kanto Group of Plaintiff Lawyers], http://www.asbestoslawsuit.jp/kanto2012.

one of the defendants, the plaintiff alleged that her late husband had been exposed to asbestos at his workplace during his employment period from 1963 to 1984 and that Kansai Hoon Kogyo is liable for damages under Articles 415 and 709 of the Civil Code because it breached its obligation to pay attention to his safety.

In 2004, the Tokyo District Court found that the asbestos industry and Kansai Hoon Kogyo could have foreseen that asbestos dust has serious adverse effects on human life and health by 1965 at the latest. In addition, the asbestos industry and Kansai Hoon Kogyo could have foreseen that asbestos exposure caused the risk of developing mesothelioma by 1974 at the latest. In conclusion, it held Kansai Hoon Kogyo liable under Articles 415 and 709.[78] It was the first case where a court recognized the employer's liability in mesothelioma case in Japan. In 2005, the Tokyo High Court dismissed the appellant claims but decreased the amount of plaintiff's damages from ¥57 million to ¥47 million.[79]

Litigations on Para-Occupational Domestic Exposure. There are only two cases dealing with para-occupational domestic exposure. Both defendants were originally the same company.[80]

The first case (*Misawa Resort Case*) was brought by the bereaved family of a child who allegedly died from mesothelioma caused by asbestos brought home on the work clothes and masks of his father. His father died from lung cancer caused by asbestosis and was covered by the Workers' Accident Compensation Insurance System. The plaintiffs argued that the defendant company were subject to tort liability under Article 709 of the Civil Code because it failed to exercise due care in providing safety training regarding danger of asbestos to its employees and preventing employees' family from para-occupational domestic exposure. The Tokyo District Court found that because the deceased was exposed to asbestos before 1968 and the Ministry of Labor issued the notification which required employers to instruct asbestos workers not to take their work clothes home in 1976, the defendant company could not foresee the

78. *Kansai Hoon Kogyo Co., Ltd. Case*, 1882 *Hanrei Jihō* 70 (Tokyo D. Ct., Sept. 16, 2004).

79. *Kansai Hoon Kogyo Co., Ltd. Case*, 897 *Rōdō Hanrei* 19 (Tokyo H. Ct., Apr. 27, 2005).

80. Misawa Resort Co., Ltd. was the successor of Japan Eternit Pipe Co., Ltd. Resort Solution Co. Ltd. is the successor of Misawa Resort Co., Ltd.

danger of para-occupational domestic exposure. The court held that the defendant company had no duty of care and is not subject to tort liability.[81] The plaintiffs appealed; the Tokyo High Court affirmed[82] and it became the final judgment.

The second case (*Resort Solution Case*) was brought by the families of former asbestos workers. Plaintiffs were allegedly exposed to asbestos by washing their family members' work clothes, which were covered by asbestos from the defendant factory, at home. Because plaintiffs lived near the factory, they also alleged the possibility of neighborhood exposure. Plaintiffs argued that the defendant company is subject to contractual liability because it breached the duty to pay attention to its workers' safety, as well as tort liability under Articles 709 and 717 of the Civil Code. Takamatsu District Court tried this case (*Resort Solution Asbestos Case II*) with the other case brought by former asbestos workers from the same defendant factory (*Resort Solution Asbestos Case I*). The court found that the plaintiffs were exposed asbestos before 1969 when the factory was closed and that the danger of health problems caused by para-occupational domestic exposure and neighborhood exposure became foreseeable around 1975, and that based on the evidence of medical findings, administrative policies, and laws and regulations, the defendant was not subject to contractual liability or tort liability under Article 709 of the Civil Code. The court also held that the defendant factory was not liable under Article 717 of the Civil Code, finding that the factory had no defects in the installation or preservation of its structure.[83] On September 28, 2009, both cases reached a settlement for a total of ¥542 million. [84]

Litigation on Building Exposure. In 1999, during the repair work at the Sashigaya Public Nursery School, sprayed asbestos from the ceiling flew inside the school, exposing the children to asbestos. Three children and their families sued Bunkyo Ward (municipal government) and the repair company and argued that the defendants were subject to tort liability for

81. *Misawa Resort Asbestos Case*, 1210 *Hanrei Taimuzu* 150 (Tokyo D. Ct., 2004).

82. *Misawa Resort Asbestos Case*, 1210 *Hanrei Taimuzu* 145 (Tokyo H. Ct., 2005).

83. Unpublished opinion.

84. Plaintiffs of Resort Solution Asbestos Case, Defendants of Resort Solution Asbestos Case, and Kagawa Office of the All Japan Construction, Transport and General Workers' Union, Seimei [Statement] (Oct. 1, 2009), http://analyticalsociaboy.txt-nifty.com/yoakemaeka/files/seimei09928.rtf.

the plaintiffs' future health risk caused by asbestos exposure. On April 27, 2004, the case reached a settlement. Bunkyo Ward formally apologized and paid a total amount of ¥2.4 million, and the repair company paid ¥600,000.[85]

Asbestos Litigations after "Kubota Shock"

Cases with New Legal Issues

Kajima Takenaka Case: Liability of Construction Companies. This was the first asbestos lawsuit brought by construction workers against a construction company. On February 1, 2006, a former construction worker brought a lawsuit for damages of ¥33 million against two major construction companies, Kajima Corp. and Takenaka Corp. The plaintiff alleged that he had worked at construction sites for 30 years since 1964, that he was heavily exposed to dust including asbestos during that period, and that he developed asbestosis and secondary bronchitis in 1997. The main issue in this case was the nature of the plaintiff's job. Because construction workers typically work at various construction sites under subcontract or sub-subcontract with various construction companies, it is difficult for them to identify where and how they were exposed to asbestos. During the trial at the Osaka District Court, the presiding judge recommended a settlement plan, stating that "companies are in the position to instruct and supervise sub-contract workers, and they should have taken preventive measures (against asbestos exposure)."[86] On November 6, 2009, following the recommendation by court, both companies settled with the plaintiff for ¥15 million.[87]

Kintetsu Case: Operator/Owner Liability of Asbestos-Containing Building. In 2006, the bereaved family of a shop manager who worked at

85. Nikkei BP, Asubesuto Higai wo Uketa Enjira to Bunkyō-ku ya Kensetsu Gaishara to ga Wakai [Settlment among Kindergarten Children Exposed by Asbestos, Bunkyo-ku, and Construction Companies] (May 24, 2004) http://www.nikkeibp.co.jp/archives/309/309130.html.

86. Kyodo News, Ishiwata Higai no Sagyōin to Wakai: Motouke 2 sha ga 1500 Manen de [Settlement between Asbestos Worker and Two Prime Contractors for 15 million] (Nov. 12, 2009), http://www.47news.jp/CN/200911/.

87. Osaka Lawyers Advocacy for the Victims of Pneumoconiosis & Asbestos Disease, Kajima Takenaka MH Jiken: Shōri Wakai [Successful Settlement in Kajima Takenaka NH Case], http://www.asbestos-osaka1.sakura.ne.jp/act/rupo5.html.

a building containing sprayed asbestos sued the lesser-owner of the building. The plaintiff alleged that the deceased was exposed to asbestos for more than thirty-two years at the building, and contracted mesothelioma, which became his motive to commit suicide. The plaintiff argued that the lesser-owner of the building is subject to contractual liability due to the breach of a duty to ensure the safety of the building and to tort liability under the Articles 709 and 717 of the Civil Code. In 2009, the Osaka District Court dismissed the contractual liability claim because it found that the defendant could not foresee the danger of asbestos before 1987 and that even if the defendant could foresee such danger after 1987, the plaintiff had been exposed to asbestos for seventeen years prior to that date and the defendant could, therefore, not prevent the development of the plaintiff's mesothelioma. It held, however, that the defendant was liable as the indirect owner of the building for ¥50 million in damages.[88] Likewise, on March 5, 2010, the Osaka High Court held the defendant liable as the operator of the building for ¥60 million in damages.[89]

Watanabe Industries Case: Tort Liability for Family Member of Asbestos Victim. In 2007, a former factory worker (X1) and her daughter (X2) brought a lawsuit against Watanabe Industries. X1 alleged that she had been making asbestos materials at one of the factories of Watanabe Industries for 21 years between 1962 and 1984 and that she developed various lung diseases, including asbestosis. X2 alleged that, due to the substantial burden of care for X1, she was forced to adjust her working conditions, which led her to a decrease in salary and health loss. In 2010, the Osaka District Court held the defendant liable for X1's damage under the breach of its obligation to pay attention to X1's safety as well as under Article 709 of the Civil Code, and, moreover, it ordered that the defendant was liable for X2's pain and suffering under Article 709.[90]

88. *Kintetsu Asbestos Case*, 1311 *Hanrei Jihō* 183 (Osaka D. Ct., 2009).

89. Unpublished opinion. For more details on this case, see Matsumoto Katsumi, "Tatemono Fukitsuke Asubesuto to Tatemono Chintainin no Tochi Kōsakubutsu Sekinin: Osaka Chisai 2009 (Heisei 21).8.31 Kintetsu Jiken Hanketsu no Kentō wo Chūshin ni [The Spraying Asbestos Building and the Building Owner's Liability: With a Focus on the Review of the Judgment on the Kintetsu Case Delivered by the Osaka District Court on August 31, 2009]," *Ritsumeikan Hōgaku* 327–28 (2001): 880.

90. *Matsumoto v. Watanabe Industries*, 2099 *Hanrei Jihō* 62 (Osaka D. Ct., 2010).

Cases against the Government

Sennan Asbestos Case. From 1907 to 2005, there were many small asbestos spinning and weaving factories in the Sennan area, Osaka. Most of these factories were household industries typically operated by families and a few employees and have since closed their businesses. Even if the former managers are still alive, they lack the financial ability to compensate former employees. Furthermore, the asbestos disaster in Japan has been deemed, like other past environmental pollution cases, as the result of government failure; that is, the State should have prevented this asbestos disaster earlier on.

As a result, eight asbestos victims filed lawsuits against the State as a sole defendant with the Osaka District Court on May 26, 2006. The number of plaintiffs in the suit has increased to thrity-one as of June 2010. These plaintiffs include those who worked at asbestos spinning and weaving factories from 1939 to 2005, their families, and the neighbors of these asbestos factories. Moreover, a secondary lawsuit was filed by nine plaintiffs on September 24, 2009. The number of plaintiffs in this case has similarly increased to seventeen as of June 2010. Although each plaintiff is seeking ¥33 million in damages, it is too early in the Sennan Asbestos Lawsuits to estimate what damages will ultimately be awarded. There may be a comprehensive political resolution for all asbestos victims in the Sennan area in the expectation that a favorable ruling for the plaintiffs will occur.

On May 19, 2010, the Osaka District Court found that because the Ministry of Labor collected medical findings on asbestosis by 1959, it could have recognized the needs to take measures to prevent asbestosis by 1959. This court held that the Minister of Labor should have set up a ministerial ordinance to require employers to take control measures against asbestos dust (i.e., installing ventilators) by the enactment of the Pneumoconiosis Act of 1960. The danger of asbestosis would have, therefore, been reduced, and the damage caused by asbestos would have been substantially prevented. The Minister, however, did not do so until the Ordinance on Prevention of Hazards Due to Specified Chemical Substances in 1971.[91]

The court ordered the government to pay a total of ¥435 million to all plaintiffs except a former worker who left his factory prior to 1960

91. Sennan Asbestos Case, 2093 *Hanrei Jihō* 3 (Osaka D. Ct., 2011).

and two neighbors of asbestos factories. After the decision, plaintiffs and plaintiff lawyers have been requesting the Ministry of Health, Labor, and Welfare and the Ministry of the Environment not to appeal the ruling.[92] On June 1, 2010, however, the State appealed to the Osaka High Court, and all the plaintiffs followed.

Tokyo Metropolitan Building Asbestos Lawsuits. Three hundred and eighty-eight construction workers and bereaved families of workers brought lawsuits against the Japanese government and forty-five asbestos-containing building material makers to the Tokyo District Court on May 16, 2008 and to the Yokohama District Court on June 30, 2008 (Tokyo Metropolitan Building Asbestos Litigation). The main legal issues are (1) whether the Government is liable for not exercising their power to regulate asbestos and (2) whether building material makers are liable under Article 719 of the Civil Code and the Product Liability Law.

In addition to the above cases, cases are pending at the Osaka District Court, the Sapporo District Court, and the Kyoto District Court.

Experiences from Past Public Interest Litigation

Generally, plaintiff's lawyers of asbestos litigations in Japan have developed strong backgrounds in other public interest litigation. In other words, they have considerable experiences on how to organize plaintiffs and their supporters to fight against the Government. One example is the Osaka Lawyers Advocacy for the Victims of Pneumoconiosis & Asbestos Disease. It was reorganized from the Osaka Lawyers Advocacy for the Victims of Pneumoconiosis, which had been active since the 1980s, by drawing in environmental lawyers soon after the "Kubota Shock" in August 2005. Their financial sources include a part of the attorneys' fee from the legal services for certification practice, donations from the settlement money in the *Mitsubishi Materials Kenzai Co. Ltd. Case,*[93] and plaintiffs'

92. Osaka Lawyers Advocacy for the Victims of Pneumoconiosis & Asbestos Disease, Sennan Asubesuto Higai Kyūsai Kokkai Tsūshin [Communication with Diet on Remedy for Sennan Asbestos Disaster] No. f3 (May 21, 2010), http://www.asbestos-osaka1.sakura.ne.jp/%E5%9B%BD%E4%BC%9A%E9%80%9A%E4%BF%A13%E5%8F%B7.pdf.

93. Throughout the negotiations, former workers, their bereaved families, and neighbors of Miyoshi Asbestos Industry Co. Ltd. received a total of ¥123.7 million for their damages from Mitsubishi Materials Kenzai Corp., which is the successor of Miyoshi Asbestos Industry Co. Ltd, on September 11, 2008. "Mitsubishi Materiaru

expenses. They generally do not take counseling fees or retainer fees and work on a voluntary basis.

On November 10 2005, with the support from Japan Federation of Democratic Medical Institutions, lawyers and doctors cooperated to conduct a medical and legal checkup session in the Sennan area and found lung abnormalities among more than 60% of those who received X-ray examinations. These checkup sessions have been held regularly since. Moreover, Sennan victims and their lawyers have been supported by labor unions, citizen groups, and the Environmental Pollution Lawyers Association. In addition to organizing several symposiums on the *Sennan Asbestos Case*, they have been conducting a signature-collecting campaign and lobbying for the reform of the asbestos relief system. After the conclusion of the trial on November 11, 2009, they held local meetings, media briefings, and Diet members' meetings, in addition to conducting demonstrations once a every week in front of the Osaka District Court. These actions were intensively conducted, especially after the district court's decision. Though the Government finally appealed, these actions attracted a great deal of public attention.[94]

IV. Some Observations

Possible Reasons for Belated Asbestos Regulations

As mentioned above, the asbestos disaster in Japan is now regarded as a government failure. Through environmental pollution cases (e.g., Minamata Disease cases), medical-related health disaster cases (e.g., HIV-tainted-blood products cases),[95] and some other mass tort cases, the "no exercise of regulatory power" theory has been developed in the Administrative Law arena.

Kenzai Kabushiki Gaisha to no Wakai Seiritsu ni Atatte no Seimeibun [Statement on the Reached Settlement with Mitsubishi Materials Kenzai Co. Ltd.]" (Sept. 11, 2008), http://www.asbestos-osaka.sakura.ne.jp/siryo-mitubishimateriaru.html.

94. More information is available at the website of Osaka Lawyers Advocacy for the Victims of Pneumoconiosis & Asbestos Disease, http://www.asbestos-osaka1.sakura.ne.jp/.

95. For more details, see Eric A. Feldman, "HIV and Blood in Japan: Transforming Private Conflict into Public Scandal", in Feldman and Bayer, eds., *Blood Feuds: AIDS, Blood, and the Politics of Medical Disaster* (New York, 1999).

In 2004, the Administrative Case Litigation Act[96] was amended to allow a "mandamus action" (Art.3(6)) with an "action for the declaration of illegality of inaction" (Art.3(5)) in case any serious damages were likely to occur if a certain original administrative disposition is not made and there are no other appropriate means to avoid such damage (Art. 37-3 (1) (i) and 37-3(3)(i)). Moreover, the Act was also amended to allow courts to make provisional orders of mandamus (Art. 37-5 (1)). Before these amendments, courts had been taking a passive attitude toward the mandamus action. As a result, it must have been difficult for general Japanese public to force the Government to prevent the asbestos disaster before they learned how hazardous asbestos was in the wake of the "Kubota Shock."

Be that as it may, why did it take Japan so long to regulate asbestos in the first place? It may be because asbestos has been an economically advantageous material in comparison with other, safer materials of the same nature as asbestos. Asbestos products were widely used in Japan even after they could be replaced by safer but high cost products.

Asbestos regulations imposed an economic burden on all the industries that used asbestos at that time, even though they would surely reduce its use in the future. As a matter of course, not only the asbestos product makers but also the industries that use asbestos products array themselves against asbestos regulations, and the Government, giving economic growth top priority, delayed the implementation of asbestos regulations as a consequence.

Additionally, workers sometimes put their employment before their health. When the Social Democratic Party of Japan, the predecessor of the Social Democratic Party, tried to pass a bill banning the production and use of asbestos in principle from 1992 to 1994, not only the Japan Asbestos Association but also the labor unions of eight asbestos building materials companies and the Japanese Trade Union Confederation (JTUC) fought against the bill.[97] It should be noted that there was an information disparity on asbestos.[98] Again, not only the general public but

96. Gyōsei Jiken Soshō Hō, Law No. 139 of 1962.

97. Asahi.com, Rengō, Ishiwata Kisei Hoan ni Hantai, "Koyō Fuan" Riyū ni 94 nen [The Japan Trade Union Confederation against the Asbestos Ban Bill for Employment Insecurity in 1994] (Aug. 5, 2005), http://www.asahi.com/special/asbestos/TKY200508040494.html.

98. Mesothelioma - Pneumoconiosis - Asbestos Center, *Asubesutoka wa Naze Hirogattanoka: Nihon no Sekimen Sangyō no Rekishi to Kuni no Kan'yo [Why the Asbestos*

also most marginal workers and their families did not really understand the hazardous nature of asbestos until the "Kubota Shock" occurred. There were substantial number of workers who had no choice but to take asbestos-related jobs for their living, even if they knew the risk of suffering asbestos related disease a few decades later. Indeed, the JTUC expressed this employment insecurity when it opposed the bill stated above.

Furthermore, it might be attributed to the Government's vertical administrative structure. Asbestos industries in Japan have been placed under the supervision of the Ministry of Commerce and Industry (1925–1949), the Ministry of International Trade and Industries (1949–2001), and the Ministry of Economy, Trade, and Industries (2001–present). On the other hand, the safety of workers has been placed under the supervision of the Ministry of the Interior (1873–1947), the Ministry of Labor (1947–2001), and the Ministry of Health, Labor, and Welfare (2001–present). Moreover, the regulatory power over environmental problems was scattered among various ministries and agencies before and even after the establishment of the Environmental Agency in 1971, which was later reorganized into the Ministry of the Environment in 2001. This sectionalism has disturbed information-sharing among ministries and agencies. For instance, as mentioned earlier, the Department of Health under the Ministry of the Interior conducted the research on asbestos health damage in several places, including the Sennan Area from 1937 to 1940. It found out that 80 out of 650 (12.3%) asbestos workers contracted asbestosis; however, the result did not affect the national policy on asbestos.[99]

Prospects for the Future

According to one study, an estimated 58,000 people in Japan are predicted to die from mesothelioma from 2000 to 2029.[100] The biggest problem is how to deal with asbestos-containing construction materials. The Ministry of the Environment estimates that the volume of asbestos emitted

---

Disaster Became Outspread: The History of Asbestos Industry in Japan and the State's Involvement] (Tokyo, 2009), 204–06.

99. Hiroyuki Mori, "Asubesuto Saigai to Kōkyo Seisaku: Senzen kara Kōdo Seicho Ki ni kakete [Asbestos Disaster and Public Policy: from World War II to the High Economic Growth Period]," *Seisaku Kagaku* 16-1 (2008): 23–24.

100. Takehiko Murayama, Ken Takahashi, Yuji Natori, and Norio Kurumatani, "Estimation of Future Mortality from Pleural Malignant Mesothelioma in Japan Based on an Age-Cohort Model," *American Journal of Industrial Medicine* 49, No. 1 (2006): 1–7.

from demolition work will peak from 2020 to 2040.[101] Moreover, if demolition waste containing asbestos is inappropriately treated as general demolition waste, it will be reused under the Construction Material Recycling Act.[102] Therefore, the risk of exposure to asbestos could continue among construction workers as well as neighbors of construction sites.

So what will happen in the future? The troubles that future asbestos victims will have are attributed to the latent nature of the asbestos-related diseases. Causation will surely be the biggest legal hurdle; however, the most difficult problem will be missing defendants, due to bankruptcy or closure. Even if potential defendants continue their businesses decades into the future, their financial ability to compensate those affected by their use of asbestos will be a serious problem for potential plaintiffs. To respond to the increased number of asbestos victims out of the workers' compensation system, it will be necessary to improve the current relief program under the Law on the Relief of Health Problems Caused by Asbestos in the near future. The contents of review include the purpose of the program (relief or compensation), contribution of cost, and eligible diseases.[103] Sooner or later, the people of Japan must be prepared for a tax increase to cover the state contribution for the program.

V. Conclusion

Japan, like other leading industrialized countries, has been developing environmental and worker safety laws and regulations to a certain extent. The Japanese Government and Legislature, however, have not properly responded to health risks posed by asbestos, among others. As a result, asbestos victims now rely on the Judiciary, with help from lawyers with

101. Committee for Preventing Airborne Asbestos during Demolishing Waste Treatment Facility, etc., *Haikibutsu Shori Shisetsu Kaitaijitō no Ishiwata Hisan Bōshi Taisaku Manual [Manual for Preventing Airborne Asbestos during Demolishing Waste Treatment Facility, etc.]* (March 2006).

102. Kensetsu Kōji ni kakaru Shizai no Saishigenkatō ni kansuru Hōritsu, Law No. 104 of 2000.

103. According to a report by the International Agency for Research on Cancer, a part of the World Health Organization, "sufficient evidence is now available to show that asbestos also causes cancer of the larynx and of the ovary." Kurt Straif et al., on behalf of the WHO International Agency for Research on Cancer Monograph Working Group, "A Review of Human Carcinogens—Part C: Metals, Arsenic, Dusts, and Fibres," *The Lancet Oncology*, 10-5(2009): 453–54.

substantial experiences of past public environmental and workers accident litigation.

VI. Appendix

After the completion of this article, there were several important developments in asbestos regulation and litigation.

From March 1, 2012, by the revision of the Enforcement Order of the Industrial Safety and Health Law, the manufacture, import, supply, and use of all materials containing more than 0.1 wt% asbestos was banned with no exception.

Regarding the Sennan Asbestos Case, the Osaka High Court overruled the district court judgment and dismissed the case on August 25, 2011.[104] The plaintiffs/appellees appealed to the Supreme Court. Moreover, regarding the secondary lawsuit of the Sennan Asbestos Case, the Osaka District Court held that the State is partly liable for plaintiffs' damages on March 28, 2012.[105] Both parties appealed to the Osaka High Court.

Regarding Tokyo Metropolitan Building Asbestos Lawsuits, the Yokohama District Court dismissed the case on May 25, 2012.[106] The plaintiffs appealed to the Tokyo High Court.

There are many lawsuits against Kubota Corporation. Among them, the Kobe District Court found that Kubota is liable for damages sustained by one of the neighbors of the former Kanzaki plant on August 7, 2012.[107] Both parties appealed to the Osaka High Court.

104. Sennan Asbestos Case, 2135 *Hanrei Jiho* 60 (Osaka H. Ct., 2011).

105. Sennan Asbestos Case II (Osaka D. Ct., 2012), http://www.courts.go.jp/hanrei/pdf/20120619165619.pdf.

106. Tokyo Metropolitan Building Asbestos Lawsuit at Yokohama, 5 *Rodo Hanrei Journal* 24 (Yokohama D. Ct., 2012).

107. Kyodo News, "Sekimenka, Jūmin no Kenkō Higai Hatsu Nintei: Kubota ni Baishō Meirei [Court First-ever Found Neighbor's Health Damage by Asbestos Disaster: Ordering Kubota to Pay for the Damage]" (Aug. 7, 2012), http://www.47news.jp/CN/201208/CN2012080701002327.html.

The Law and Practice of the Venture Industry in Japan: A Period of Transition

Zenichi Shishido[1]

I. Introduction

In this article, I will try to explain how law matters to the practice of the venture industry in Japan, particularly by influencing the incentive bargain between monetary capital providers and human capital providers. This will be done by comparing the legal regulation of the Japanese venture industry with its Silicon Valley counterpart.

In general, the firm is an ongoing joint project requiring both financial and human capital. Like other joint projects, the firm cannot maximize the value added without achieving an efficient incentive bargain among indispensable capital providers, i.e., shareholders and creditors as monetary capital providers, and management and employees as human capital providers.

Law is a part of the infrastructure of the incentive bargain of the firm. We need to draw the whole picture of the incentive bargain of the firm by focusing on interrelationships and complementarities among different institutions such as markets, social norms, and laws.

I will analyze how old and new Japanese laws matter in incentivizing bargains between monetary capital providers and human capital providers and in the practice of the venture industry by dividing it into two areas: investments into venture capital funds and investments into start-up companies. The incentive bargain of the former is made between investors as limited partners and venture capitalists (VCs) as general partners. The incentive bargain of the latter is made between venture capitalists and entrepreneurs.

1. Professor, Graduate School of International Corporate Strategy, Hitosubashi University.

Part II draws a picture of the Silicon Valley model from the viewpoint of incentive bargaining. In Part III, the paper focuses on the last decade, during which rapid changes to the institutional infrastructures occurred that affect venture capital investments in Japan. Part IV draws a picture of the incentive bargaining practice in Tokyo compared with the Silicon Valley practice. In Part V, the paper points out complementarities among exit options, both for entrepreneurs and for VCs, and the method of venture financing. Part VI picks up with the problems of Japanese law, which affect the practice of VC investments, in three categories of law: corporate law, tax law, and employment and trade secrets law. Part VII will conclude the paper.

II. Incentive Bargains in Silicon Valley

The incentive bargaining practice in Silicon Valley is a typical two team bargaining scenario between the team of monetary capital providers and the team of human capital providers. Also, such bargaining is two-tiered. The first tier bargaining is between institutional investors and venture capitalists, and the second tier bargaining is between venture capitalists and entrepreneurs. In Silicon Valley, not only human capital providers but also monetary capital providers organize their teams. All players share the equity incentive.

To solve the two-sided agency problem,[2] entrepreneurs cede control to VCs and obtain the opportunity to receive "sweat equity," by which entrepreneurs can keep a greater share of equity than their monetary capital based share.[3]

2. If VCs feel too much risk, they will hesitate to invest their monetary capital. On the other hand, if entrepreneurs feel too much risk, they will hesitate to invest their human capital. For maximizing their own payoff, both VCs and entrepreneurs need to reduce not only their own risk but also that of their counterpart's by bargaining for agreements specifying specific control- and value-sharing commitments. See Zenichi Shishido, "Why Japanese Entrepreneurs Don't Give Up Control to Venture Capitalists," (Working Paper for Business Law and Innovation Conference at Columbia Law School, 2008).

3. A typical example of sweat equity practice is as following: In November 2010 (Founders' round), 1.2M shares of common stock were issued to founders at $0.10, and 470K shares of common stock were issued to employees at $0.20–.30. In March 2011 (Series A round), 2M shares of Series A preferred stock were issued to VCs at $2.00. As a result, there are 3.67M shares and their valuation is $7.34M. The founders' group share

Figure 1. Incentive Bargains in Silicon Valley

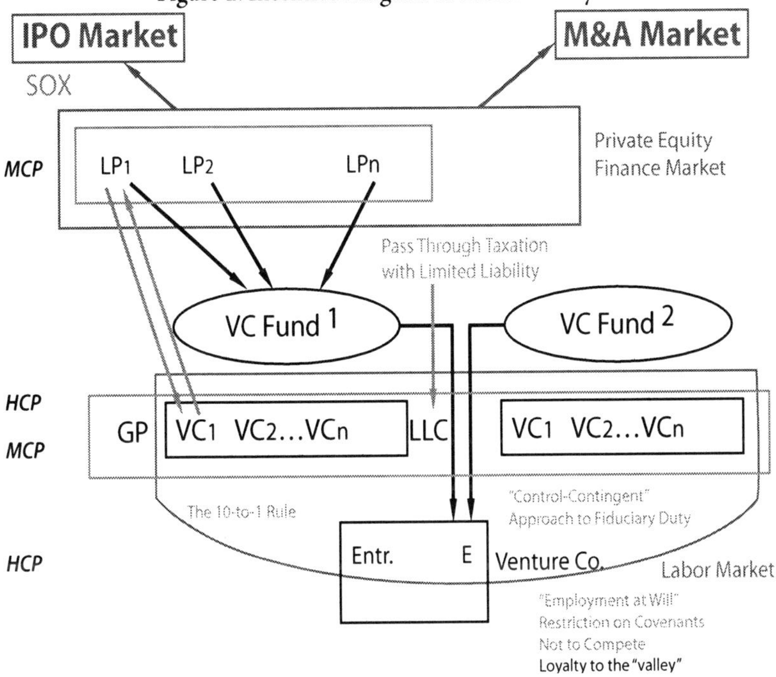

Liquid external labor markets and players' loyalty to the venture community make Silicon Valley one of the most successful industrial clusters in the world.

III. The Last Decade as a Transition Period in Japan

The first decade of the twenty-first century was a transition period for the Japanese venture industry, both in law and practice.

First, several IPO markets for emerging growth companies have emerged since the Tokyo Stock Exchange created the "MOTHERS" market in 1999. Now there are several IPO markets for emerging growth companies, which are competing against each other for new public listings.[4]

---

is 45.5% and the VCs' share is 54.5%. See Michael Halloran, et al., *Venture Capital and Public Offering Negotiation*, 3rd ed., Supp. (New York, 2009), 6–12.

4. Mothers-Tokyo Stock Exchange (http://www.tse.or.jp/listing/mothers/index.html) and JASDAQ (http://www.ose.or.jp/jasdaq) are the two major IPO markets in Japan. There are three local IPO markets: Centrex-Nagoya Stock Exchange (http://www.

Second, many NPOs for supporting entrepreneurs have been organized and the venture community has been gradually developed in Tokyo. Professionals, such as venture capitalists, lawyers, and accountants that are specialized for start-up companies, have been gradually increasing and provide an infrastructure to assist these companies. There has also been growth in expatriate entrepreneurship with VC funding in Japan.[5]

And third, the law of "vehicles" has been formulated both for VC funds and start-up companies. Since 2001, and particularly since 2005, Japanese corporate law has been significantly, and purposefully, deregulated to stimulate the venture industry.

In the 2005 reformation, Japanese corporate law changed its nature from a mandatory law to an enabling law. First, the area of freedom of contract liberalization for charter creations was expanded. Second, alternative forms of corporate governance for closely-held corporations were increased, including the LLC. Third, preferred stock and stock options were totally deregulated. Accordingly, investment contracts have gradually changed. And fourth, the tools for M&A were implemented as in the U.S., such as stock swap and cash-out merger. Now almost all legal structures available in Silicon Valley are possible in Japan.

Table 1. Founder Family Shareholding at IPO (average)

	JASDAQ/NEO	Mothers	Hercules and others
2009	72.1%	58.8%	N/A
2008	66.4%	50.4%	59.0%
2007	63.3%	53.7%	55.2%
2006	66.5%	59.0%	54.8%
2005	57.3%	58.0%	60.6%
			Data by PRONEXUS

nse.or.jp); Ambitious-Sapporo Stock Exchange (http://www.sse.or.jp/pdf/about_amb.pdf); and Q-Board-Fukuoka Stock Exchange (http://www.fse.or.jp/). In 2009, the Tokyo AIM Exchange for professional investors was established as a joint venture between the Tokyo Stock Exchange and the London Stock exchange, and later turned into Tokyo Pro Market (http://www.tse.or.jp/english/rules/promarket/index.html) after being merged into the Tokyo Stock Exchange in 2012. There have been, however, only three companies listed as of September 2012.

5. See Shishido, "Japanese Entrepreneurs."

Still there are big differences between Japan and the U.S. One difference is the founders' tendency to maintain majority shareholding. As the Table 1 shows, on average in Japan, the founding family maintains majority shareholding even after an IPO.

IV. Incentive Bargains in Japan

The incentive bargaining practice in Tokyo is generally not a genuine two-tiered, two-team bargaining scenario as is typical in Silicon Valley.

In the first tier, investors, who are limited partners of VC funds, are generally VC companies' parent financial institutions and business corporations, which are often their cross holding partner companies. They are not genuine investors but have market research purposes with weak incentives to monitor human capital providers, i.e., venture capitalists. Institutional investors, such as pension funds, which are major investors in Silicon Valley VC funds, rarely invest in VC funds in Japan. Venture

Figure 2. Incentive Bargains in Tokyo

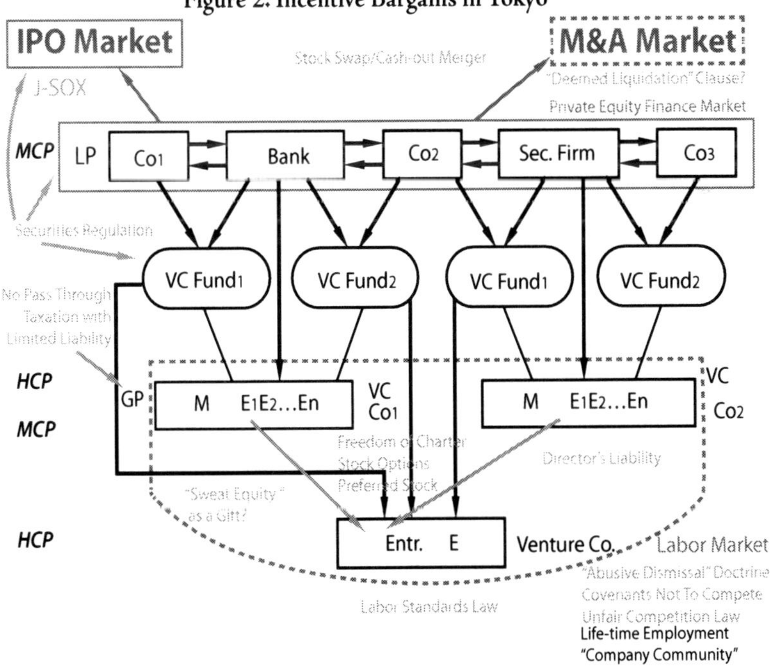

capitalists, who are VC company employees, typically have no equity incentive.

In the second tier, entrepreneurs seldom cede control to VCs. Monetary capital providers, VC funds, which invest in the same start-up company, do not coordinate their teams. Each VC company individually bargains with the entrepreneur separately and creates a unique contract. Syndicate financing among VCs is still not standard. External labor markets are not liquid and players have loyalty to their own "company communities." Employee spin-offs from large companies are few, and information sharing is hard to achieve.

V. Complementarities among Exit Options and the Method of Venture Financing

There are complementarities between the method of venture financing and exit options for both human capital and monetary capital. Entrepreneurs and VCs are each capable of imposing hold-up costs. Entrepreneurs may pursue private benefits and may reject an IPO proposition or M&A deal that would benefit the VC. VCs may squeeze out entrepreneurs and may exit at timing unfavorable for entrepreneurs. The availability of an exit option determines which party needs protection.[6]

Exit options for human capital are complementary to the method of venture financing. Liquid labor markets facilitate risk sharing and enable entrepreneurs to cede control to VCs. Open labor market institutions should be seen as transferring risk from entrepreneurs to VCs, which VCs, in turn, limit by bargaining for control.[7]

Exit options for monetary capital, such as the IPO and M&A markets, are also complementary to the method of venture financing. Although several IPO markets have been created, the M&A market is still incomplete in Japan. That may be a reason why Japanese VCs choose a bank-like financing method, such as a stock buyback agreement.

6. See Augustin Landier, "Start-up Financing: From Banks to Venture Capital" (2003), http://pages.stern.nyu.edu/~alandier/pdfs/bank_vc.pdf.

7. See ibid.

VI. Law Plays an Important Role

Corporate Law

Although the rapid deregulation of Japanese corporate law since 2001, particularly the reformation of 2005, has gotten rid of most obstacles for Japanese entrepreneurs and permits local VCs to introduce the Silicon Valley model, differences in corporate law between the U.S. and Japan might be one of the reasons why Japanese VCs seldom acquire formal control via stock acquisition or via board representation.[8]

Japanese corporate law is based on the shareholder choice doctrine, while American corporate law is based on the management choice doctrine.[9] In Japan, shareholder meetings are used as a tool to decide almost all issues faced by the company. This includes charter amendments, regardless of whether the board of directors cooperates.[10] Conversely, board control becomes less important in Japan than in the U.S.[11] Interestingly, when looking at the role of the board, Japanese law is less regulatory than American law.[12]

8. The following observations are based on Shishido, "Japanese Entrepreneurs."

9. See Stephen Bainbridge, *The New Corporate Governance in Theory and Practice*, (Oxford and New York, 2008), 53; Mitsuhiro Fukao, *Financial Integration, Corporate Governance, and the Performance of Multinational Companies* (Washington D.C., 1995), 4; Zenichi Shishido, "Japanese Corporate Governance: The Hidden Problems of Corporate Law and Their Solutions," *Delaware Journal of Corporate Law* 25 (2000): 189, 198.

10. Corporate Code § 295. See Kenjiro Egashira, *Kabushiki-Kaisha Hō [Laws of Stock Corporations]*, 3rd ed. (Tokyo, 2009), 294. Under Delaware law, only the election of directors and amendment of the bylaws do not require board approval before shareholder meetings can decide. See Bainbridge, *The New Corporate Governance*, 54.

11. See Bainbridge, *The New Corporate Governance*, 53; Jesse Fried and Mira Ganor, "Agency Costs of Venture Capitalist Control in Startups," *New York University Law Review* 81 (2006): 967, 976.

12. In the U.S., several business decisions must be made by the board and even amendments to the bylaws cannot grant the shareholders such decision making powers. The board manages the business and affairs of the company, initiates charter amendments, and completes fundamental transactions, such as mergers, IPOs and liquidations. Shareholders, on the other hand, usually cannot initiate fundamental transactions even when their approval is required to effectuate the transaction. Del Code Ann Tit. 8, § 141(a) (2001); Cal Corp Code § 3000(a) (West 1990); Revised Model Bus. Corp. Act § 8.01 (1984). See Fried & Ganor, "Agency Costs," 976. In Japan, shareholder meetings are the tool used to make decisions in areas including dividends and executive compensation—issues outside of the control of shareholders in the U.S. Shareholders can even initiate charter amendments and mergers. Corporate Code §§ 295, 466, 783.

Japanese written law plainly states that directors have fiduciary duties to the company and requires directors elected by class-voting to be loyal to the company, not to their electing body.[13] Some Japanese lawyers may be concerned about possible fiduciary duty violations by their venture capitalist clients, who inevitably have conflicting interests, and that courts may recognize their gross negligence, although there has been no such legal case so far.[14]

In answer to this problem, Delaware courts have adopted a "control-contingent" approach to fiduciary duties.[15] This precedent provides venture capitalists with an additional economic incentive to use preferred stock[16] and gain board control.[17]

The biggest difference between U.S. and Japanese law exists when considering potential liability to third parties, i.e. creditors. Japanese written law dictates that directors are liable for damages to a third party that are caused as a result of their gross negligence in the course of executing their duty to the company.[18] Because of this corporate law statute and its accompanying case law, taking on a directorship at a start-up company,

13. Corporate Code § 355.

14. See Tatsuhiro Takahara, *Torishimariyaku no Sennin-kengen no Bunpai to Torishimariyaku no Sekinin [Sharing Board Seats and Liability of Directors]*, in Zenichi Shishido & Venture Law Forum eds., *Benchā Kigyō no Hōmu-Zaimu Senryaku [Law and Finance of Venture Companies in Japan]* (Tokyo, 2010) chap. 11, at 408. Issues arise when both sides meet to discuss and eventually determine important factors including company valuation, a decision to sell the venture, liquidations, mergers, and so on. The question becomes whether venture capital directors can use their voice to cast a vote that favors the venture capital interest without violating the fiduciary duties attendant to their directorship positions within one of their fund's portfolio firms.

15. Fried and Ganor summarized the case law as follows: "[A] common-controlled board is free to serve the interests of common shareholders at the expense of the preferred shareholders and aggregate shareholder value. In contrast, a preferred-controlled board can make business decisions that serve the preferred at the expense of common, as long as those decisions can be defended as in the best interests of the corporation." Fried and Ganor, "Agency Costs," 993. See also *Equity-Linked Investors, L.P. v. Adams*, 705 A.2d 1040 (Del. Ch. 1997); *Orban v. Field*, No. 12820, 1997 Del. Ch. LEXIS 48 (Apr. 1, 1997). But see, in re Trados Incorporated Shareholder Litigation, No. 1512-CC (July 24, 2009).

16. Other than for tax reasons, another advantage for VCs use of preferred stock are "deemed liquidation" clauses. The validity of these clauses is still ambiguous in Japan. It may be a reason why the use of preferred stock has not yet become widespread.

17. Fried and Ganor, "Agency Costs," 993.

18. Corporate Code § 429.

which generally has a higher risk of bankruptcy and thus potential liability claims by third party creditors, continues to be a risky venture.

Tax Law

Although corporate law is deregulated and there are now only a few obstacles to introducing Silicon Valley-style legal structures, tax law is still a problem.

In particular, the so called "sweat equity" practice in Silicon Valley may be taxed as a gift or donation in Japan.[19] In the U.S., VCs allow the entrepreneur more equity than her monetary capital contribution simply because it will bring them more pay off by giving the entrepreneur stronger incentive to work hard. It has been an established practice that the IRS will not challenge such a scheme of sweat equity. In Japan, tax treatment of sweat equity is unpredictable. The National Tax Agency might challenge the practice of sweat equity as a gift or donation because of the transfer of value from the VCs to the entrepreneur without consideration. This unpredictability itself distorts the incentive of entrepreneurs and VCs to use a sweat equity scheme. As a result, sharing cash-flow rights cannot be complementary to sharing of control, and the two-sided agency problem is not yet solved.[20]

A tax problem on the VC side is that there is still no way for individual venture capitalists to gain both limited liability and pass-through taxation, like the use of the LLC as a general partner vehicle in the U.S.. Although it is not a problem for bank-related or securities firm-related VCs because their general partners are VC companies and pass through taxation has no merit for their employee venture capitalists, it is a big problem for Silicon Valley type independent VCs because venture capitalists have to take the risk of non-limited liability for gaining pass-through taxation.

Two tax non-neutralities are partly responsible for the incomplete M&A market in Japan. First, a higher capital gains tax rate is applied to

19. On the sweat equity practice, see note 2.

20. See Zenichi Shishido, "Sweat Equity as a Gift," (Working Paper for the Sho Sato Conference at UC Berkeley Law School, March 9–10, 2009, http://www.law.berkeley.edu/8364.htm). After serious negotiations between the Ministry of Economy, Trade, and Industry (METI) and the National Tax Agency, in October, 2011, a footnote was included on the METI website that states, in effect, that the exercise price of a qualified stock option for common stock could be based on the price of a preferred stock issued before the stock option. It is a small but significant step toward the establishment of the practice of issuing sweat equity in Japan.

closely-held stock than to listed stock. Entrepreneurs have a disincentive to sell their controlling stock before the IPO. Second, tax deferral in a stock swap is not available for foreign companies.[21]

Employment and Trade Secrets Law

There is a big distinction between Silicon Valley and Tokyo in employment law. While "employment at will" and restrictions on covenants not to compete in Silicon Valley have supported its liquid labor market and clustering of information,[22] in Japan, very strong regulations on employment termination, which is called the "abusive dismissal" rule,[23] and the "rule of reason" regulation of covenants not to compete,[24] together with life-time employment and company community norms,[25] have discouraged employee spin-offs from big companies.

Another distinction related to employee spin-offs exists in legal practice rather than in the written law of trade secrets. While trade secrets suits are considered to be difficult to win and harm the reputation of the companies that bring them in California,[26] not a small number of trade secrets suits are raised in Japan.[27] The possibility of a suit being raised is an obstacle to employee spin-offs.[28] Thus, information sharing is hard to achieve.

21. See Michael Korver, "Egujito toshiteno M&A [M&A as an Exit]," in Zenichi Shishido and Venture Law Firm eds., *Benchā Kigyō no Hōmu-Zaimu Senryaku [Law and Finance of Venture Companies in Japan]* (Tokyo, 2010), chap. 12, at 472.

22. See Ronald Gilson, "The Legal Infrastructure of High Technology Industrial Districts: Silicon Valley, Route 128, and Covenants not to Compete," *New York University Law Review* 74 (1992): 575.

23. See Sugeno Kazuo, *Rōdō-Hō [Labor Law]*, 9th ed. (Tokyo, 2010), 489.

24. See Kosuke Sato, "Supin-Ofu Kigyō no Sai no Hōritsu Mondai [Legal Problems of Spin-off Ventures]," in Zenichi Shishido & Venture Law Firm eds., *Benchā Kigyō no Hōmu-Zaimu Senryaku [Law and Finance of Venture Companies in Japan]* (Tokyo, 2010), chap. 13, at 489.

25. See Zenichi Shishido, "Japanese Corporate Governance," 201.

26. See Alan Hyde, *Working in Silicon Valley: Economic and Legal Analysis of a High-Velocity Labor Market* (2003): 38.

27. See Sato, "Supin-Ofu Kigyō," 503.

28. The Japanese firms that had been expected to dominate the manufacture of hard disk drives (as they had memory chips) missed this opportunity because no Japanese incumbent had spun-off a new HDD firm, nor did employees job-hop among companies. See Hyde, *Working in Silicon Valley*, 32.

VII. Conclusions

As I briefly reviewed, the law and practice of the venture industry in Japan has changed a lot in the last decade. The Japanese venture industry has, however, not yet actually taken off. Tokyo has not yet become a successful venture habitat like Silicon Valley. Although its role may be complementary, law definitely matters. We need to study complementarities among the legal environment, the market, social norms, and business practices in order to derive appropriate policy implications.

Although Japanese corporate law has been reformed to accept the Silicon Valley-type VC investment, tax law, labor law, and labor market norms are still in need of reform in order to support liquid external labor markets, a sweat equity practice, and an active market for M&A. These reforms are necessary in order to expand the role of venture capital in the Japanese economy and to promote a culture of entrepreneurship that can leverage Japan's technical prowess in the twenty-first century.

Privacy Issues in Japanese Law—The Development of Privacy Protection Law in Japan and the Future

Junichiro Makita[1]

I. Overview of the Circumstances of Privacy Protection in Japan[2]

Beginnings of Privacy Protection in Japanese Law

The Civil Code of Japan enacted in 1896 had a provision stipulating that a person who installs windows or other facilities in a building at a close distance from the boundary with neighboring land, allowing the observation of that land, must put up a privacy screen. While there have been some slight revisions to the distance, this provision still exists (Civil Code Article 235). In addition, in the Penal Code enacted in 1907, the opening of a sealed letter without justifiable grounds was a punishable offense. This provision also still exists today (Penal Code Article 133).

After the end of World War II, the Constitution of Japan emulated the United States Constitution by providing provisions for the privacy of communications (Article 21 (2)), the right to be secure in your home against entry (Article 35), and the right to be free from compulsion to testify against him or herself (Article 38 (1)). These had the function of protecting privacy.

Protection by Tort Low Against Public Disclosure of Embarrassing Private Facts

Debate over privacy began in earnest in Japan during the 1960s. Published in 1962, *Puraibashii kenkyū [Study of Privacy]* by Michitaka Kaino and Masami Ito introduced, among others, Prosser's so-called "four privacy torts" in U.S. tort law. This led to the public disclosure of embarrassing private facts to be considered a tort prescribed by the civil code.

1. Attorney at Law, Harago & Partners Law Offices, Tokyo, Japan.

2. See Masao Horibe, *Puraibashii to kōdojōhōkashakai [Privacy and Advanced Information Society]*, 43 et seq.; Hiroshi Miyake and Ikuko Komachiya, *Kojinjōhō hogohō [Act on Protection of Personal Privacy]* (Tokyo, 2003), 58 et seq.

In a famous court case, the 1964 decision in the *After the Banquet (Utage no Ato)* case[3] recognized the publication of a novel based on a recognizable model to constitute a tort, infringing the right to privacy through a public disclosure of embarrassing private facts.

As requirements for establishing infringement of privacy, the *After the Banquet* decision maintained that: (a) the contents publicized must be facts from private life or matters that had the likelihood of being interpreted as facts from private life, (b) when placed in such circumstances, a private individual of ordinary sensitivities would not wish these matters to be publicly disclosed, (c) these matters were not yet known to the general public, and (d) the victim suffered discomfort and distress as a result of the disclosure.

These requirements are referred to even now when reviewing the possibility of an infringement of privacy. Of the four separate branches of Prosser's privacy torts, this came under the "public disclosure of embarrassing private facts."

Following this, the Supreme Court in 1994 released the following decision in a case concerning the propriety of a tort claim for damages in the event that the previous conviction, etc., of a person was publicized in nonfiction material using his real name:

> The interest of not publicizing the fact concerning the previous conviction, etc. could deserve legal protection, but there are also cases where this disclosure should be allowed. Whether or not the publication of the fact concerning the prior conviction, etc. of a person in a novel using the real name of that person constitutes a tort should be judged by considering not only the living situation of that person since that time, but also the historical or social significance of the criminal case itself, the importance of that person as a party in the case, the social activities of that person and his influence, together with the significance and necessity of using his real name in light of the objectives and characteristics, etc. of the work. If, as a result, the legal interest of not publicizing the fact concerning the prior conviction, etc. surpasses the reason for publicizing it, that person may claim compensation for the mental anguish that he suffered from the publication.[4]

3. Tokyo District Court decision of Sept. 28, 1964 (385 *Hanrei Jiho* 12)

4. My translation of the Supreme Court decision of Feb. 8, 1994 (*Saikō Saibansho Minji Hanreishū* 48, No. 2: 149).

By using the approach of balancing privacy interests against the freedom of expression, the claim for damage compensation was recognized.

This 1994 Supreme Court decision did not use the word "privacy," calling this "the interest of not publicizing the facts (*kōhyōsarenai rieki*)." In a case concerning an article published in a weekly magazine that mentioned the plaintiff by an easily identifiable pseudonym and described aspects of a crime he committed as a minor, in addition to other private information such as his previous record of delinquency and circle of friends, however, the Supreme Court rendered a decision in 2003 clearly indicating that the infringement of privacy is a tort:

> Regarding the violation of privacy, when the legal interest of not publicizing the facts is balanced against the reason for publication, if the former surpasses the latter, this constitutes a tort. Therefore, it would be necessary to specifically deliberate each individual circumstance concerning the legal interest of not publicizing the fact and the reason for publicizing it, and reach a decision by weighing the circumstances including the age and social position of the plaintiff at the time this article was published in the magazine; the contents of the act of crime; the scope of distribution of information pertaining to the privacy of the plaintiff and the extent of specific damages that the plaintiff will suffer through disclosure of the fact; the purpose and significance of this article; the social circumstances at the time of publication; and the necessity of publicizing the information in this article.[5]

Protection by Tort Law Against Other Privacy Torts

Japan's debate on privacy has centered around the public disclosure of embarrassing private facts, but tort protection against acts other than this public disclosure of embarrassing private facts categorized in Prosser's four privacy torts is also generally considered to be provided regardless of whether it can clearly be argued that these constitute violations of privacy.[6]

5. My translation of the Supreme Court decision of March 14, 2003 (*Saikō Saibansho Minji Hanreishū* 57, No. 3: 229).

6. Categorization of "publicity which places the plaintiff in a false light in the public eye" is not clear in Japan, but it is discussed as defamation or infringement of privacy. "Appropriation, for the defendant's advantage, of the plaintiff's name or likeness," is almost exclusively discussed as the right of publicity as a property interest, such as one's name.

For example, in a case that could be considered as an example of an "intrusion upon the plaintiff's seclusion or solitude, or into his private affairs," a company had management continuously monitor the actions of a specific employee inside and outside of the workplace, following him after work, and even opening his locker without permission and taking a photograph of his personal diary. In 1995, the Supreme Court ruled that this was an infringement of the right to privacy and constitutes the tort of infringement of personal interests.[7]

It could be said that, in this way, tort law provides broad protection against the infringement of privacy.

Protection by the Constitution

Lagging somewhat behind tort protection, claims of infringement of privacy centering on cases of crime began to surface in the process of contesting the crime or the legality of criminal investigations, which led to the issues concerning the Constitution's protection of privacy.

In a case concerning the constitutionality of police officers taking photographs on a public road during a criminal investigation, the Supreme Court in its decision of 1969 stated:

> As one freedom in the private life of an individual, people should have the freedom to not have their face or appearance (hereafter "face, etc.") photographed without their consent or without good reason. Setting aside the question of whether this right can be called the right of portrait, it must at least be said that for a police officer to photograph an individual's face, etc. without justifiable reason goes against the purport of Article 13 of the Constitution and is unacceptable.[8]

In addition, in a case where a person refused to be fingerprinted for alien registration, the 1995 Court decision was as follows:

> An individual's fingerprint is a pattern on the individual's fingertip, and the fingerprint itself does not represent any information on the individual's private life or his/her inner mind, such as his/her personality, thought, creed and conscience. However, due to its nature, an individual's fingerprint is unique throughout the world and it is permanent throughout the individual's life, and there is the risk that the

7. Supreme Court decision of Sept. 5, 1995 (*Hanrei Times* 891: 77).

8. My translation of the Supreme Court decision of Dec. 24, 1969 (*Saikō Saibansho Keiji Hanreishū* 23, No. 12: 1625).

> individual's private life or privacy would be infringed depending on how his/her fingerprints taken by the authorities will be used. In this sense, the fingerprinting system has close relevance with the people's freedom in private life.
>
> Since Article 13 of the Constitution can be construed to stipulate that the people's freedom in private life shall be protected from the exercise of state power, each individual, as one of his/her freedoms in private life, has the freedom of not being compelled to be fingerprinted without due cause, and it is against the purport of said Article and therefore impermissible for the state organ to compel any individual to be fingerprinted without just cause...[9]

This shows that Article 13 of the Constitution was construed by the Supreme Court as providing for a certain amount of protection of privacy.

Information Society and Protection of Personal Information

With the advancement of the information society, it has become easier to collect and store personal information. Consequently, there are now increased risks of data matching and larger leakages of sensitive information, and it has come to be believed that traditional judicial relief based on the Civil Code and Constitution will not be sufficient to protect privacy.

In 1970, the government began reviewing the introduction of a common individual code number for use in administrative procedures, but this died out after strong criticism by the public that this is a "national numbering system." In the same year, Professor Koji Sato advocated for the right to control one's own information in his manuscript, "*Puraibashii no Kenri (Sono Kōhōteki Sokumen) no Kenpōteki Kōsatsu (1) (2) [A Constitutional Study of the Right to Privacy (from the aspect of public law) (1) (2)]*.[10]

In 1980, the OECD (Organisation for Economic Co-operation and Development) Recommendation of the Council Concerning Guidelines on the Protection of Privacy and Transborder Flows of Personal Data was adopted. As this called for member nations to enact State laws based on

9. Supreme Court decision of Dec. 15, 1995 (*Saikō Saibansho Keiji Hanreishū* 49, No. 10: 842); Translation by Judicial Research Foundation found at http://www.courts.go.jp/english/judgments/text/1995.12.15-1990.-A-.No..848.html.

10. *Hōgaku Ronsō* 86, No. 5, and 87, No. 6.

the so-called eight principles of the OECD,[11] there was heightened debate in Japan as well concerning legislation for the protection of privacy.

In 1981, the Supreme Court ruled on an infringement of privacy concerning a case in which, during a dispute between a company and its employee on the justification of dismissing the employee, the company's attorney, through the bar association, requested information from a government office on the criminal record of the said employee. The government office negligently gave out all the information it possessed on the previous convictions of the employee without giving careful thought to the purpose of use. In his concurring opinion, Supreme Court Justice Masami Ito indicated the importance of protecting personal information:

> The collection and storage of personal information by the State and local public entities are increasing due to necessities of the public interest such as administrative requests. At the same time, however, there is a rising necessity for strict management of information so that issues such as the infringement of privacy do not arise through disclosure of the collected information without due cause.[12]

The Ordinance for Protection of Personal Information in the city of Kasuga, Fukuoka Prefecture, and other local government-level ordinances for the protection of personal information were enacted starting from 1984. On the national level, the Act on the Protection of Personal Information Pertaining to Electronic Data Processing Held by Administrative Organs (formerly the Act on the Protection of Personal Information Held by Administrative Organs) was enacted in 1988. In 1997, the then Ministry of Trade and Industry announced the Guidelines for the Protection of Personal Information Pertaining to Electronic Data Processing Held by the Private Sector (Notification No. 98).

As the result of revision to the Residential Basic Book Act in 1999, the Juki Net residency registry network system was introduced starting in 2002. This institutionalized a system in which each citizen is given

11. The eight privacy protection principles of the OECD had a strong influence on Japan's current Act on the Protection of Personal Information. The principles are (1) collection limitation principle, (2) data quality principle, (3) purpose specification principle, (4) use limitation principle, (5) security safeguards principle, (6) openness principle, (7) individual participation principle, and (8) accountability principle.

12. My translation of the Supreme Court decision of April 14, 1981 (*Saikō Saibansho Minji Hanreishū* 35, No. 3:20).

a different resident code and a residency registry ID card that serves as personal identification. Protests arose that this system constituted an infringement of privacy.

Following this, responding to opportunities opened up by the EU Data Protection Directive and through the introduction of the Juki Net system, the Act on the Protection of Personal Information, Act on the Protection of Personal Information Held by Administrative Organs, and Act on the Protection of Personal Information Retained by Independent Administrative Agencies and Others were enacted in 2003. The Act on the Protection of Personal Information not only has specific provisions that commonly apply in the private sector but also prescribes the responsibilities of the State and local public entities. It is thus unique in that it possesses the quality of a basic act, laying down matters serving as basis for the Act on the Protection of Personal Information Held by Administrative Organs, the Act on the Protection of Personal Information Retained by Independent Administrative Agencies and Others, and ordinances to protect personal information, which apply to the public sector. Regarding the private sector, in addition to the Act on the Protection of Personal Information, which is a general law, forty guidelines based on this Act have been formulated for twenty-six fields including health care and finance (as of July 29, 2010; Consumer Affairs Agency announcement).

In a case in which Waseda University, without the consent of the applicants, gave the police information on the student ID number, name, home address, and telephone number of students applying to attend a lecture organized by the University, the Supreme Court recognized tort protection in their 2003 decision:

> Student ID number, name, address, and phone number constitute simple information used by Waseda University for identification and other such procedures, and, within this scope, the need for confidentiality of the information is not necessarily high. The same can be said for the students who applied to attend this lecture. However, even for such kinds of personal information, it is natural for a person to not want to have this information disclosed without due cause to someone he/she does not care to share this with. As such expectations should be protected, it must be said that personal information in this case should be subject to judicial protection as information related to the privacy of the appellants.

> The actions of the university in disclosing this personal information to the police without the consent of the appellants went against the reasonable expectations of the appellants for the appropriate management of privacy information that they had willingly presented. Since this is an infringement of the privacy of the appellants, it must be said that this act constitutes a tort.[13]

In this way, the protection of personal information due to the development of the information society has begun in Japan, albeit belatedly.

Overview of the Act on the Protection of Personal Information[14]

The purpose of the Act on the Protection of Personal Information is stipulated as follows in Article 1:

> The purpose of this Act is to protect the rights and interests of individuals while taking consideration of the usefulness of personal information, in view of a remarkable increase in the use of personal information due to development of the advanced information and communications society, by clarifying the responsibilities of the State and local public bodies, etc. with laying down basic philosophy, establishment of a basic policy by the Government and the matters to serve as a basis for other measures on the protection of personal information, and by prescribing the duties to be observed by entities handling personal information, etc., regarding the proper handling of personal information.

As noted in Article 1, the opening section of the Act on the Protection of Personal Information calls for the State and local public entities to formulate and implement measures to protect personal information, but specific provisions for administrative organs are provided in other laws. The Act on the Protection of Personal Information Held by Administrative Organs provides for the State, the Act on the Protection of Personal Information Retained by Independent Administrative Agencies and Others provides for independent administrative entities, and ordinances to protect personal information provide for local governments.

The following sections of the Act on the Protection of Personal Information lay down the general duties that must be observed by the private sector. The main duties of the private sector are stipulated to be

13. My translation of the Supreme Court decision of Sept. 12, 2003 (*Saikō Sanbansho Minji Hanreishū* 57, No. 8: 73).

14. See materials in English at http://www.caa.go.jp/seikatsu/kojin/index_en.html.

(1) Restriction by the Purpose of Use, (2) Proper Acquisition, (3) Security Control Measures, (4) Restriction of Provision to Third Parties, and (5) Disclosure, Correction, and Stopping the Use. These duties were decided based on the aforementioned eight principles of the OECD. More detailed regulations exist for finance, health care, and other individual fields in the private sector through guidelines determined by the relevant ministries and agencies. These duties do not apply to small-scale entities or for personal use, or to media reports, research, religious activities, and political activities.

In order to ensure that the private sector observes these obligations, each industry draws up its own guidelines for the protection of personal information, and a separate, authorized organization for the protection of personal information handles any complaints concerning the handling of personal information made against an entity handling personal information. And if the entity does not uphold its obligations, the competent minister holding jurisdiction over the entity can take measures to improve the situation, such as ordering that it correct or stop the violations. If the entity does not comply with the order for correction or cessation, they will be sentenced to imprisonment of not more than six months or to a fine of not more than ¥300,000.

II. Issues in Japan's Protection of Privacy

Technological Advancements and Delay in Response

Although the Act on the Protection of Personal Information has been enacted, the issue of privacy has yet to be sufficiently resolved. In society today, technological advancements have made it possible to easily grasp, store, and analyze an individual's history of behavior. For instance, web page view history and search history on the Internet is collected and analyzed. Behavioral data is grasped by attaching cookies to the browsers of website visitors, which allows revisits to the site by the same cookie to be recognized as visits by the same individual. This is not regulated by Japan's Act on the Protection of Personal Information because the operator only has a history of visits by cookies and not information that can identify the visitors, such as names. But with the accumulation of information such as browsing history, it will become easier to identify whose information this is; even if identification is not possible now, it is likely that technological progress will make this possible in the future.

The United States is more advanced than Japan in online behavioral advertising, a form of advertising that collects and analyzes web behavior to send advertisements tailored to the tastes of an individual. In response to this, the industry is imposing self-regulations and there are also studies underway on regulatory bills. Meanwhile, in Japan, self-imposed regulations by industry have just begun, and there are no concrete plans for regulations. But the biggest problem is that the public is hardly aware that such actions to track behavior are being conducted.

Technological progress has not only facilitated the monitoring of behavior on the Internet but behavior in the real world as well. Improved performance of recording devices has made it easier for surveillance cameras to be installed, and these devices are now being introduced to not only street corners but taxis and trains as well. Facial recognition systems will soon make it possible to automatically identify specific individuals from their photographed facial features. In addition, the police are currently increasing the number of cameras installed along main roads in Japan for the N-system. These cameras can read and record the license plates of all vehicles that pass by and store the data. But regarding such monitoring of our behavior, much about the current state and the rules for the storage and use of the photographed images has not been clarified. These changes are occurring without the knowledge of the public.

Introduction of a Common ID Numbering System

Amid such advancements in gathering information on an individual's history of behavior, the government is now stepping up its work to introduce a common numbering system to be used for both taxes and social security purposes. According to the government's agenda, the bills necessary for this legislation will be drawn up by around this fall, followed by distribution of the numbers in June 2014. You need not even look at the US Social Security Number (SSN) system to realize that this number will, for all intents and purposes, become a national ID number.

In Japan, the Juki Net residency registry system was launched in 2003 as a national ID system, but due to concerns over privacy, it was prohibited for the private sector to ask for this number. In addition, there are hardly any cases requiring the presentation of this number to receive public services. Because of such circumstances, there is hardly anyone who knows his or her own number. Meanwhile, however, if an ID number is used for tax collection purposes, it would have to be presented to the other party in the event of monetary transactions, making it clear that this will come to be used in the private sector.

If this national ID is broadly used in the private sector, it could serve as the key to collecting personal information, and, as in the United States, lead to the development of an industry dealing in personal information. There are concerns that our society will become one in which a single piece of information can provide the means to retrieving large amounts of information about an individual.

The Japanese government explains that the purpose of introducing this common numbering system—despite such potential risk of invasion of privacy—is to bring together the bits of information that had been handled separately by the various sections of government, and, by having the authorities know that such information concerns the same individual, allow the provision of more efficient administrative services as well as fair taxation and social security benefits. The separate management of information would, however, be a more preferable scheme from the perspectives of security and privacy. It would probably be technically possible to integrate separate information only when the necessity arises, without having to introduce a common ID number. The common numbering system, which carries great privacy risks, is not the only solution available. It would be essential to build a system for information integration that gives full consideration to privacy.

Society Heading Toward a Panopticon

It could be said that living in a society where new technological advancements can put your personal information on display to others, notably the government and big companies, would be like being imprisoned in a Panopticon prison building. A Panopticon prison is designed so that the prisoners in their cells are unable to tell if the observers in the observation tower are watching them or not. Imagine how it would be to have your personal information known to a person in control but you are not able to see that person. If this situation continues, you would begin to feel that you were being monitored at all times even when no one is actually observing you; this would discourage you from acting differently from other people. This kind of chilling effect, in turn, leads to a loss of autonomy. It is an issue that cannot be overlooked as it shakes the foundation of democratic society, which is built on the premise of a collective body of autonomous individuals.

The German Federal Constitutional Court expounded on the importance of privacy as the foundation of a democratic society in its 1983 population census decision. It concluded that a person who cannot foresee with sufficient certainty how much of his or her information is known to certain segments of society, and who is not able to assess to a certain degree the knowledge of his/her communication partners, may be essentially limited in his/her liberty to plan and make decisions. A society in which the citizenry cannot learn who came to know what about them and when and at what opportunity this took place would stand against the right to informational self-determination; this also follows for the legal order that made this possible.

The decision goes on to say that individuals who are concerned that behavior differing from others can always be recorded, accumulated forever as information, used, and communicated, would avoid attracting attention to themselves by taking that kind of action. For example, people who know that there is the possibility of danger in participating in a meeting or civil movement, which will be recorded by the authorities, would probably not exercise their basic rights such as the freedom to meet and the freedom of expression. This sentiment not only damages the development of each individual personality but also the public interest; the reason being that self-determination, which forms the basis for citizens to act on their own decision and supports their capability to cooperate with others, is the basic condition necessary for a free and democratic community to function.[15]

Moreover, the Act on the Protection of Personal Information has brought Japanese society closer to a Panopticon. In a Panopticon, the flow of information between prisoners in their individual cells is obstructed. In much the same way, the Act of Protection of Personal Information has been inhibiting the flow of personal information in the private sector in a general and comprehensive manner. The provisions of Japan's personal information act are, in principle, directed toward controlling the flow of all personal information. Based on this, all possessors of personal information—mostly the government and large companies—can easily refuse to provide information on the basis of the protection of personal information. And those who want information—mostly the general public,

15. Tsuyoshi Hiramatsu, *Kojinjyōhō Hōgo—Riron to Un'yo [Protection of Personal Information: Theory and Application]*, 26.

media, and researchers—are not able to obtain useful personal information even on rational grounds unless they act aggressively and devote an enormous amount of time and effort. As a result,there is an increasingly uneven distribution of personal information.

Solidarity between people is being hampered because name lists cannot be created. There have also been an increasing number of cases where the names of public officials involved in scandals are not revealed under the pretext of personal information. Speaking from my own experience, I once requested an insurance company provide me with a document that was prepared by a doctor upon their request concerning the injury of a client of mine, but they refused to give this to me on the grounds that it contained personal information on the doctor.

In this way, through the advancement of technology and the Act on the Protection of Personal Information, a trend can be seen in Japan for certain powers to have the bulk of personal information, making it appear that Japan is heading toward becoming a Panopticon.

III. The Path Japan Should Take

I now wish to propose some steps that Japan should take to avoid becoming a Panopticon.

Redefining the Value of Privacy

I believe that the time has come for us to think once again about the value of privacy. Developments in technology change how privacy should be protected. For example, Article 35 of the Japanese Constitution, which provides for the protection of all persons in their home against entries, searches, and seizures, can also be considered as aiming to protect the privacy of the residence, but if there are technologies that can eavesdrop on conversations or see inside the house from outside, limits will be reached in protection under Article 35. Much of our privacy has been protected merely by existing physical elements, such as the exterior walls of a house. In a society where the advancement of technology has made the walls of a house no longer able to live up to their role of protecting privacy, aggressive measures to protect privacy become necessary to replace these walls. In considering what form this should take, it is necessary to pursue the meaning of privacy protection, namely, to discern what kind of values privacy has been attempting to protect.

I believe that the value of privacy lies in protecting the autonomy of people. Thus it would be necessary to analyze privacy issues and, notably for those cases that make autonomous decision-making difficult, take aggressive measures to rectify the situation.

Privacy by Design

Many people feel that technological advancements will result in the loss of privacy. It is true that technology is making astounding strides, and it is also true that legislation is unable to keep pace with individual technologies. It is possible, however, to also use this technology to protect privacy.

One example would be using the aforementioned cookies. Cookies can be used to refuse the use of cookies that track user behavior on the Internet. For surveillance cameras as well, there are technologies that can store footage as blurred images when there is nothing out of the ordinary and restore this to sharp images when the need arises. There is also a method in which the camera begins to record images only when abnormal actions are detected such as a person suddenly running.

In this way, in the debate on protection of privacy hereon, it would be important to have technologies that are less privacy-invasive deliberately developed and adopted from the design stage. Special efforts to maintain privacy should not have to come from the side of the public; they need to be made by the developers of systems that could infringe on privacy.

This kind of thinking was broadened in scope by the concept of Privacy by Design. Privacy by Design proposes the design of technologies or systems that consider privacy. Privacy considerations include minimum use of personal information, maximum implementation of security, and strengthening the individual's power to control his or her information. In order to protect privacy within an environment undergoing significant technological advancements, it is believed necessary to also determine a comprehensive doctrine of this kind and, within each individual case, weigh the interests and necessity of personal information against the protection of privacy, rather than having separate, specific conduct controls.

Google, Facebook, and other Internet services with large numbers of users were introduced to Japan from North America. Due to the efforts of non-governmental organizations for privacy protection and the Federal Trade Commission (FTC) of the United States, as well as the

Privacy Commissioner of Canada, these services reflect to some extent the concept of Privacy by Design, and constant improvements are also being made. It is actually because of this situation that there has been little opportunity in Japan for people to take the initiative in thinking about protection of privacy on the Internet. (They tend to take protection of privacy for granted, with little interest in the methods taken to protect privacy.) I believe that in the near future, however, value will be placed on products and services excelling in privacy protection—just like environmental protection is today. Thus, it is necessary to quickly popularize the concept of Privacy by Design in Japan so that when this age comes, Japan will not find itself unable to sell its new products and services to the world because they lack techniques to protect privacy.

In Japan, the Act on the Protection of Personal Information assumed a life of its own, and there is little public awareness of this as a law protecting personal information for the protection of privacy. The purpose of this act is also noted only as "to protect the rights and interests of individuals," with no clear indication as to what rights or interests it is protecting.

The Act on the Protection of Personal Information was a method to protect areas of privacy that had become difficult to protect through the traditional framework for privacy protection due to advancements in information technology. But in Japan, the word "privacy" was not even included in the purpose of this law on the grounds that the concept of privacy is vague and has not gained a common understanding. Consequently, evaluation standards were lost, and the flow of personal information was obstructed in an all-encompassing way, bringing about an inconvenient situation in which the government and large companies can monopolize personal information.

Professor Tsuyoshi Hiramatsu of Himeji Dokkyo University Law School, who studied Germany's act on protection of personal information, states that the objectives of this act are to make it possible for the citizens to predict who has their personal information and how it is used, to remove fears over judgment by the government or toward building human relations with other people, to make it possible for each individual person to make decisions and take actions autonomously based on their own conscience, and to make it possible for people to create good human relations with everyone and to cooperate with all people by allowing individuals to select what parts of their personal information can be given to each of the parties they interact with.[16]

This kind of meaning of privacy should be reflected in law. Personal information that can be considered as not directly affecting autonomy should be made more readily available for circulation, and the flow of personal information that would directly impact autonomy should be strictly controlled. Any issue that arises should be solved by an individual weighing of interests on its impact on autonomy.

The government has established an investigative committee specializing in the protection of personal information under the Consumer Commission of the Cabinet Office and is now reviewing revision of the Act on the Protection of Personal Information. The Japan Federation of Bar Associations is also advocating revision in the above-mentioned direction.

Establishment of a Third-Party Entity for Privacy Protection

One of the reasons that can be given for why Japan is lagging behind in privacy protection is that there has been no organization to comprehensively handle Japan's privacy issues.

Studies were conducted on the establishment of a privacy commissioner when the Act on the Protection of Personal Information was enacted, but due to the bureaucratic silo organization of the ministries and agencies, it was decided that the respective ministers would be responsible for overseeing the protection of personal information in the private sector. A system for oversight by a minister who is not an expert in privacy issues is not effective. In addition, although the independent Review Board for the Protection of Personal Information reviews complaints concerning the disclosure of personal information in the possession of the government, the head of the relevant administrative organ makes decisions concerning the collection and management of personal information, rendering this system ineffective as well. The aforementioned investigative committee specializing in the protection of personal information has, since its establishment in 2010, only held a few hearings to revise the Act on the Protection of Personal Information and has made no specific solution proposals.

Meanwhile in the United States, for example, the Federal Trade Commission has been working on protecting consumer privacy since

16. Ibid., 154, 158.

1970. Last year, after holding a series of public round-table discussions, the FTC released a report in December proposing concepts such as Privacy by Design, which prevents privacy infractions by designing privacy protection in the systems when they are being built, and the Do Not Track mechanism, which allows the consumers to choose if they want to refuse the collection and analysis of their browsing history.

The Japanese government is not taking aggressive initiatives like these to protect privacy. Even today, after the introduction of the Act on the Protection of Personal Information, the lives of citizens are inconvenienced by situations such as the unavailability of emergency telephone chains and name lists, which had previously been prepared by schools and local communities, and the hindering of community activities because essential personal information is not provided or shared (so-called "overreaction"); there is also insufficient protection of personal information by private companies. Moreover, it cannot be said that swift and appropriate actions are being taken in response to new issues of privacy that routinely surface through the advancement of technology, such as Google Street View.

Proactive efforts should be taken to build a social infrastructure that will minimize the risk of infringement of privacy. A third party entity should, after establishing the basic concepts for privacy protection in digital society, monitor how administrative organs are implementing concrete policies based on these concepts (e.g. privacy impact assessment). It would also have the function of giving guidance, advice, counsel, and orders concerning the situation of privacy protection, promoting the spread of this basic concept among the private sector, and implementing specific policies in line with this concept.

This third party entity needs to be established not just on the national level but on the local level as well. These third party entities should, in addition, play the role of bodies providing simple and fast solutions for privacy disputes with the government and private sector and serve to promote awareness among the public on the true circumstances of personal information circulation and use, as well as the methods taken to protect privacy.

Recent Issues in Medical Ethics and Law in Japan

Manabu Wagatsuma[1]

Introduction

We are fast developing innovative and revolutionary technologies in the fields of medical science and treatment. From birth to death, medical ethics and law are intertwined with our daily lives. This chapter focuses on two specific areas of rapid technological change, reproductive technology and organ transplantation, both of which are closely connected to Japanese culture. It is necessary to consider these innovations not only from medical and biological viewpoints but also from ethical, regional, moral and legal positions.

I. Reproductive Technology

Assisted reproductive technology (ART) refers to the use of reproductive technology to treat infertility. Currently, no law in Japan regulates the use of ART.

As ART advances and more people turn to the technology to treat infertility,[2] the legal and ethical issues surrounding the technology also proliferate. For example, when, if ever, should ART be permitted? What is the legal status of a child born through ART?[3]

1. Professor, Faculty of Law, Tokyo Metropolitan University.

2. In 1999, there were 284,800 people being treated for infertility (165,000 used fertility drugs, 35,500 used artificial fertilization, 17,700 used in-vitro fertilization (IVF), 14,500 used micro-fertilization and 51,600 used other treatments (The Special Report by Department of Health, The Attitude Survey to Medical Doctor and People with regards to assisted reproductive technology, conducted in 1999 by Professor Takumi Yauci at Showa University).

3. In one case, the Osaka District Court declared that a husband could deny his paternity of a child if he did not clearly consent to the use of artificial insemination with a donor's semen (AID). Decision of the Osaka District Court, December 18, 1998, 51-9 *Kasai Geppou* 71. Most AID in Japan is performed at Keio University Hospital and most

In 1998, an Obstetrician in Nagano successfully produced twins through in-vitro fertilization, using a husband's sperm and an egg from his wife's sister. This technique violated the guidelines of the Japan Society of Obstetrics and Gynecology and the obstetrician was expelled from the Society.

In 2000, the Special Committee on Medical Technology for Reproductive Treatment presented its "Report on Ideal Reproductive Treatment Using Donor Sperm, Eggs and Embryos." It concluded that surrogate pregnancy should be prohibited because it uses the surrogate mother only for reproduction, violating her dignity. Moreover, surrogate pregnancy endangers the life of the surrogate mother and may also cause disputes between the surrogate mother and the infertile couple. The report also claimed that surrogate pregnancy was against the interests of the child born to the surrogate.[4]

Based on this report, the Committee on Assisted Reproductive Technology Treatment conducted an investigation in order to develop a regulatory framework for ART. In 2003, it summarized its findings in its "Report on the Development of a System for Assisted Reproductive Technology Treatment using Donor Sperm, Eggs, and Embryos." In offering proposals for regulation, the report considered the need to protect the welfare and dignity of both surrogates and children born through ART, and public opposition to eugenics and the commercialization of the surrogate market.

The report made the following proposals: (1) ART should be permitted only for infertile couples deemed to be "legitimate";[5] (2) siblings should be prohibited from serving as surrogates and donating sperm, eggs, and embryos; (3) donor sperm and eggs should be stored for no more than two years, while embryos should be stored for no more than ten

---

sperm donors are students at Keio University. The clients should be a legitimate couple and both clients should submit written consent acknowledging that the child born using AID will be a legitimate child. Noboru Ienaga, "[AID in Japan]," in [*The Family and Medical Treatment*], ed. Koichi Bai and Minoru Ishikawa (Tokyo, 1995), at 424. This concentration has to some degree reduced pressure to resolve issues as to the legal status of child, as there are relatively few disputes.

4. The Japan Federation of Bar Associations also recommended prohibiting surrogate pregnancy (Proposal 11).

5. Gay and lesbian couples are not regarded as legitimate in Japan.

years; (4) if the donor dies, the donor's sperm, eggs or embryos should be destroyed.

The report recommended prohibiting surrogate pregnancy because it concluded that when a surrogate mother's body is used for reproduction, the pregnancy and delivery could endanger the surrogate's life and may be against the interests of the child born to the surrogate.[6]

At the same time, in 2003 the Committee on Legislation for Parenthood Relating to Assisted Reproductive Technology Treatment published a report entitled the "Interim Draft Summary on Special Cases of the Civil Code related to Parenthood of Children Born though Assisted Reproductive Technology such as those using Donor Sperm Eggs or Embryos." This report proposed designating the woman who gives birth to a child as the legal mother of that child.[7]

Advances in ART have created serious legal issues with regard to the legal status of children born with the help of this technology. The following three cases focused on issues in Japan and the U.S. concerning the relationship between parents and children. The U.S. law is implicated because of so called "fertility tourism" in which couples travel to other jurisdictions to take advantage of a more favorable medical and legal environment.

The first case involved a request for a declaration of parenthood for a child born as a result of in-vitro fertilization using the frozen sperm of a dead husband. In 2004, the Takamatsu High Court[8] determined that the child was legitimate because the dead husband was the biological father of the child and had consented to the posthumous use of his sperm through in-vitro fertilization. In 2006, the Supreme Court reversed the High Court's decision and refused to recognize the child as the legitimate descendant of the dead husband.[9] Civil law, which regulates fam-

6. A minority of the committee opposed the prohibition of surrogate pregnancy as against the constitutional right to the pursuit of happiness (Art. 13)

7. A father or mother may choose to "affiliate" with his or her child out of wedlock. Art 779 of Japanese Civil Law. However, the mother who gives birth to a child is regarded as the legal mother of that child and it is not necessary to affiliate her child. With regards to non-legitimate children, see Decision of the Supreme Court, April 27, 1962, 16-7 *Minshu* 1247. See also, Atsushi Omura, "[The Assisted Reproductive Technology and Family Law]," *Jurist* 1243 (2003): 13.

8. Decision of the Takamatsu High Court, July 18, 2004, 56-11 *Kasai Geppou* 14.

9. Decision of the Supreme Court, September 4, 2006, 60-7 *Minshu* 2563. The Supreme Court also refused to recognize the child of a dead husband in the U.S.A. as

ily relations, does not regulate relations between a deceased father and any biological children who were born after the father's death. It is necessary to discuss whether the law should recognize the family relationship using frozen sperm after the death de facto father, considering bioethics, the interests of the child and the opinions of relatives if the family relationship is admitted.

In the second case, the state refused to accept the birth certificate of a child born to a surrogate mother using a husband's frozen sperm and an egg donated by a woman in the U.S. A court in Los Angeles, California had declared that the Japanese couple was the legitimate parents of the child. The Osaka High Court refused to recognize a mother-child relationship between the commissioning female and the child because the court deemed the surrogate mother to be the legitimate mother based on the fact that she delivered the child. The Osaka High Court overturned the Los Angeles court's decision as against public policy.[10] The Japanese Supreme Court upheld the decision.[11]

In the third case, the state refused to accept a birth certificate that listed the names of a married couple as parents of twin children who were born to a surrogate mother in the U.S. using the couple's sperm and egg. This was a high profile case in which the couple was television personalities and the wife had lost her womb to cancer.

The Tokyo High Court agreed with the Nevada State Court that the commissioning father and mother should be regarded as the legal father and mother of the children born to the surrogate.[12] But in 2007 the Japanese Supreme Court[13] reversed this decision and declared that the mother giving birth to the children should be regarded as the legal mother according to the Japanese Civil Code (Art. 772). The Court declared that the judgment of the Nevada State Court was against the public policy of Japan (Art. 118 of Code of Japanese Civil Procedure). It also declared that the Civil law does not include provision for surrogate pregnancy. The Civil law, in the Court's view, should be interpreted so that only a female who is pregnant and gives birth can be regarded as a mother of a child. Therefore the female who only provides an egg should not be regarded

legitimate. Decision of the Supreme Court, September 8, 2006 (unpublished).

10. Decision of the Osaka High Court, May 20, 2005, 1919 *Hanrei Jiho* 107.

11. Decision of the Supreme Court, November 24, 2005 (unpublished).

12. Decision of the Tokyo High Court, September 29, 2006, 1957 *Hanrei Jiho* 20.

13. Decision of the Supreme Court, March 23, 2007, 61-2 *Minshu*, 619.

as a mother. But the Court declared the necessity of a legislative solution regulating surrogate pregnancy based on medical and family law as soon as possible.

After the Court had rendered its decision, the Family Court granted the married couple's application for a special adoption.[14]

Adoption remains a little-used legal device in Japan, and adoption permits have been declining since 2005. In 2009, only 1,314 permits were granted.[15] Although the precise number of ART births in Japan has not been published, the number is surely higher than the number of adoptions. There are two reasons why adoption in Japan is rare. First, many couples refuse to raise a child that does not share their blood.[16] Second, adoption requirements remain extremely strict.[17] The reasons why the number of adoption is decreasing are both that there is a decline in available children for adoption and development of ART.[18]

The Ministry of Justice, together with the Ministry of Health, Labor and Welfare, responded to growing public demand for guidelines on ART by making a joint request to the President of the Science Council of Japan for clarification. The Assisted Reproductive Technologies Review Committee examined the medical, ethical, social and legal dimensions of surrogate pregnancy, and in 2008 it published "The Report on Issues Related to the Assisted Reproductive Technologies Centered on Surrogate Pregnancy."

Aiming to protect the health and welfare of surrogate mothers and the children that they bear, the Committee made the following proposals. First, surrogate pregnancy should be largely prohibited, except in certain

14. Special adoption is permitted only if both biological parents of the child to be adopted are incapable of or unfit to care for the child or there are other special circumstances and it is found that a special adoption is necessary to protect the best interests of the child. Art. 817-7 of Japanese Civil Code.

15. General Secretariat of the Supreme Court, *Annual Report of Judicial Statistics for 2010* Volume 3, Table 2 at 7 (Tokyo, 2010).

16. Tomoko Takahashi et al, "[Roundtable: The regulation of reproductive treatment and parent-child relation law]," *Horitujiho* 79 (11) (2008) (opinion by Yasunori Yoshioka), 16.

17. Ibid. at 16 (opinion by Azumi Tsuge).

18. Yukiko Terado, "[The Examination of Special Adoption]," *Jurist* 1059 (1995): 138.

narrow circumstances when it should be strictly regulated. Second, surrogate pregnancy for profit should be criminalized.[19]

Third, the government should consider supporting tightly controlled clinical trials for surrogate pregnancies as long as the trials give due regard to protecting the welfare of surrogate mothers and their children. Some have criticized the Committee for failing to specify the scope of these clinical trials.[20] Fourth, clinical trials should be overseen by a new public administrative organization composed of specialists in medicine, law, and other areas.

Fifth, the surrogate mother should be regarded as the legal mother of the child born through the surrogacy. The legal status of a child is generally based on biological relationships, but we should also consider whether social relationships, such as those developed through raising a child, provide a stronger basis for recognition.[21] Sixth, married couples that use a surrogate to bear their child can establish parenthood over that child through adoption or special adoption.

The difference between adoption and special adoption is that for ordinary adoption, the relationship between the birth parent and the child is not severed by the adoption. Severance of the relationship is possible by consent (Art. 811 of Japanese Civil Code). These adoptions have a long tradition in Japan, and mostly are undertaken for succession and support. In contrast, special adoption extinguishes the relationship between real parent and child (Art. 817-9 of Civil Code).Therefore the requirements for special adoption are much stricter and it can only be undertaken through an order of the family court (Art. 817-2 of Civil Code). To become a special adoptive parent, one must be married (Art. 817-3 of Civil Code). A person who has not attained 25 years of age may not become a special adoptive parent; unless he or she is over 20 years of age and married to someone who is older than 25 who is joining the application for special adoption (Art. 817-4 of Civil Code). No person who has attained 6 years

19. Agents who facilitate surrogate pregnancy for profit should be punished even if the surrogate mother freely volunteered to serve as a surrogate. Noriko Mizuno et al., "[Roundtable: Reproductive medicine]," *Jurist* 1359 (2008) (opinion by Saku Machino): 33.

20. Mizuno et al., 26.

21. Toyohiro Nomura, "[The Assisted Reproductive Technology and the Decision of Parent and Child]," in Minoru Ichikawa, Jun Nkagawa and Akira Yonekura, eds., *[The Issues of Reform of Family Law]* (1993): 337.

of age at the time of the application can be subject to special adoption; provided that this shall not apply if he/she has not attained 8 years of age and has been continually cared for by a person to be an adoptive parent since before the child attained 6 years of age (Art. 817-5 of Civil Code). There were 374 such adoptions in Japan in 2011.[22]

Seventh, the welfare of the child should be the chief concern in determining the breadth of any right to obtain identifying information about the surrogate. In 2009, the Japan Society of Obstetrics and Gynecology regulated 616 institutes that conducted in-vitro fertilization.[23] It is difficult to keep accurate records of the number of children born through surrogates[24] because parents often hide the fact that they used a surrogate.[25]

Eighth, the Committee acknowledged, but did not discuss, other difficult issues, such as the use of donor eggs or of frozen sperm from deceased husbands. Ninth, the Committee made clear that the welfare of the child should be given the highest priority in determining any issues related to surrogate pregnancy and other ART.

The Judgment of the Supreme Court suggests the need for the Diet to legislate as soon as possible. At the time of this writing, these reports have not led to any legislation regarding reproduction in Japan. The fertility tourists still have reason for concern.[26]

22. General Secretariat of the Supreme Court, supra n. 15, Table 2 at 7.

23. Institutes performing in-vitro fertilizations must be registered and report all deliveries.

24. Noriko Mizuno, "[Looking Back at the Japanese Parent and Child-Related Law from Reproductive Medicine]," *Hoso Jiho* 61, no. 5 (2000) at 27. Most parents do not tell their children about AID and clinics do not always maintain accurate records (Mizuno et al., supra note 19 at 7 [Opinion by Yoshimura].

25. Japanese Penal Code Art. 161-2 criminalizes false birth certificates. A false birth certificate cannot serve as the basis for an adoption. Decision of the Supreme Court, December 28, 1950, 4-13 *Minshu*, 701 .

26. For example, in 2008 a married couple entered into a contract with a surrogate mother in India using the husband's sperm and the egg of an unidentified Indian woman. The couple divorced before the child was born. Upon delivery, the baby became stateless and was prohibited from entering Japan. The Japanese government later issued a visa for the child to enter Japan. Hiroko Ito, "[The Present State of Surrogate Pregnancy and the Status of Born Child]," *Koseki Jyoho* 631 (2008): 24.

II. Brain Death and Organ Transplantation

Brain Death and Organ Transplant

In 1968, the first heart transplant in Japan was performed at Sapporo Medical University by Professor Juro Wada. The successful operation was clouded by the suspicious circumstances surrounding the donor's death and by concerns that the donor was not given proper medical treatment. Furthermore the condition of the recipient might not have been sufficiently critical to warrant a heart transplant. Although the state initiated criminal charges against the recipient, the charges were later dropped for lack of evidence. The public has remained distrustful of the transplant industry ever since.

In the past, the first heartbeat marked the beginning of life, and the cessation of the heartbeat and breathing, together with bilateral dilated pupils, marked its end. These definitions have become inadequate now that cardiopulmonary resuscitation (CPR) and prompt defibrillation allow doctors to restart breathing and the heart. It is a pity that public resistance to using organs from brain-dead patients has led to opposition to using brain-based criteria for determining death.

In 1992, the Prime Minister's Special Committee on Brain Death and Transplantation (*rinji noshi oyobizoukisyokutyousakai*) presented its final report.[27] The opinion of the committee was divided over the definition of "death." The majority concluded that death should be defined based on objective medical and biological criteria. In particular, the majority decided that brain death constituted the death of a human being.

A minority of the committee opposed using brain death as a criterion for a human death because they claimed that it lacked a rational basis and no social consensus supported the definition. The minority also feared that this definition might lead to more human rights violations.

The committee also held that the state should respect an individual's decision to donate his or her organs upon death. The minority agreed that this decision should be respected, provided that the definition of "brain death" is narrowly construed, the organ recipient is selected fairly, and the consent of the donor is clear.

In 1994, the Diet considered an organ transplant bill that would have permitted doctors to remove organs from brain-dead patients as long

27. Ichiro Kato et al., "[Roundtable: With regards to the Report of Prime Minister's Special Committee on Brain Death and Transplantation]," *Jurist* 1001 (1992): 9.

Table 1. Number of organ donors and transplants in Japan

Year	1999	2000	2001	2002	2003	2004	2005	2006	2007	2008	2009	2010	2011	Total
cadaveric	85	71	71	59	75	90	82	102	92	96	98	81	68	1070
brain death	4	6	8	6	3	5	9	10	13	13	7	32	44	160
Total organ donors	89	77	79	65	78	95	91	112	105	109	105	113	112	1230
Total organ transplants	163	159	176	143	142	190	182	227	230	259	213	293	329	2706

Source: The Japan Organ Transplant Network

as the patient's family consented and the patient had not clearly refused to donate his or her organs. In the face of unexpectedly strong public criticism, the bill was revised to require individuals to clearly consent to organ donation, but even this revised bill could not get through the Diet.

In 1997, the Diet settled on a compromise with the passage of the Organ Transplant Law. There was a strong fear that life support for patients would be terminated once they were declared brain dead, leading to a view of organs and tissues as merely as potential donations. The law did not provide a single definition of human death. The object of transplant must come from a dead body, including brain death as a definition. The definition of brain death is a person who is going to have organs removed for transplant and the irreversible end of all brain activity including brain stem (Art. 6, para. 2).

It was criticized that brain death is regarded as death only for purpose of facilitating transplants. That is why the transplant is impossible without the consent of the donor. Professor Machino criticized that the transplant law admits that the concept of death is cardiac death including brain death and the concept of death will be chosen by the patient.[28]

The law had strict requirements of a donor's prior documented consent to organ transplant, as well as family consent for transplant. By 2009, only 84 transplants from brain-dead donors had been performed in Japan (Table 1). Guidelines on organ transplantation prohibit anyone younger than fifteen from consenting to donate their organs. This is based on

28. Saku Machino, "[Organ transplant]," [*Collected Articles for Memorial of Professor Tamiya*], 1 (2001): 17. See also Koichi Bai, "[The Discussion of Brain Death is Ended?]," *Horitujiho* 69 (1997): 76.

the Japanese Civil Code (Art. 961) law that declares the only individuals older than fifteen possess sufficient independence of mind for their will to be respected by law. Accordingly, no child under 15 can donate his or her organ in Japan. Because of the shortage of donors in Japan, some people have begun seeking donor organs in foreign countries. (Table 2). There has been increasing criticism of this trend.[29]

Table 2. Number of Japanese heart transplants in foreign countries by age.

Year	1–9 Years	10–17 Years	Over 18	Total
1988	1	0	0	1
1989	0	0	1	1
1990	0	2	2	4
1991	2	1	0	3
1992	1	1	0	2
1993	0	0	3	3
1994	2	1	2	5
1995	1	2	6	9
1996	1	0	3	4
1997*	**1**	**0**	**4**	**5**
1998	3	1	2	6
1999	2	1	1	4
2000	4	3	2	9
2001	3	1	4	8
2002	4	2	1	7
2003	1	2	4	7
2004	3	3	3	9
2005	4	5	6	15
2006	1	2	4	7
2007	4	1	4	9
2008	3	3	3	9
2009	3	3	3	9
Total	44	34	58	136

*Organ Transplantation Law in Japan enacted.

Source: The Japan Society for Transplantation

Living Donor Transplant

There is strong public resistance in Japan to harvesting organs from brain-dead patients. In contrast, many support transplants from living organ donors, though concerns remain regarding so-called "transplant tourism," whereby poor individuals from impoverished countries sell their organs to patients in the first world.

The Organ Transplant Law regulates only brain-dead donors. It contains no provisions with respect to living donors. The only rules governing living donors are contained in the Japan Society's ethical guidelines. These require that organ donation should be voluntary and organ trading for profit is prohibited.

29. The Declaration of Istanbul on Organ Trafficking and Transplant Tourism in 2008.

A living donor must be a "relative" of the recipient, as defined by Article 725 of the Civil Code in Japan.[30] A relative is defined as (1) a relative by blood within the sixth degree; (2) a spouse; or (3) a relative by marriage within the third degree. Most transplants from living donors involved blood relatives in the first or second degree. Accordingly, in Japan living donor transplants are characterized as a private or family issue.

According to a survey conducted by the Japan Liver Study Group in 2004,[31] most donors are positive about their experience (65.5%). Some donors worry about their future health (38.9%), while others do not undergo regular medical examinations (26.8%).[32]

Over four hundred liver and kidney transplants from living donors are performed every year (Table 3), far more than the number of transplants from brain-dead donors. Although the requirements to transplant from brain dead donors are very strict, the success rate of liver transplants from living donor is actually higher than that of the dead.

Table 3. Liver Transplants in Japan

Year	1999	2000	2001	2002	2003	2004	2005	2006	2007	2008	2009	Total
Living Donor	251	327	417	434	440	551	566	505	433	464	464	2986
Cadaveric (including brain-death)	2	6	6	7	2	3	4	5	10	13	7	30

Source: Japanese Liver Transplantation Society

In 1994, a father donated his kidney to his son, but the son died of pulmonary edema following the transplant. The parents sued the hospital, alleging that it had violated its duty of care to their son. The Tokyo

30. Donors are limited to relatives not only because of the higher liklihood of organ compatibility, but also on the theory that the restriction reduces opportunities for coercion. Eiji Maruyama, "[Donor Requirements for Living Transplants]," in Yuji Shiroshita, ed, [*The Living Transplant and Law*] (2009): 93.

31. The Japan Liver Study Group, [Report of the Survey of Living Liver Donor] (2005): 17.

32. Ibid. at 18.

District Court[33] found for the parents and ordered the hospital to pay the non-economic damages of the donor. But the Tokyo High Court[34] reversed the decision and denied the non-economic damages of a donor losing his kidney when the organ transplant had failed. It only allowed the non-economic damage for a parent losing their child.

In 2006, police in Uwajima arrested a donor and recipient on charges of illegal organ trading.[35] The common-law wife of the recipient falsely claimed that the unrelated donor was her sister, and the hospital, failing to check the family registry, did not discover the lie. The recipient paid the donor ¥300,000 (ca. US$3,750) and gave her a car worth ¥1,500,000 (US$ 18,750) as a gift. The court found both the donor and recipient guilty.[36]

No charges were brought against the operating surgeon, however. Because the surgeon was not a member of the Japan Society for Transplantation, the Society's guidelines did not apply to him. In 2006, the Society's guidelines were amended to require that the relationship between recipient and donor be confirmed by official documents. If there is a suspicion of paying money or providing benefits for the transplant, the surgery should be cancelled. In 2007, the guidelines of the organ transplant law were amended so as to cover all surgeons, including those who are not members of the Society for Transplantation. Doctors can use organs from living donors only in exceptional cases because of the danger the operation poses to donors. Doctors must explain to the donor in writing all of the risks related to the operation, along with the success rate for transplants of the organ the donor is providing, and obtain the written consent of the donor. Doctors must also explain to the recipient the nature of the operation, any foreseeable effects of the transplant, and any related dangers. If the donor is a relative of the recipient, this relationship must be confirmed using official documents. If, for whatever reason, these documents are not available, an ethics committee must confirm the relationship based on documents.

In a second case in Uwajima, the donor and the recipient engaged in an adoptive marriage in order to undertake a kidney transplant. The

33. Decision of the Tokyo District Court, February 28, 2000, *Hanrei Times* 1108, 230.

34. Decision of the Tokyo High Court, February 6, 2001, *Hanrei Times* 1109, 198.

35. Decision of the Matsuyama District Court, December 26, 2006.

36. Decision of the Matsuyama District Court at Uwajima branch, December 26 in 2006.

recipient was a physician and an owner of a clinic. He paid a gangster ¥10 million (ca. US$125,000) as a commission to find a donor. The transplant, however, did not proceed because the gangster asked for more money. The recipient and his wife then asked another gangster to find a new donor. This search was successful, and the recipient and donor undertook the adoptive marriage in order to conduct the kidney transplant. The transplant was conducted on July in 2010. Both the donor and the recipient were subsequently arrested for trading in organs.

The Japan Society for Transplantation is considering reforms to its ethical guidelines in order to strengthen the Society's commitment to consent at the decision of transplant.[37]

Reform of the Organ Transplant Law

In 2000, the Diet considered several proposals for revision to the Organ Transplant Law. The debate centered on three issues.[38] First, how clearly must individuals declare their intention for their organs to be donated upon their death. Second, whether children under 15 could donate their organs. Third, is there any priority for donation to the brain dead donor's family member. The debate also revealed that the definition of brain death remained an extremely controversial question.

Taro Nakayama proposed a bill that defined human death as brain death. He proposed that a patient could also be found to be legally dead if the patient's family consented to the donation, provided that the patient had not made a written refusal to donate. Nakayama also proposed that doctors be able to use organs from brain-dead children under fifteen if their families consent, and that priority be given to donations to the brain dead donor's family member.

Keiichiro Ishi also proposed defining death as brain death. His bill would have lowered the age of consent from 15 to 12. The draft B also proposes a priority donation for family members of the donor.

Tomoko Abe called for a clearer definition of brain death. He also sought to regulate tissue transplants and organ donations from living donors.

37. Announcement of the President of the Japan Society for Transplantation, August 1, 2011.

38. Katsunori Kai, "[The Significance and Problem of the Reform of the Transplant Law]," *Hougakukyoushitsu* 351 (2009): 38; Katsunori Kai, "[Roundtable: The Significance and Problem of the Reform of the Transplant Law]," *L &T* 45 (2009): 10.

Takumi Nemoto proposed permitting transplants from children under 15 if their families consented and a third party confirmed the consent.

In 2009, after much debate, the Diet adopted Nakayama's bill by a vote of 263 to 167 and it was enacted the following year. The law contains no provisions regarding living donors or tissue transplants.

The revised law defines brain death as the irreversible end of all brain activity including brain stem as it deletes "the person who is going to remove organ for transplant" of former paragraph 2 of Art 6 of former law. This is a more general definition of brain death, responding to some of the criticism of the previous law.

Professor Kai has observed that after implementing the Organ Transplant Law, the "social norm"[39] among people not to oppose the concept of brain death may emerge. But Professor Machino criticizes the paragraph 3 of Art 6 of the reform of transplant law still limits the decision of death to organ transplant. Because the decision of brain death is only conducted for organ transplant and the family has a right to deny.[40]

The revised law also permits organ donation from brain-dead children under 15, provided that doctors obtain their families' consent.[41] Brain-dead donors under 18 who died because of abuse are not eligible to become donors (Supplementary provision 4 of the reform of transplant law).[42]

The law also implements a system of priority donation to a brain-dead donor's family member (new Article 6-2).[43] The "family member" is

39. Professor Kato criticized the concept of the social agreement is conservative theory not to admit the brain death as it is impossible to confirm the social norm (Ichiro Kato, "[The Social Agreements of Brain Death]," *Jurist* 845 [1985], 43).

40. Professor Machino points out the concept of brain death should be applied generally not based on the decision of brain death. Machino, "[The Development of Brain Death]," *Criminal Journal* 20 (2010), at 7.

41. No. 1 of the revised guideline with regards to operation of organ transplant law.

42. No. 3 of the revised guideline with regards to operation of organ transplant law.

43. In 2001, the donor not only declare for transplantation but also both kidneys to two relatives. The Department of Health and Labor supported that decision. The Committee of Transplants (*Koseikagakushingikai shipeitaisakubukai zoukiisyokuiinnkai*) discussed the issue of prior declaration of recipient by donor. It is divided and announces not to permit such kind of decision by the rule is established.

defined in Civil law Art. 725 as follows; a relative by blood within the sixth degree, a legitimate spouse and a relative by marriage within the third degree. But the definition of a"family member" in the guideline is limited to parents, children and a legitimate spouse in order to limit priority donation.[44] Common law spouses are excluded and only special adoption is permitted It is not permitted to limit or exclude a specific person. The priority donee is determined not only by the will of donor but also by the medical conditions (compatibility requirements). If there is no family member to match the recipient, other people will be recipient. Finally, it is possible to donate from a person who commits suicide but it is not eligible for priority donation in order to prevent suicide.

Professor Higuchi has criticized the law's narrow definition of a family member, seeking to promote transplants and respect for the decisions of the donor. (Art. 2 of transplant law).[45] It is also necessary in his view to consider the fairness of opportunity of transplant (Art. 2 of the reform of transplant law) and medical adaptation.

The new law also urges state and local governments to make greater efforts to educate the public about transplants (Art. 17-2). A family's consent is based on the opinions of a spouse, parents, children, grandparents and grandchildren, though it is desirable for the family to speak through a family representative.

Japan's resistance to transplanting organs from brain-dead donors is rooted in the country's cultural, philosophical and religious conceptions of life and death. For example, few families consent to autopsies because of a deep-seeded respect for preserving the sanctity of the corpse.

Most Japanese are not yet not willing to donate their organs. But with regards to the needs of transplant for a family member, the desire to be the living donor and priority donation from brain death donor will be strong.

These attitudes may be changing, however. The number of transplants from brain-dead donors increased dramatically in 2010 and the total number of transplants also increased, but the number of organ donations has been stable from 2006 to 2011 (Table 1).

44. No. 2 of the revised guideline with regards to operation of organ transplant law.

45. Norio Higuchi, "[Reform of Transplant Law]," *Jurist* 1393 (2010), 45.

Conclusion

Advances in assisted reproductive technology have outpaced Japan's efforts to regulate the field. Despite years of discussion on reproductive technology and transplants from living donors, no legislation exists. Legislators are reluctant to regulate these areas because they are regarded primarily as family issues. In devising any legislation on ART, we must consider not only the medical, biological and legal dimensions of the technology, but also its ethical, moral, and cultural implications.

While more regulation of ART is necessary, domestic legislation alone cannot solve every problem. For example, if Japan prohibits surrogate pregnancy, Japanese couples will inevitably look abroad for surrogate mothers. Thus it is critical for Japan to coordinate with other countries as it develops a regulatory framework.

CPSIA information can be obtained at www.ICGtesting.com
Printed in the USA
BVOW041224250213

314002BV00002B/7/P

9 781882 239207